CW00595098

Validation, Verification and Test of Knowledge-based Systems

Validation, Verification and Test of Knowledge-based Systems

Edited by

Marc Ayel and **Jean-Pierre Laurent**
Université de Savoie, France

JOHN WILEY & SONS
Chichester · New York · Brisbane · Toronto · Singapore

Copyright © 1991 by John Wiley & Sons Ltd.
Baffins Lane, Chichester
West Sussex PO19 1UD, England

All rights reserved.

No part of this book may be reproduced by any means,
or transmitted, or translated into a machine language
without the written permission of the publisher.

Other Wiley Editorial Offices

John Wiley & Sons, Inc., 605 Third Avenue,
New York, NY 10158-0012, USA

Jacaranda Wiley Ltd, G.P.O. Box 859, Brisbane,
Queensland 4001, Australia

John Wiley & Sons (Canada) Ltd, 5353 Dundas Road West, Fourth
Floor, Etobicoke, Ontario M9B 6H8, Canada

John Wiley & Sons (SEA) Pte Ltd, 37 Jalan Pemimpin 05-04,
Block B, Union Industrial Building, Singapore 2057

Library of Congress Cataloging-in-Publication Data:
Validation, verification and test of knowledge-based systems / edited
  by Marc Ayel and Jean-Pierre Laurent.
    p. cm.
  Includes bibliographical references and index.
  ISBN 0 471 93018 0
  1. Expert systems (Computer science) I. Ayel, Marc.
  II. Laurent, Jean-Pierre.
  QA76.76.E95Y353 1991
  006.3'3—dc20   91-22277
                                                            CIP

*A catalogue record for this book is available from the British
Library*

Printed in Great Britain by Courier International, East Kilbride,
Lanarkshire

Contents

5. SACCO–SYCOJET: Two Different Ways of Verifying Knowledge-based Systems   63

M. Ayel and J.-P. Laurent

6. The Use of Object-oriented Process Specification for the Validation and Verification of Decision Support Systems   77

P.J. Krause, P. Byers, S. Hajnal and J. Fox

PART C   COHERENCE CHECKING   93

7. MELODIA: Logical Methods for Checking Knowledge Bases   95

E. Charles and O. Dubois

PART D   TESTING

8. Consistency, Soundness and Completeness of a Diagnostic System

V. Guibert, A. Beauvieux and M. Haziza

9. Design Knowledge Validation Through Experimentation: The SYSIFE System

P. Mazas

13.   CONKRET: A Control Knowledge Refinement Tool   191
B. Lopez

14.   Judging Knowledge-base Quality   207
S. Craw

Authors of Papers

EDITORS

Marc AYEL   Laboratoire d'Intelligence Artificielle
Jean Pierre LAURENT   Université de Savoie

REFEREED PAPERS

Marc AYEL   *Université de Savoie*
Jean Pierre LAURENT   *Laboratoire d'Intelligence Artificielle*
                                     B.P. 1104
                                     73011 CHAMBERY CEDEX
                                     FRANCE

Paddy BYERS   *Department of Mathematics and*
                                     Computing Science
                                     Surrey University
                                     Guildford
                                     SURREY

Evelyne CHARLES   *Electricité de France*
                                     Direction des Etudes et Recherches
                                     IMA-TIEM
                                     1 Avenue du Général De Gaulle
                                     92140 CLAMART
                                     FRANCE

Susan CRAW

Robert Gordon's
Institute of Technology
Aberdeen
SCOTLAND AB1 1HG

Luc DE RAEDT
Gunther SABLON
Maurice BRUYNOOGHE

Katholieke Universiteit Leuven
Department of Computer Science
Celestijnenlaan 200 A
B-3001 HEVERLEE
BELGIUM

Olivier DUBOIS

LAFORIA
Université Pierre & Marie Curie. CNRS.
4 place Jussieu, Paris 6
75005 PARIS
FRANCE

Sorin GRUNWALD

Darmstadt University
Department of Computer Science
Alexanderstr. 10
D-6100 DARMSTADT
GERMANY

Vincent GUIBERT
Alain BEAUVIEUX

IBM Scientific Center
Place Vendôme
75001 PARIS
FRANCE

Marc HAZIZA

MATRA Espace
Z.I. du Palays
Rue des Cosmonautes
31077 TOULOUSE Cedex
FRANCE

Thomas HOPPE

Mommsentr. 50
1000 BERLIN 12
GERMANY

Paul J. KRAUSE
Saki HAJNAL
John FOX

Biomedical Computing Unit
Imperial Cancer Research Fund
Lincoln's Inn Fields
LONDON WC2A 3PX

Philippe LAFON

EDF
Direction des Etudes et Recherches
1 Avenue du Général De Gaulle
92140 CLAMART
FRANCE

Beatriz LOPEZ

Centre d'Estudis Avançats, CSIC
Cami de Sta. Bàrbara, s/n
17300 BLANES
SPAIN

Philippe MAZAS

Service des Systèmes Experts
D. S. C. I. T. - Régie Renault
860 Quai Stalingrad
Bat J4-D14
92109 BOULOGNE BILLANCOURT CEDEX
FRANCE

Daniel E. O'LEARY

School of Business
University of Southern California
Los Angeles CA 90089-1421
CALIFORNIA USA

L.F. PAU

Digital Equipement Corporation
Route de crêtes
BP 129
Sophia Antipolis
06561 VALBONNE Cedex
FRANCE

Jaak TEPANDI

Tallin Technical University
Akademia tee 1
Tallin, Estonia, USSR 200108
USSR

Foreword

This book contains the best contributions presented at the "First European Workshop on Validation, Verification and Test of Knowledge-based System" which was organized during the ECAI 90 Conference in Stockholm.

Validation is one of the main concerns in Software Engineering for classical and conventional programs (procedures). This is a problem which is not totally solved and which is still under investigation.

Many studies have been made, as much in academic contexts with more formal approaches as in industrial ones with a more pragmatic emphasis. Their common goal is to assert and even to guarantee the "good quality", the "correctness" of a piece of Software. From all these studies various methods, techniques, and recommendations have emerged, especially at the development phase level, in order to prevent the building of bad programs. Some results (but not so many in fact) have also been obtained for checking the correctness of an already written procedure (formal proofs and testing methods).

In the field of Knowledge Engineering, the problem of Validation of a Knowledge-based System (KBS) has not yet been very thoroughly investigated. The complexity of this problem may explain in a way why AI researchers did not deal with it sooner. In fact this problem consists in trying to validate approximative systems which use approximate information for approximate reasoning, in order to solve problems which are themselves often only approximately defined.

Thus it is a very difficult challenge, still more difficult indeed than classic software validation.

But at a time when knowledge-based systems are penetrating every field in Industry and Business, how can it be possible to remain in the situation where receipt of an expert system remains nothing less than an act of faith, of mutual confidence between a developing team and a customer?

The emergence of methods for validating Knowledge-based Systems has become an obvious necessity and it corresponds to a relatively new Research field called "VVT" : "Validation, Verification and Test". (The differences between the three concepts are clarified later in this foreword.)

For three years workshops on VVT of KBS have been organized during AAAI or IJCAI (Detroit, 89) Conferences. At Stockholm, during the ECAI 90. Conference the "First European Workshop on VVT of KBS" was organized and it was a great success, attracting about thirty European "pioneers" in the field.

This workshop was very useful in establishing links between European researchers (academics and those working in industry working on this topic, and also the contributions were of very high quality. This is why we have decided to gather these contributions in a more formal form in the present book.

This collection of papers provides a good idea of the European state of the art in the VVT field. Of course it can only show the results of the first steps in an emerging area. But we are sure that the clarification of the concepts that it contains will be very useful and that the description of the different approaches that are presented will give both information on what has been done and ideas on what remains to be done.

CONCEPTS OF VALIDATION, VERIFICATION AND TEST

These three concepts are quite different, but very often they are not clearly distinguished.

The IEEE definitions (No. 729-1983) are :

- Verification : the process of determining whether or not the products of a given phase of software development meet all the requirements established during the previous phase.
- Validation : the process of evaluating software at the end of the development process to ensure compliance with software requirements.

These definitions are well founded for classical software with a waterfall life-cycle. It is not obvious that they can be easily adapted to Knowledge-based Systems, first because the life-cycle is more specific. So we will not try, in this foreword, to set up definitions of these concepts but to have a different point of view and different approaches to them.

The validation process and the verification process can be distinguished according to the persons who use them (figure 1).

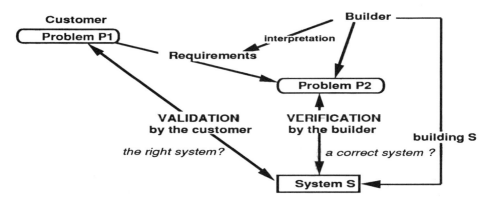

Figure 1 : Differences between the validation process and the verification process.

The "customer", that is the person placing the order and/or the future user(s), is concerned with the validation process. For him the question is as follows : "Is the system provided by the builder the right product? Does it actually solve my problems (P1)?"

The customer looks for Usability, Competencies, Performances, Reliability of the product. The validation process is directly concerned with the behavior of the Knowledge-based System.

With Knowledge-based Systems the notion of "builder" covers different kinds of specialists, different functions (the computer scientist, the knowledge engineer and the experts who cooperate during development). It should be noted that these different functions can be assumed by the same person or by several persons. The builder is concerned with the verification process. For him the question is : "Have I built a correct product?" Does it solve the problem of the customer, so far as I have understood it from our discussions, that is the problem P2? The verification process is concerned with the code (Inference Engine, interfaces), the knowledge and the meta-knowledge.

Let us point out that, unlike the validation process, the verification process is based on the builder's thorough knowledge about the product he has developed. This knowledge is mainly concerned with technical details about the product and with its components. The verification process stems from this kind of knowledge.

The builder looks for syntactic properties, Coherence, Completeness, Correctness, Robustness but also Performance.

Distinctions must also be made at another level, between Knowledge-based Systems Validation or Verification and Knowledge based Validation or Verification. In the first case software is concerned, in the second only a set of knowledge, not software. But this knowledge contains an important part of the power of the future software. The goals of the process for validation or verification may not be the same for the two kinds of product.

For example, verifying a Knowledge-based System means:

- verifying its Inference Engine,
- verifying its Knowledge Base,
- verifying its "good working order"

while verifying the Knowledge Base only, when this Knowledge Base is composed of facts and rules, means:

- ratifying each fact, each rule,
- checking the properties of the sets of deduced facts,
- checking the properties of the rule set,
- checking the good potential behavior of each rule and of the whole rule set.

Testing is a technique used during a validation or a verification process. This technique is well suited for verifying the good working order of a Knowledge-based System or for evaluating the performances of the Knowledge-based System.

The first technique used by developers and customers is testing because there always exists some test cases. There may exist historical test cases when a Knowledge-based System replaces classical software or handmade procedure. During the acquisition process test cases may also be described. With testing the main problem is the representativity of test cases : How to be sure that the Knowledge-based System is sufficiently tested ?

THE FRAMEWORK OF THE WORKSHOP

We can distinguish five parts in this framework:

- General problems of validation
- Verification and Validation processes
- Coherence Checking
- Testing
- Completeness and reliability

General problems of validation

The paper by D.E. O'Leary, "Design, Development and Validation of Expert Systems : A Survey of Developers" is a good introduction to this book because it provides empirical evidence of the need for validation methods. It presents a survey of expert systems developers on designing, developing and validating expert systems by means of an enquiry sent to 80 users or developers.

L.F. Pau in "Validation, Evaluation and Maintenance of Knowledge-based Systems", focusses on the life cycle of the Knowledge-based System in which the validation process, and especially testing methods, have to take place. Industrial development of Knowledge-based Systems requires a life-cycle adapted to this kind of software. Such a life-cycle takes into account the building of mock-ups and prototypes. L.F. Pau presents guidelines as requirements for the Knowledge-based System development process.

T. Hoppe in "Aspects of Incremental Knowledge Validation", has focused his paper on the validation of Knowledge Bases. Two points of view are presented: first, the validation process is parallel with the acquisition process and both must be incremental. The second point of view concerns the necessity to take into account the customer's intention during the validation process. These customer's intentions cannot be expressed within one state of the Knowledge Base. All the KB developed during the life-cycle of a Knowledge-based System must conform to these intentions.

Verification and validation processes

The Verification and Validation of the Knowledge-based System process may, at the coarsest level, be divided into two approaches :

- considering the Knowledge-based System as a whole;
- studying the different parts of the Knowledge-based System and the behavior of this set of parts.

J. Tepandi, in "Comparison of Expert System Verification Criteria" shows the distinction between the structural (internal) and functional (external) aspects of verification. The first is characterized by syntactical properties or logical properties of the Knowledge Base. The second is concerned with the behavior of the Knowledge-based System and testing is appropiate.

M. Ayel and J.P. Laurent, in "SACCO and SYCOJET: Two different ways of verifying Knowledge-Based Systems", illustrate these two approaches with two systems, SYCOJET as a testing method and SACCO a coherence checking tool for the second approach. They show that these tools can be used both for verification and for validation.

A coherence checking method is not sufficient to provide a complete validation of the Knowledge-based System; some other forms of validation are needed. For example it is necessary to validate the software which controls the manipulation and accessing of the Knowledge Base.

The work presented by P.J. Krause, P. Byers, S. Hajnal and J. Fox in "The Use of Object-Oriented Process Specification for the Validation and Verification of Decision Support Systems", is concerned with this last topic. Their solution is to define a formal specification of the intended behavior and properties of the system.

Coherence checking

We have already, seen, with M. Ayel and J.P. Laurent, the SACCO system for the detection of incoherence in Knowledge-based Systems. Now with E. Charles and O. Dubois in "MELODIA : Logical Methods for Checking Knowledge Bases", we can discover Boolean techniques for detecting inconsistencies, redundancies and hidden theorems in Knowledge Bases using rules and integrity constraints.

Testing

Testing is more often used than other techniques. V. Guibert, A. Beauvieux, and M. Haziza in "Consistency, Soundness and Completeness of a Diagnosis System" show us an application of testing in the domain of troubleshooting and controlling a satellite. In that application, the set of test cases is given.

With P. Mazas, in "Design Knowledge Validation Through Experimentation", the set of test cases has to be generated. The application domain is a conception domain with many numeric constraints.

COMPLETENESS AND RELIABILITY

P. Lafon in "A Descriptive Model of Predicates for Verifying Production Systems", is concerned with the completeness and the consistency of a Knowledge Base. The predicates are the means of expressing both completeness properties and consistency properties. He observes that these predicates are very often implicit knowledge added to the Knowledge Bases, but this knowledge is very important to the verification point of view.

S. Grunwald in "Estimation of Failure Potential in Knowledge Bases" studies the reliability of a Knowledge Base. He defines an entropy as the measure of the failure potential of the predictive inference. He assumes that this entropy is related to the incompleteness of the Knowledge Bases, and its analysis leads to identification of the weak points of the Knowledge Bases.

L. de Raedt, G. Sablon and M. Bruynooghe in "Using Interactive Concept-Learning for Knowledge Base Validation and Verification", use the interactive concept-learning environment CLINT to redefine, from examples, all the concepts of the Knowledge Base. This technique allows each concept to be verified one after another, but also the behavior of the Knowledge-based System on the set of examples.

"CONKRET : A Control Knowledge Refinement Tool", the paper by B. Lopez, presents a tool for refining a set of meta-rules. In this case it is necessary to assume that the domain knowledge has already been checked. CONKRET uses a library of cases, a library of traces and strategies expected to be followed by the system for a given case.

S. Craw in "Judging Knowledge Base Quality" defines a metric for Knowledge Base quality based on "performance" which is obtained from statistics for rules which are responsible for incorrect diagnoses. A refinement generator may suggest all possible refinements to correct a faulty diagnosis.

CONCLUSION

This set of 14 papers is quite an extensive overview of the research and development in the Validation, Verification and Test domain. It is not, however, an exhaustive overview of both academics and industrial companies which are working on this domain.

After this first European workshop we observe that the number of European companies which are working in this domain is increasing year after year. Success in world competition for AI products depends on the capability to possess good development methodologies and Validation tools.

Marc AYEL
Jean Pierre LAURENT
April 1991

PART A

GENERAL PROBLEMS OF VALIDATION

1

Design, Development and Validation of Expert Systems : A Survey of Developers

Daniel E. O'LEARY

ABSTRACT

This paper discusses a survey of developers of expert systems. Although previous researchers have developed frameworks and performed case studies, there is little empirical work on developers, views about the two primary development methodologies (prototyping and traditional software engineering), determining who performs the validation effort, the relationship between the validation budget and actual expenditures, and the use and effectiveness of various validation processes.

Prototyping is found to yield more robust models, without requiring more effort, than alternative methods. In addition, prototyping is found to be amenable to incorporation of activities such as requirements definitions, milestone setting and establishing completion dates.

It also is found that the effectiveness and the use of validation techniques are highly correlated. Interestingly, roughly 98% of the validation appears to be done using test data, direct examination of knowledge bases and parallel use of systems. Validation budget areas are used and sometimes exceeded, thus, indicating that validation is a critical activity that is performed by most developers.

As in knowledge acquisition, human participation in the validation process appears to be a major bottleneck. Experts appear to be the source of roughly 50%

21/10/98

use of techniques

of the validation effort. This suggests the need to develop techniques that allow greater leveraging of expertise. Finally, in an assessment of a wide range of potential problems, the completeness, correctness, and accuracy of knowledge bases were found to be the most important problems. This indicates where to focus validation resources and efforts.

1. INTRODUCTION

Much of the expert systems research [4] is theoretical or single case study oriented (e.g., the development of a single system). Little empirical work has been done beyond the analysis of single systems. The purpose of this paper is to mitigate that gap by investigating two basic sets of issues: design and development of expert systems (primarily through and examination of the acceptance and use of the prototyping approach) and validation of expert systems. This was done using a survey of developers.

Promulgate = to spreed widely (2) to use

1.1 Design and development of expert systems

There has been substantial research in the area of prototyping general information systems [9] and decision support systems. The extensive bibliography of [7] illustrates that wide-ranging literature. The work on prototyping research in information systems has ranged from theoretical to empirical. For example, [2] compared prototyping information system to more   structured life-cycle approaches.

Many expert systems and artificial intelligence researchers was promulgated the use of prototyping [6] and others have examined the uses and controls appropriate for prototyping of expert systems [12]. Still, as expert systems have moved out of the research lab and into practical settings, the implications for implementation of prototyping in a "real world" setting have not been explored. For example, does the prototype approach interfere with the validation process ?

In addition, other researchers have begun to emphasize the use of more traditional software engineering approaches [3]. However, unlike general information systems, there has been little empirical research to compare the acceptance and use of those two methodologies in the development of expert systems. Mitigating that limitation is one objective of this paper.

Situation   *study*

1.2 Validation of expert systems

Closely associated with the development of an expert system is the validation of that system. Validation researchers have developed frameworks for the validation process [12, 13] provided case studies of the validation process [15] and analyzed the need for validation efforts in the development of expert systems [11].

Unfortunately, there is little evidence to indicate that any given validation approach is more effective or even which approaches are used.

In addition, there are a number of other implementation issues that have not been addressed in the literature. For example, do developers of expert systems have budgets for validation, and what is the relationship to actual expenditures.

Similarly theoretical analyses have been developed for who should perform the validation process, yet little empirical evidence exists on what is done in practice. Thus, a second objective of this paper is to gather empirical evidence as to the methods used to validate expert systems, examine the validation budget process and understand who actually performs the validation process.

1.3 Biggest problems

Since the validation process is so intertwined with the design and development processes, there is some interest in determining the relative importance of the validation process. One approach to that issue is to ask developers of expert systems to assess the importance of different potential problems that include both validation issues and more general issues of system performance. If validation issues are found to be important then their rank will either be about the same or more important than those other issues.

In addition, it is critical to be able to assess which validation issues are the most important. Since constrained resources are always an issue in a system development process, there is a need to obtain guidance on where to focus validation efforts. Unfortunately, there is little empirical evidence on what are the biggest potential system development and validation problems. This is a third objective of this paper.

1.4 Uniqueness of artificially intelligent systems and expert systems

This paper investigates the design, development and validation of expert systems. Thus, it is assumed that expert systems are different from other types of computer systems. It is not the purpose of this paper to explore those differences. However, those differences include : a focus on symbolic knowledge rather than numeric ; investigation of previously unstructured problems ; and inclusion of both symbolic and numerical information in the same program (e.g., rules of the form "if then" and uncertainty factors on the weights) ; and the general lack of a means by which to determine the quality of a solution, other than a comparison to a human's decision.

1.5 Plan of this paper

This paper proceeds as follows. The design and development and the validation are treated separately in the next two sections. Section 2 reviews the previous research on the design and development of expert systems using prototyping and software engineering approaches and summarizes the specific issues to be examined. Section 3 reviews some of the primary validation issues in expert systems and summarizes the specific issues examined in this research. Section 4 discusses the test instrument and sample that participated in the study. Section 5 discusses the findings. Section 6 briefly summarizes the paper.

2. DESIGN AND DEVELOPMENT OF EXPERT SYSTEMS

As noted above there are two basic theoretical design approaches that have been promulgated for the design and development of expert systems : prototyping [6] and [12] and software engineering [3,16]. Those studies provide a basis for the choice of some of the relationships examined in this paper.

In addition, there has been research on the use of prototyping in information systems and decision support systems. Although expert systems are unique, because they are computer systems, it is likely that some of the variables important to prototyping information systems and decision support systems will be also important for expert systems. However, this is not to say that the effects will be the same. Instead, it is likely that the unique aspects of expert systems will have an impact on the type of effect of the variables. These studies are another source of some of the variable studied in this paper.

The following summarizes the research issues addressed in the test instrument used as the basis of this paper. The subsection titles include in parentheses the questions in the research study discussed in those subsections. The questions are summarized in table 2.

2.1 Prototyping leads to robust models (1)

A critical aspect of an expert system is its "robustness". If the system is unable to respond to the demands placed upon it, then the system may not receive continued use. Thus, robustness generally would be viewed as a highly desirable characteristic. The interactive development associated with the prototyping approach would appear to lead to a more robust system since there would be constant user feedback on the quality of the system's responses.

However, Boehm et al. [2] found that prototyping yielded a slightly lower level of robustness for general information systems. There are at least two reasons why this finding probably would not hold in the area of expert systems. First, the finding may be, in part, a function of the level of the complexity of the information systems that were developed. If the systems are not complex then an initial requirements analysis may be able to anticipate the primary and additional needs of the users. Since an expert system is likely to be addressing a more complex or initially less structured problem, it would appear that the substantial user feedback associated with prototyping would contribute to the robustness of the system. Second, in the development of an expert system there is typically substantial asymmetry of expertise : the expert knows more about the domain than the developers of the system. Unless the knowledge engineer also is an expert, it would be difficult to anticipate additional user needs as may be done in more traditional information systems. Unless the system contains sufficient domain knowledge, it will not be robust. Thus, the interaction associated with prototyping could help establish a more robust system.

2.2 Prototyping facilitates development of specifications (2)

One of the differences between a traditional software engineering approach and prototyping is the generation of requirements. If the objectives and processes of the system are well known, a priori, then the development of the specifications is a relatively structured task. However, in the case of expert systems, the tasks the systems are to accomplish often are not, a priori, well structured. The notion of prototyping [6] is consistent with the iterative development of specifications. Prototypes offer a vehicle with which developer and client can use to agree on specifications. This can be particularly important when the system is being developed for some other company. The author is familiar with a consulting firm that has indicated that it uses prototypes as the basis of eliciting a set of specifications. Thus, prototypes may be a useful tool in delineating specifications in other firms.

2.3 Prototypes are difficult to manage and control (3)

Alavi [1] found that "the designers of the prototyped information system experienced more difficulty managing and controlling system experienced more difficulty managing and controlling the design process." That finding was attributed in part to the higher level of user participation and the more frequent changes in user requirements. There does not appear to be any unique aspect in assuming that expert systems should be any easier to manage and control with the prototyping process.

2.4 Software engineering as an approach for expert systems (4)

An alternative to the prototyping approach is the software engineering approach. As a result, recent researchers such as Bull et al. [3], have suggested the use of software engineering, rather than a prototyping approach. They report successful use with that approach. Thus, we would anticipate that software engineering would be a feasible tool for developing expert systems.

2.5 Management tools for prototyping (5, 6, 8)

Alavi [1] found that project managers suggested that prototyping was more difficult to manage, in part since " due to the newness of the nature of prototyping, there is a lack of know-how for planning, budgeting, managing and control". Thus, management may be more difficult because prototyping might not allow easy use of milestones, completion dates or allow for the development of formal deliverables, all part of the traditional software engineering process [16].

As a result, in a discussion on "how to prototype" Alavi suggested integrating devices of this type (milestones, completion dates and deliverables) into the prototyping process. In addition, researchers such as Bull et al. [3] have promulgated traditional software engineering development of expert systems, that include such devices. Thus, it would be expected that devices associated with the management and controlling of systems projects would be embedded into either a prototyping approach or software engineering approach and that they would facilitate management of the process.

2.6 Prototyping makes it more difficult to validate (7)

Since prototyping is less structured than more traditional software engineering methods and more difficult to control, it has been found in field studies of the use of prototyping in information systems [1] that testing activities could be bypassed or performed superficially. This would suggest that prototyping could inhibit validation.

However, in the case of expert systems, since expertise is present in the expert, the interactive approach of prototyping offers an important opportunity to validate the system. In particular, in some cases only the expert will be able to determine if the system is solving the problem correctly or solving the correct problem. As a result, the prototyping process is likely to facilitate a timely and constant validation effort.

2.7 Prototyping takes more effort (9)

In an experiment of seven software teams, Boehm et al. [2] found that prototyping yielded products that were about the same in performance as more traditional software engineering approaches, yet had 40 percent less code and 45 percent less effort. There is no apparent reason to assume that the expert system environment would be any different. Thus, prototyping of expert systems would be expected to take less effort.

3. VALIDATION OF EXPERT SYSTEMS

Researchers have developed frameworks in which to couch the validation efforts and they have provided a number of different methods to assist in the validation process. However, there is little empirical work available regarding which tools are used, how effective they are, who performs the validation efforts, do budgets exist for validation, what happens to validation budgets (are they used) and what are the primary validation difficulties.

3.1 Validation methods

O'Leary [11] identified a number of different methods for the validation of expert systems, including : testing with actual data, testing with contrived test data, direct examination of the knowledge base by either an expert or the knowledge engineer, parallel use of the system by either an expert or a non-expert, and contingency tables. Of concern are at least two sets of issues. First, to what extent are these validation tools used, if at all. Second, to what extent are these tools effective.

Testing with actual data, tests the system with the same type of requirements that it is likely to face if it is implemented. Since the validator is able to assess the system in "real life" situations (deriving some level of "comfort") and see the direct effectiveness of the system in those situations, the effectiveness may exceed the extent of the effort.

Testing with contrived data can focus the validation efforts on either extreme points or particular parts of the system of greatest concern. Unfortunately, the development of test data may take a substantial effort, while the success at ferreting out problems is not necessarily guaranteed. In fact, the difficulties of developing contrived data have led some to suggest that intelligent systems be developed to design that test data.

Direct examination of the knowledge base is another tool that can assist in the validation process. If the knowledge is in a readable form then it may prove quite useful for the expert to examine the system. Unless the knowledge engineer understands the domain a similar examination by the knowledge engineer may not yield useful insights.

Another approach that can be useful for validation of the system is to use the system in parallel with the decision maker. Such parallel usage may be done by the expert or a naive user. Since the expert typically is actively involved in the development of such systems, parallel use by the expert may not yield substantial insights. Alternatively, use by a non-expert may generate a substantial number of validation inquiries. This may called the "emperor's new clothes effect". A user unfamiliar with the system and many of the assumptions entailed may find many difficulties.

Finally, other statistical tools or contingency tables might be used to assist in the validation process. These validation methods are summarized in table 2.

3.2 Who performs the validation process

O'Leary [14] elicited a number of different potential validators including : the same expert from whom knowledge was gathered, a different expert than from whom the knowledge was gathered, the knowledge engineer, the end user, a sponsor of the system, or an independent validator. Each of these potential validators is listed in table 3.

Using the *same expert* from whom the knowledge was gathered has both advantages and disadvantages. In the first case, the expert has been a part of the project and thus, the effort has captured their expertise. In addition, the expert has thought about what it takes to structure the problem as a system. Finally, that expert is accessible. In the second case, since the expert has worked with the system this might indicate that overlooked assumptions continue to be overlooked and that the expert may be too close to the system design and development effort to note inconsistencies, incompleteness, etc.

A different expert offers advantages such as the potential for another view of the problem and an awareness of unstated assumptions in the model. However, there are also potential disadvantages such as a different model of the world (conservative vs. liberal), a lack of understanding of the problem that comes from the development of such a system or a lack of availability.

There is some evidence that the knowledge engineer becomes a "near expert" as they work on particular expert system projects [8]). This is critical to the validation effort, since if the knowledge engineer does not have an appropriate level of expertise then there may be only limited ability to validate the system. However, the knowledge engineer may be too close to the system or may have a vested interest in the system's use. In each case, these issues could influence the validation judgments of the knowledge engineer.

The ultimate *end user* may also play a part in the validation effort, depending on the extent of understanding of the problem. In many cases expert systems are developed so that decision making can be pushed down in the organization to lower level decision makers. In these cases the user may not provide substantial insight. However, for those cases where the systems are designed to assist a decision maker to ensure uniform quality or increased speed of processing, the user may provide substantial insights.

In some cases there may be a *sponsor* of the project. Again, as with the end user, the understanding of the sponsor can play a critical part. Probably the greatest independence of analysis would come from an *independent validator*. Unfortunately, there is little evidence to indicate that there is very much of that activity taking place.

3.3 Validation budget

As noted in Alavi [1], one concern with using prototyping of information systems is that testing could be either bypassed or performed in a superficial manner. A measure of whether or not an appropriate level of validation is performed are whether or not there is a budget for validation to meet or exceed budgeted expenditures.

3.4 Potential problems

In order to assess the relative importance of validation, in general, and some specific validation issues, in particular, a list of some of the more critical validation issues was developed. These validation issues, summarized in table 4, included completeness of the knowledge base, correctness of the knowledge in the knowledge base, and accuracy of the knowledge base in its interactions with the user. These issues are unique to the validation of expert systems since they all deal with the knowledge base of the system and include each of those delineated as knowledge base problems in O'Leary [13]. Inference engine issues were not included since many of the systems developed make use of existing expert system shells.

Another issue that is primarily a concern in the development of expert systems, sequencing of rules, was also included. This particular issue is a system construction issue to expert systems. It was included in order to assess the importance of such construction issues in relation to validation issues.

Finally, two generic information systems issues were also included. First, if a system is hard to use it can result in a lack of use of the system. Second, if the results generated by the system are difficult to interpret then that can also result in a lack of use of the system. These problems are often cited as major problems with information systems in general. Clearly, since these problems are critical issues. Their inclusion in the list of potential problems can provide insight into the general importance of validation issues.

4. TEST INSTRUMENT AND SAMPLE

Since there is little empirical evidence to substantiate many of the issues delineated in the previous two sections, a test instrument was developed and sent to a sample of developers of expert systems.

4.1 Test instrument

The test instrument gathered background information from the respondents, including "number of systems currently in use", "number of expert systems being developed" and industry classification".

The remainder of the questionnaire was divided into five different parts. Part 2, entitled "System Design and Development Approach," contained questions requesting a response to (-2, -1, 0, 1, 2), described as "Not True" (-2) to "True" (2).

Part 3 examined the validation budget asking the subject for the percentage of total development and the percentage of the implementation budget planned to go to validation and the percentage that actually goes to validation. Part 4 asked the user to rate eight different validation methods for the percentage of validation methods and for the percentage of validation effectiveness (e.g., testing with actual data). The percentages were required to sum to 100. Part 5 asked the subject to estimate the percentage of the total validation from whom knowledge was gathered. The percentages were required to sum to 100. Apparently, the section on validation is virtually complete, since two of the respondents reported informally that they used the instrument as a check list to assist in the validation process.

The final part asked the subject to assess "potential biggest problems". Subjects were asked to rank seven potential problems in terms of the impact on use of the system. A "1" was used to represent the biggest problems.

4.2 Sample

The test instrument was sent to 80 different subjects. The subjects were chosen because the author had accumulated either published information or private information indicating that the subjects had designed, developed and validated at least one expert system. Although this approach to choosing subjects for the test instrument was not random, it was viewed as necessary since the population of developers was small.

A single domain was chosen in order to normalize the impact of the domain. The domain, accounting and financial applications, was chosen because of the relatively large number of systems compared to other business domains, such as marketing.

The average respondent had 3.5 expert systems in use and 5.0 systems under development. If a subject responded and indicated that they did not develop expert systems they were removed from the sample. A single follow-up to the initial mailing was sent to those subjects that did not respond to the first mailing. The initial mailing was in January 1989 and the follow-up was in March 1989.

A total of 34 test instruments were received. This yielded a 42.5% response rate. Not all respondents answered each part of the questionnaire. The questions on the budget received the smallest response ; 28 respondents answered the first two sections, while 31 respondents answered the remaining portion of the test instrument.

4.3 Question construction

The questions were constructed so as to encourage response. In addition, the questions were aimed at finding out what developers do or do not do.

As a result, the questions reflect the way a trial sample of developers viewed the world. For example, three of the questions use the terms "... it is difficult, infeasible or impractical..." Although this phrase uses three terms (difficult, infeasible and impractical) all are reasons that developers gave for doing something, e.g., using completion dates. Further, professionals were gauged as not likely to take the time to answer three questions differing only by a single word (first difficult, then infeasible, then impractical).

The questions were initially developed and discussed with two developers. Then a revised questionnaire was developed. The two developers who assisted in the design were not included in the sample.

5. FINDINGS

5.1 Design and development of expert systems

5.1.1 Analysis of data

The results are given in table 1. The sign (+ or -) of all the questions was as expected, based on the discussion in section 2.

A number of the questions had relatively large average scores for a range of (-2, 2). Questions 8 (formal deliverables) and 9 (prototyping takes less effort) had absolute mean values of about 1 or greater. Questions 1 (robustness), 5 (milestones), 6 (completion dates), and 7 (validation) had absolute mean values between .59 and .79.

A t-test was used to test the statistical significance of the individual mean scores. For each question, the null hypothesis was that the mean score was equal to zero against the alternative that the score was either less than or greater than zero, depending on whether the value was respectively less than or greater than zero. If a score were potentially to take on an average value of zero this would suggest that the statement was not either "true" or "false," as would be indicated by the respective sign on the average response. All but questions 2, 3, and 4 were significant at the .01 level.

5.1.2 Interpretation

Question 1 indicates that prototyped expert systems indeed are thought to be more robust. On the other hand question 9 indicates that prototyping does not take more effort than more formal methods. Further, it appears that when prototyping is used, various management devices (milestones and completion dates) are built into the process (questions 5 and 6), as recommended by Alavi [1]. As noted in discussions with firms, it appears that prototypes are used as a basis of generating requirements (question 8). Finally, prototyped systems were not judged to be more difficult to validate (question 7).

5.2 Validation of expert systems

5.2.1 Validation methods

The results of the inquiry on validation methods are contained in table 2. The rank correlation between percentage validation effort and percentage validation effectiveness was .967. Thus, there is a very strong relationship between use and effectiveness.

The greatest percentage change of the percentage validation effort (36 %)was with parallel use of the system by a non-expert. The change on direct examination by an expert was -23%. These changes indicate that some techniques appear to provide more insight into the validation process. In the aggregate, the results indicate that roughly 49% of the validation effort is with some kind of test data, while another 30.6% is with direct examination of the knowledge base and 18.6% is with parallel use of the system.

As a result, 49.2% of the validation effort is done using human participants. Although knowledge elicitation is often called a bottleneck because of the extent of human participation, it appears that validation faces a similar concern.

Further, over 98% of the validation is with rather basic methods -- that is, not statistical or analytical. This suggests that there is substantial room for work in the development of techniques to assist in the validation of expert systems.

5.2.2 Validation budget

The respondents reported an average validation budget of 22.46%, while the actual reported validation budget averaged 23.78%. There were 14 respondents that reported that the budget and actual percentage were the same, 5 reported that the budget was less than actual and 9 reported that the budget was more than actual.

Thus, there are at least two pieces of evidence that indicate that even though prototyping was used, the validation budget was not eliminated. First, there were 28 out of the 34 respondents that reported a validation budget. Second, in 23 out of the 28, actual was at least as large as the budget.

5.2.3 Who performs the validation process

The results on the "who" side of validation are contained in table 3. These results indicate that roughly 50% of the validation effort is accomplished by experts in this domain. Clearly, this is in contrast to virtually any other kind of computer-based system. In addition, this indicates that validation is a very expensive process that could benefit from using alternative techniques, as opposed to focusing all those expert resources on the task. Finally, these results also indicate relatively minor use of end users, sponsors and independent validation.

5.3 Potential biggest problems

5.3.1 Analysis of data

The mean observations are summarized in table 4. A statistical analysis of the pairwise relationships between some of the means of the distribution of responses for each of the problem pairs is contained in table 5. A pairwise approach was used because importance is only established relative to other problems on the list and one of the primary concerns in this research is the relative importance of validation issues.

A t-test was used to compare the mean values of the responses to the average response value for problems 4 and 5 (used to represent non-validation problems). This results are summarized in table 5. For each question (1, 2, 3) the hypothesis was that the average response for problems 4 and 5 was rated as not important, while the hypothesis for questions 6 and 7 was that problems 1, 2, 3 and 7 were found to be statistically significant. This indicates that the validation problems (1, 2, 3) are viewed as being more difficult than non-validation issues to which they were compared.

5.3.2 Interpretation

The results are summarized in table 4. The three most highly ranked problems were validation problems, each of which seem relatively unique to expert systems and other intelligent technologies. "Completeness of the knowledge base" was recognized as the most difficult problem in roughly one third of the responses and the first or second problem in almost one-half of the responses. It also had the lowest average score, and thus was recognized as the major problem. "Ensuring correctness of the knowledge base" had the second lowest average and the second highest number of being either first or second ranked. "System misses some possible opportunities" had the third lowest average score and tied for third place in total number of first and second rankings.

The next two lowest ranking occurred for "System is hard to use" and "Results from the system are difficult to interpret." These two alternatives are not unique to expert systems technology, but instead are problems of systems in general.

The two remaining problems in the list given to subjects are unique to expert systems : "System presents incorrect opportunities" and "sequencing rules." These problems were found to be ranked first or second in only five of the responses. The rankings also establish the importance of validation problems, since validation issues had three highest average rankings.

6. SUMMARY

This paper has presented the results of a survey of expert systems developers on designing, developing and validating expert systems. This study supplements previous theoretical analysis and case studies.

The prototyping development methodology is found to lead to more robust systems. However, prototyping apparently does not increase the difficulty of validating systems, probably because of the increased level of communications. Prototyping seems to take less effort than a software engineering approach. Further, it does appear that some developers have built various devices (completion dates and milestones) into the prototyping process. Finally, a prototyping approach can be used as the basis for defining the deliverables.

The survey provides empirical evidence for the use and effectiveness of particular validation methods. For example, it was found that roughly 50% of the validation effort employs a test data approach. In addition, the validation process appears very labour intensive, thus possibly becoming a bottleneck, as with knowledge acquisition.

The study also found a prevalent use of budgets for managing the validation process. Based on self-reporting in the study, those budgets are roughly adhered to.

Further, the study indicated who performs the validation process. Roughly 50% of the validation effort is performed by experts. This indicates that validation is an expensive process that could benefit from the development and use of validation tools.

In addition, the paper finds that validation problems are among the biggest problems facing developers. The issues of completeness, correctness and accuracy of the knowledge base are viewed as the most difficult.

Table 1
System Design and Development Approach[*]

No. Ques	Expected Sign	Mean	Std. Dev	Questions
1	+	0.76	1.059	We have found that prototyping leads to more robust expert systems than more formal software engineering approaches.[&]
2	+	0.32	1.489	We use prototyping development methodologies for expert systems because it is difficult, infeasible, or impractical to develop "specifications" for AI/ES projects.
3	+	-0.17	1.294	We have found that prototyping an expert system is a more difficult approach to manage than software engineering approaches.
4	-	-0.505	1.304	We have found that traditional software engineering methods just don't work in the development of AI/ES projects.
5	-	-0.59	1.308	We use prototyping development methodologies for expert systems because it is difficult, infeasible or impractical to develop "milestones" for AI/ES projects. [&]
6	-	-0.61	1.358	We use prototyping development methodologies for expert systems because it is difficult, infeasible, or impractical to develop completion dates for AI/ES projects. [&]
7	-	-0.79	1.022	We have found that prototyping expert systems, rather than using traditional software engineering methods leads to systems that are more difficult to validate. [&]
8	-	-0.97	0.923	We don't use prototyping because it doesn't allow for formal deliverables, which makes it difficult to know when the system is complete or when formal sign-of. can be made. [&]
9	-	-1.03	1.175	We have found that prototyping takes more effor than more formal methods to develop the same typc of system. [&]

Not True				True	
-2	-1	0	1	2	

[*] Subjects were asked to "circle a number between -2 and 2.".
[&] Significantly different from 0 at .01 level.

Table 2
Validation Methods

Method	%Validation Effort	%Validation Effectiveness	Increase (Decrease)
Testing with actual data	31.1	33.5	2.4
Testing with contrived data	17.9	16.3	(1.6)
Direct examination of knowledge base by expert	17.6	17.1	(0.5)
Direct examination of knowledge base by knowledge Engineer	13.0	10.0	(3.0)
Parallel use of system by expert	11.6	12.1	0.5
Parallel use of system by non-expert	7.0	9.5	2.5
Decision tables/ contingency tables	1.4	1.1	(0.3)
Other	0.3	0.3	0.0
Total	99.9◊	99.9◊	

Table 3
"Who Generally Performs the Validation Process ?"

Percentage	Job Category
29.6	Same expert from whom knowledge was gathered
20.3	Knowledge engineer
20.1	Different expert than from whom the knowledge was gathered
12.4	End user
9.5	"Sponsor" of the project
7.5	Independent validator
.3	"Other"
99.7	Total (difference from 100 due to rounding error by some respondents)

◊ Differences due to rounding error by respondents.

Table 4
"Potential Biggest Problems" (subjects were asked to rank the problems from 1 to 7 with 1 used to denote the biggest problem).

Problem Number	Average Rank	First	Ranked Second	Ranked Problem	
1	3.10	10	5		Determining cmpleteness knowledge Base
2	3.12	5	7		Difficult to ensure that the Knowledge in the system is correct
3	3.21	5	6		System does not present some possible opportunities to the user
4	3.89	8	3		System is hard to use
5	4.11	3	5		Results from the system are difficult to interpret
6	4.32	1	5		System presents some incorrect opportunities to the user
7	4.78	1	4		Difficult to sequence rules correctly

Table 5
Pairwise Level of Significance of Test of Similarity of Distributions for "Potential Biggest Problems"

Problem	Problem 4	Problem 5
1	0.025	0.01
2	0. 01	0.01
3	0.05	0.01
4	NA	NS
5	NS	NA
6	NS	NS
7	0.025	0.05

NS = Not significant and NA = Not applicable, otherwise significantly different at the specified.

REFERENCES

1.   ALAVI M., (1984) : *An Assessment of the Prototyping Approach to Information Systems Development*, Communications of the ACM, Vol. 27, No. 6, June 1984, pp. 556-563.
2.   BOEHM B., GRAY T., SEEWALDT T., (1984) : *Prototyping Versus Specifying : A Multiproject Experiment*, IEEE Transactions on Software Engineering, Vol. SE 10, No. 3, May 1984, pp. 290-303.
3.   BULL M., DUDA R., PORT D. AND REITER J., (1987) : *Applying Software Engineering Principles to Knowledge-base Development*, Proceedings of the First Annual Conference on Expert Systems in Business,   New York, November 10-12, 1987, pp. 27-38.
4.   CHANDLER J., LIANG T., (1990) : *Developing Expert Systems for Business Applications*, Merrill Publishing, Columbus, Ohio.

5.   GOLDBERG A., (1986) : *Knowledge-Based Programming : A Survey of Program Design and Construction Techniques*, IEEE Transactions on Software Engineering, Vol SE 12, No. 7, 1986, pp. 752-768.

6.   HAYES-ROTH F., WATERMAN D., AND LENAT D., (1983) : *Building Expert Systems*, Addison-Wesley, Reading, Massachusetts.

7.   JENKINS M., FELLER R., (1986) : *An Annotated Bibliography on Prototyping*, Institute for Research on the Management of Information Systems, Indiana University, June.

8.   LETHAN H., JACOBSEN H., (1987) : *ESKORT -- An Expert System for Auditing VAT Accounts*, Proceedings of Expert Systems and Their Applications, Avignon, France.

9.   NAUMANN J., JENKINS M., (1982) : *Prototyping : The New Paradigm for Systems Development*, MIS Quarterly, September 1982, pp. 29-44.

10.   O'LEARY, D., (1990) : *Validation of Expert Systems*, Decision Sciences, Vol. 18, No. 3, 1987, pp. 468-486, in Chandler and Liang.

11   O'LEARY, D., (1990) : *Soliciting Weights or Probabilities From Experts for Rule-Based Systems*, International Journal of Man-Machine Studies, Volume 32, pp. 293-301.

12.   O'LEARY, D., (1988-a) : *Expert Systems Prototyping as a Research Tool*, in Applied Expert Systems, E. Turban and P. Watkins, (eds) North-Holland.

13.   O'LEARY, D., (1988-b) : *Methods of Validating Expert Systems*, Interfaces, November-December, 1988-b, pp. 72-79.

14.   O'LEARY,D., (1987) : *Validation of Expert Systems*, Decision Sciences, Summer 1987, Vol. 18.

15.   O'LEARY D., KANDELIN N., (1988) : *Validating the Weights in Rule-Based Expert Systems : a Statistical Approach*, International Journal of Expert Systems, Volume 1, N° 3, pp. 253-279.

16.   PRESSMAN R., (1987) : Software Engineering, 2nd edition,   McGraw-Hill, New York.

2

Guidelines for Prototyping, Validation and Maintenance of Knowledge-based Systems Software

L.F. PAU

ABSTRACT

chapter reports the results of evaluating

This paper provides some guide lines useful for the prototyping, validation, evaluation and maintenance of knowledge-based systems software. The major concerns addressed by these guide lines are to achieve final operational use of the *system* software, in terms of :

i   speed performance
ii memory occupation
iii reliability of the results
iv consistency of knowledge base
v   user friendliness
vi updating capabilities

These concerns are addressed within the framework of using a software life - cycle sequence.

The guidelines serve standardization and requirements specification work in industry and government.

ABREVIATIONS :

AI	Artificial Intelligence	SCD	Software Control Document
ATN	Augmented Transition Network	SM	Software maintenance
KA	Knowledge Acquisition	SRD	Software Requirements Document
KB	Knowledge Base	SW	Software
KBS	Knowledge Based Systems	URD	Users Requirements Document

1. INTRODUCTION

In terms of software development, KBS exhibit some features, which alone or combined pose some significant challenges to their prototyping, testing, validation :

i   KBS operate in domains in which the precise effect of an action is not always predictable;

ii   KBS operate in incomplete domains, in that data crucial for a decision may be missing or uncertain, or

iii   KBS operate in domains so large that it may not be practicable to establish the precise effect of an action.

The challenges resulting from these features are :

i   the ability of KBS to explore large domains on the basis of heuristics, and evolution of the heuristics over time;

ii   dependence of KBS on a formal conceptual model of the application domain;

iii   inclusion of an explanatory and of an interactive display component.

This paper surveys the programming process, specific for KBS, by systematizing some steps and automating others [29] in the KBS software systems life - cycle.

This paper does not present specific research techniques, but on the contrary specific operational validation and test requirements on KBS, as enforced in large real-life projects and contracts [20]. Also, the guidelines are the basis for standards work, and have been tested out on a variety of large projects.

2. KBS PROTOTYPE SPECIFICATION STUDY

A KBS project starts with a specification study, during which the potential application is considered with particular attention to its suitability for KBS techniques, and also during which the user requirements are compiled. At the end of this phase, two documents will be published, both concerning the prototype. The first one will be URD (Users Requirements Document); it will identify the domains of expertise, and the main functions of the KBS.

The second document will be a draft SRD (Software Requirements Document); the SRD will identify the source(s) of expertise (human experts, books, ...) and will define the hardware and software environment in which the prototype will be developed, (tested) and executed; the relationship with the operational environment will be established and described as in regular software certification standards [30, 11].

The production of the URD is quite straightforward; the case is different with the SRD, because the AI part of the software (knowledge base, reasoning, ...) does not lend itself very well to being specified in that phase; it will be the main objective of the feasibility phase (see below) to consolidate the SRD. This is the reason why only a draft SRD is asked for at the end of the preliminary study, to be finalised at the end of the next phase. This draft SRD will deal mainly with those parts of the KBS which can be considered as conventional software (e.g. user's interfaces, data base interface, file transfer, archiving, documentation,....), and partly only with the AI part (e.g. : requirements on a shell,...).

Never forget that the process of writing specifications is at least as error-prone as the process of programming; thus, substantial incremental checking must be done on the specifications themselves during the subsequent phases. It is here that the URD interacts with the SRD, because valid transformations on formal specifications need not be a true representation of the needs of the user [12].

3. KBS PROTOTYPE FEASIBILITY PHASE

The aims of the feasibility phase are to confirm the feasibility of the KBS, to take a number of decisions concerning knowledge representation and structure of the knowledge base, to evaluate the size of that base, to select an inference engine, to identify the constraints on the hardware and basic software to be used for the prototype, and finally to complete the software requirements document SRD for the prototype. In order to archieve these goals, a representative sub-domain will be selected, and implementation trials (also called feasibility demos) will be performed in an ad - hoc existing software development environment.

The main output of the feasibility phase will be the final SRD; the URD may also be updated at the light of the experimental results. The SRD may be rewritten using a domain-specific specification language.

Developing a demo should be considered more as an experiment than as a software project; in particular, no requirements document will be issued. The manpower necessary for this phase should be small; for this purpose, there will be no other user interface than the one offered by the environment (hardware and software) in which the feasibility demo is developed; for the same reason, no hardware interface will be provided; finally the demo will not be a formal deliverable item. The demo development will be made in successive iterations, reopening issues until the objectives described earlier are met satisfactorily. Then the prototype requirements documents (SRD, URD) will be finalised.

4. KBS PROTOTYPING PHASE

The prototype is the first full-scale implementation of the KBS addressing the complete domain identified in the URD. The objective of this phase is to evaluate the KBS functions before developing an operational system. The main decisions made in the preceding phase will be implemented. The interface will allow to evaluate the KBS to be evaluated in good conditions, i.e.:

- the user interfaces will provide an easy and friendly access to the KBS capabilities (pseudo-natural language for consultation, clear explanation of the reasoning path,...);

- the hardware interfaces will at least simulate the operational I/O, so that the evaluation can be carried out on realistic data.

The prototype will be developed in the hardware and software environment as defined in the preceding phase; in some cases, it might be necessary that this environment be identical (or compatible) to the target system to be used for the operational KBS.

The prototype will be developed iteratively, each cycle involving some modification of the knowledge base, and then testing and evaluating the KBS. It will be important to control the knowledge-base configuration with respect to the tests which have been performed.

The prototype will be a software system (possibly including hardware) to be delivered to the client. The delivery will include an adequate documentation set, which will comprise

- all documents concerning the prototype. These will treat not only the software development as such, but also the knowledge acquisition and the knowledge base;

- an evaluation and validation report, which will describe the results of the experiments undertaken with various configurations of the knowledge base (see Section 5);

- if needed, an update of the URD and SRD applicable to the operational system.

To increase the reliability of the KBS prototype, it is advisable to use correctness preserving transformations during prototype development. Also, declarative statements must be separated from procedural statements, and declarative statements must be fully explained.

5. KBS TESTING

5.1 KBS testing

The classical benchmarking approach does not generally apply to KBS, as different inputs are possible for different user queries and user defined information [5 , 17].

Concerning the inferences procedures, testing can be carried out in many cases though accessibility evaluation in state transitions.

Concerning the knowledge base, testing is always carried out after KB organization into segments ("Worlds", "Methods" or "Flavors"). Rules and facts are formally sorted in each segment by lexicographic techniques. Word count statistics are produced, especially to check on imbalance between the extent of the rules and facts involving specific symbols (assumed physically meaningful). When logic programming is used, constraints are propagated throughout to detect loops, loose leaves, etc.

Testing should detect incorrect rules or facts in the knowledge base, by a series of test sessions which allocate results in equivalence classes of validity. Such incorrect rules/facts can be either missing, supplementary, or wrong. Coverage analysis (percentage of rules fired) can detect most wrong rules and some missing rules after validation classes allocation. Supplementary rules are detected by their non-use in coverage analysis.

Concerning the user interface, evaluation criteria are specified. The users grade the interface. The set of grades are analysed by multivariate statistical analysis to show basic correlated deficiencies [19].

Concerning inference and updating speeds, counts are maintained on :

i   number of inferences for each specific reasoning procedure and test KB ;
ii   speed for the inferences i ;
iii variance of i, or range ;
iv   variance of ii, or range ;
v   size of compiled KBS code (if compiled), and number or lines of source ;
vi   size of compiled KB, number of KB segments, and number of lines of source.

Concerning inference results, whenever possible, decision tables [19] are prepared to compare the KBS output against that of an expert, and separately against user performance. Such tables are confusion matrices : $M = (m_{ij})$ where m_{ij} is the frequency by which the KBS system generates assumption (j) whenever the expert (or user) selected assumption (i). Non-diagonal terms give false explanation, and non-explanation probabilities.

Inference is further tested by convergence testing methods requiring functional or structural test sessions; these can be developed for logic programming environments [23].

5.2 KB testing

The key to the KBS testing is the hierarchical decomposition of the knowledge base. This is done by decomposing the KB into its three functions :

- stating knowledge ;
- using knowledge ;
- maintaining and deleting knowledge.

From the KBS specifications SRD, it must be established which segments in KB are used, and how, and when. Then the KB memory must be segmented/paginated and formatted accordingly, so that at any given time, the inference engine does not have to search through a KB segment which is not relevant anyway. A mechanism to achieve this is to have a tree of files, where the extend of information access grows with the level in the tree.

The KB decomposition is evaluated through counts of the frequencies by which the branches in the tree are accessed.

When the knowledge base is written so as to obey a context-free grammar with terminal and non-terminal symbols (which may also be represented as an AND/OR tree), the validation includes the following tests :

i   accessibility of any terminal symbol from non terminal symbols, by tree search (bottom up, left to right); cycles must be those detected;
ii   agreement between the non-terminals appearing in the rules, and the list of such symbols as used to define the grammar;
iii validation of incorrect user input during KBS operations, that is entry of incorrect facts by the user; such validation may use session drivers and syntactic controls;
iv   validation of the attribute calculation procedures, by a test of algorithmic completeness and detection of indeterminism [7].

5.3 KB testing metric

The KB test procedures i-iii of Section 5.3 allow, together with the KB editor grammar or KB language grammar G, the implementation of calculations of the Levenshtein distance between knowledge base segments x and y :

$$d(x,y) = Min (n_s, n_d, n_i)$$

which is the smallest number of transformations to derive y from x in agreement with G, following :

- n_s substitutions of terminal symbols ;
- n_d deletions of terminal symbols ;
- n_i insertions of terminal symbols ;
after exclusion of rule separators.

This has , for example, been extensively tested in financial KBS [21].

6. KBS VALIDATION AND EVALUATION

6.1 Evaluation and validation criteria

When reaching the final KBS development stage, evaluation and validation criteria must be specified in detail. Among them are :

* Speed performance : inference
* Speed performance : editing
* Speed performance : support calculations, typically numeric
* Dynamic access to different segments of knowledge base (see Section 5.2)
* I/O rates to disk
* I/O rates to external peripherals or data links
* SW portability
* Software completeness (knowledge base, inference engine)
* Software accuracy (inference engine, user interface, utilities)
* Knowledge base consistency
* Contents/format ergonomics
* Self-descriptiveness (explanation facilities display)
* Modifiability (knowledge base editor, reasoning procedure editor)
* Software metrics

6.2 Validation procedure

(A) To validate the KBS, one may use from the beginning a formal specification tool or notation (like Z, VDM, or PROLOG procedural flowgraph representations by logic assertions). At each stage, mathematical proofs are used to check the software design; most of these proofs relate to checks on graph representations of causalities, flows and structure by finite state automata tools [18].

It should be noted that flowgraph methods do not apply to languages like LISP, SMALLTALK; however, irreducible or primes can be used in a similar way to map causalities, flows and structures (especially relational).

(B) Because of this limitation, software metrics should be used. Depending on the AI language selected, complexity and granularity measures are defined as related to structure and coding compactness. Complexity composition rules can be defined (R. Prather, V. Basili, N. Fenton).

Metrics and program verification are typically easier for PROLOG and ADA [16]. Metrics help match software complexity over time with the computing resources available.

(C) To validate the inference part of the KBS, irrespective of KB contents and organization, it is useful to relate the inference source code to its control-flow graphs. The flowgraphs may be represented in set notation, composed from and decomposed into prime components, e.g. in the Z specification language [9]. Graph theoretic metrics then can be applied to the control-flow graphs, to answer requirements from Sections 6.1 and 6.2 (B).

D) To validate KBS outputs, irrespective of combinatorics hereof, path-oriented complexity should be reduced by linearizing methods and by mapping the logic flows.

(E) Some commercial KBS validation services exist relying on conventional software testing, but few on KBS intricacies. This includes regression test systems and test completeness assessment for LISP and PROLOG. None of these services addresses KB validation, nor the testing of hybrid KBS involving symbolic conventional languages, and pipes or communications protocols.

7. DOCUMENTATION

Any software development must include the writing of documentation, to be the subject of reviews. This statement is applicable to KBS, but the list and contents of these documents will depart from the standard in several aspects :

- The SRD must specify the knowledge to be contained in the system, and this before that knowledge is acquired. The SRD will be used, at the end of the prototype phase, to perform the validation/acceptance tests (comparing the software with its specifications).

- The iterative development of the prototype, and the progressive build-up of the knowledge-base, imposes a strict software configuration control; an additional document will be produced for that purpose, a Software Control Document (SCD); it will identify the state of the KBS as a function of time, the tests performed on it and the conclusions reached.

- The knowledge which is stored in the knowledge base should be listed in the documentation and in the code itself in a specific way, including :

    i   the date at which the knowledge was introduced ;
    ii   the knowledge author's name (expert) ;
    iii   a comment explaining the purpose of the knowledge.

Other modifications to a standard documentation set [11] might be identified in the course of the early developments.

8. MAINTENANCE

Maintenance applies to the operational phase, where the KBS is implemented in the target environment, and where it will be used by its final users. Because developing the operational system will be closer to classical software engineering than to knowledge engineering, KBS maintenance is closer to regular software maintenance, again with the exception of KB maintenance.

8.1 KB maintenance

(a) Three stages must be distinguished :

(1) Refinement of facts and rules/procedures, through rule editors; the key issue here is the generality and flexibility of this rule editor.

2) Redesign, by structural change.

3) Reformulation by change of concepts. For 1 and 2, structured object oriented programming, with graphic support utilities (graph paint) are required for overview and check on completeness.

b) Automatic logs must be generated for all changes (substitutions, deletions, insertions).

c) Going one step further, knowledge based KBS software maintenance is useful as a guide to the code maintenance engineer in understanding the effects of changes, and to suggest causes of errors (see following Section 8.2).

8.2 Knowledge-based software maintenance

A software maintenance (SM) knowledge-based system, serves the three following purposes : (1) assisting a software programmer or analyst in his application code maintenance tasks, (2) generating and updating automatically software correction documentation, (3) helping the end user register, and possibly interpret, observed errors in the successive application code versions. The SM knowledge based system described in [22] is written in PROLOG II, and is largely applicable to application codes written in different programming languages, including KBS software, provided code descriptors can be retrieved. The SM knowledge-based system does not address any of the syntactic, input-output, or procedural errors normally detected by the syntactic analyser, compiler, or by the operating system environment.

8.3 Quality management

General software quality management measures apply to KBS development.

They include :

   (a) periodic project reviews and reports ;
   (b) external code auditors, baseline comparators, path analysers ;
   (c) cost/benefit evaluation of changes ;
   (d) ANSI/IEEE standard 730 software quality assurance planning
      standard ;
   (e) subcontractor control.

9. CONCLUSION

As many real KBS today no longer employ any symbolic language exclusively, and even use C, ADA, etc. for the KB and inference parts, the issue of KBS validation, verification and test is not just a matter of symbolic language code validation.

Guidelines serve as requirements for the KBS development process. These guidelines are supplemented by test series of software carrying out many of the detailed tasks involved (e.g. Sections 5.2, 5.3, etc.), and which have been developed in this group. The test can in turn readily be incorporated into a knowledge-based software maintenance system as in [22], for specific knowledge - based test/validation/verification needs.

REFERENCES

1.   AYEL M., PIPARD E., ROUSSET M.C., (1986) : *Le contrôle dans les bases de connaissance*, Proc. J. Nat. sur l'Intelligence Artificielle, CEPADUES Editions, Toulouse.

2.   ANSI/IEEE, Standard for software test documentation, ANSI/IEEE Std. 829, 1983

3.   BARR A., FEIGENBAUM E.A., (1981) : *Handbook of AI*, Morgan Kaufman Publ., Los Altos, CA.

4.   BARSTOW D., (1979) : *Knowledge based program construction*, Elsevier, N.Y.

5.   BARSTOW D., (1987) : *Artificial intelligence and software engineering*, Proc. ICSE 9, Monterey, CA.

6.   BOYER R., MOORE J., (1981) : *The correctness problem in computer science*, Academic Press, N.Y.

7.   COURANT M., GUEVEL G., (1986) : *Validation d'une base de connaissances hybride avec objets et règles de production*, INRIA Rept. 579, Nov.

8.   COCHRAN E.L., HUTCHINS B.L., (1987) : *Testing, verifying and releasing an expert system*, Proc. 3rd IEEE Conf. on AI applications, Orlando, pub. by IEEE Computer Society.

9.   FENTON N., (1986) : *The use of Z to specify the structural decomposition of control-flow in programs*, Alvey project PRJ/SE/069/Ic, Polytechnic of the South Bank, London.

10.   FRENKEL K.A., (1985) : *Toward automating the software development cycle*, Comm. ACM, Vol. 28, 1985, 578-589

11. Handbook of standards and certification requirements for software,
        Rept. ECR-182, Elektronikcentralen, Denmark
12. HANSEN H.L. (Ed.), (1984) : Software validation, North-Holland, Amsterdam.
13. HAYES ROTH F., et al., (1983) : *Building expert systems*, Addison Wesley, Reading, MA.
14. INCE D., (1985) : *The validation, verification and testing of software*,
        Oxford Surveys in information processing, Vol 2, Oxford Univ. Press, Oxford.
15. LISKOV B., GUTTAG J., (1986) : *Abstraction and specification in program developement*, M. I.
        T. Press, Cambridge, MA.
16. MC GETTRICK A.D., (1982) : *Program verification using ADA*,
        Cambridge Univ. Press, Cambridge.
17. MILLER E.F., HOWDEN W., (1984) : *Software testing and validation techniques*,
        IEEE Computer Society, Washington DC.
18. O'LEARY T., et al., (1990) : *Validating expert systems*,
        IEEE Expert, Vol. 5, no 3, June 1990, pp. 51-58
19. PAU L.F., (1981) : *Failure diagnosis and performance monitoring*, Marcel Dekker, N. Y.
20. PAU L.F., (1987) : *Prototyping, validation and maintenance of knowledge based systems
        software*, Proc. 3rd Annual Expert Systems in government conference, IEEE Computer
        Society, 19-23/10/1987, Washington DC, IEEE Catalog 87 CH 2467-9, pp. 248-253
21. PAU L.F., GIANOTTI C., (1990) : *Economic and financial knowledge based systems*,
        Springer-Verlag, Berlin.
22. PAU L.F., KRISTINSSON J.B., (1990) : *SOFTM : a software maintenance expert system in
        PROLOG*, J. of Software Maintenance, Vol. 2, no 2, June, 87-112.
23. PAU L.F., NEGRET J.M., SOFTM (1985) : *A knowledge based software maintenance expert
        system*, Battelle Institute, Geneva.
24. Proc. Workshop on software testing, IEEE Computer Society Press, July 1986
        (ISBN = 0-8186-0723-8)
25. Relevant TSCE IEEE Software engineering standards
        P 1016.2   Guide to software design descriptions
        P 1059   Guide for software verification and validation
26. RICH C., WATERS R.C., (1986) : *Readings in artificial intelligence and software engineering*,
        Morgan Kaufman Publ., 1986 (ISBN = 0-934613-12-5)
27. R. L : GLASS, Software reliability guidebook, Prentice-Hall, N. J. , 1979
28. SCHOITSCH E. , (1987) : *Software Qualitätssicherung*, Springer Verlag.
29. SMITH D.R., KOTIK G.B., WESTFOLD S.J., (1985) : *Research on knowledge based software
        environments at Kestrel*, IEEE Trans-Software Engng. Vol. SE. 11, 1985, pp. 1278-1295
30. Software engineering standards, European Space Agency ESA BSCc 1984, Vol. 1, no 1.

3

Aspects of Incremental Knowledge Validation

Thomas HOPPE

ABSTRACT

Any knowledge acquisition system has to ensure that the acquired knowledge is correct with respect to the user's intention. Incremental knowledge acquisition systems have to take into account the fact that the intention of the user can change. Obviously, an integration of incremental acquisition methods and knowledge validation requires incremental knowledge validation methods. Thus methods should be developed which address the problems of validating a formalization as well as validating the user's intention. We will analyse the possibility of building an incremental functional validation system and determine further requirements necessary for such a system.

1. INTRODUCTION

Experience indicates that successful expert systems are developed and maintained incrementally over a long period of time, during which the knowledge base is refined and extended, and the intended application domain of the expert system changes [1].

In the field of knowledge acquisition it was also recognized that the acquisition process is incremental and evolutionary. Morik [21] introduced the notion of "sloppy modelling" where, in the acquisition process and on the basis of an incomplete and ill-structured formalization, a domain theory is incrementally refined, extended and corrected. As Morik [22] points out, not only is the formalization evolving in this process, but also the model the user has in mind.

Not only in knowledge acquisition [22], but also in knowledge validation [2, 23] researchers found closer integration of validation and acquisition methods. On the one hand such an integration would make the acquisition process more effective, while on the other hand a closer integration is needed to support the whole development - life - cycle of a knowledge base. Obviously, a closer integration of incremental knowledge acquisition and knowledge validation requires incremental validation methods.

We have argued in [9] that knowledge validation integrated into an incremental acquisition process not only has to take changes of the knowledge base into account, but also that the intention of the user can change, and that users make errors. Thus incremental knowledge validation has to address two subproblems :

Validation of the formalization to determine whether a formalization is "right" with respect to the actual user's intention.

Validation of the user's intention serves the purpose of determining whether the user's intention is "right" with respect to the actual formalization.

We will analyse the possibility of building an incremental functional validation system and determine further requirements necessary for building such a system. Section 1 gives a brief overview of knowledge validation and introduces the notion of "user intention". In section 2 we describe an approach to default reasoning which can be adopted for functional knowledge validation and which (unlike an earlier approach) has interesting properties. Section 3 addresses a particular problem, the adopted incremental validation system, on the basis of an example and introduces as a consequence the notions of "validated knowledge base states" and "development history".

2. KNOWLEDGE VALIDATION

Knowledge validation as a new and young research field of "artificial intelligence" has attracted a fair amount of researchers in the last few years. The construction of solutions for isolated validation problems [7, 28], the integration of validation and refinement methods [6, 18, 29] and the construction of specialized validation tools for specific knowledge-based systems [28, 31] were the first issues researchers addressed. Current topics in this field are the discussion of a common terminology [2, 8, 17], the theoretical foundations of knowledge validation [9, 20], the extension of the applicability range of validation methods [8], and the development of validation tools which can be used to validate classes of knowledge based systems [17, 19].

Although different terminologies were proposed, we can distinguish at least two types of validation methods [8, 17, 19]. Structural validation methods are used to ensure that the structure of a system fulfils necessary logical properties, whereas functional validation methods ensure that the behavior of a system is "right".

The functionality of a system is usually validated by testing its I/O - behavior, we can distinguish two major testing approaches, the ad - hoc construction of test cases and the selection of testcases. For both types of approaches two problems arise because usually we do not know which and how many test cases are needed to ensure that the system behavior is "right".

As we have argued in [8] the problems with testing can be avoided by systematic validation experiments. Each class of models covered by a theory should be validated, and for each class of models at least one test case is needed. The classes of models covered by a theory can be determined systematically by "partial deduction"[1] and can be used as hypotheses for validation experiments.

We have determined in [9] some problems connected with partial deduction for determining experimental hypotheses. One of the most serious problems is the complexity of the partial deduction approach. Although the theory used in the partial deduction process reduces the number of possible hypotheses, a large number of hypotheses can be deduced. In the worst case determination of hypotheses for non-recursive theories is an exponential problem.

We will argue that we can reduce the number of hypotheses generated by partial deduction if we distinguish different types of clauses. While we do not like to give up clauses, we should reject those we cannot prove to be right. But before we introduce this distinction and before we address the problem of incremental knowledge validation, we introduce some definitions useful for the further discussion.

2.1 User intention

We assume a first-order language L built out of variables, constant symbols, function symbols, predicate symbols, the usual logical connectors and quantifiers. Literals, clauses and so on have their usual meaning. We call a set of clauses in language L a theory Th. We follow the model-theoretical approach to give our theories semantics [5]. Thus we say a conceptualization[2] C is a triple which consists of a universe of discourse, a functional basis set and a relational basis set. A theory Th is given a semantics by an interpretation function f which maps L into C.

The conceptualization represents facts that are supposed to be true. Of special interest are facts that are organized into test cases. A test case is a tupel (I, O) with I a set of input facts and O a set of output facts specifying the required (or intended) input/output - behavior.

The notion of "intended interpretation", normally used in the field of "logic programming" [16, 29, 30] and "machine learning" [29], is based on the assumption that the user interprets knowledge with a fixed interpretation

---

[1] Komorowski [11] introduced "partial evaluation" in the field of logic programming. He argues in [12] that the term "partial deduction" is more adequate in the context of logic programming.

[2] Following [5] we do not commit ourselves as, to whether the objects, functions and relations used in a conceptualization really exist or whether they do not necessarily have an external existence. Any conceptualization is accommodated as long as it is useful for the purposes of the user.

function. We introduced in [9] the notion of a changing interpretation function, called "user intention", which seems to be more adequate for incremental knowledge validation.

Definition 1 Given a first-order language L, a conceptualization C and a time interval T, we call a function f_u user intention, if $f_u : L \dashrightarrow C$ and f_u changes in T.

On the basis of the user intention we define "correctness", "completeness" and "rightness" :

Definition 2 A theory Th is correct at

$$t_{i'} \in T \text{ w.r.t. } f_{u'} \text{ iff } M(Th) \subseteq f_{u_{t_i}}(Th)$$

Definition 3 A theory Th is complete at

$$t_i \in T \text{ w.r.t. } f_{u'} \text{ iff } M(Th) \supseteq f_{u_{t_i}}(Th)$$

Definition 4 A theory Th is right at

$$t_i \in T \text{ w.r.t. } f_{u'} \text{ iff } M(Th) = f_{u_{t_i}}(Th)$$

where $M(Th)$ represents the set of models covered by theory Th.

These definitions have, on the one hand the advantage that we can easily integrate theoretical results and methods based on "intended interpretations" into incremental knowledge validation tools[3]. We just have to assume that the user intention does not change in a validation step. On the other hand, these definitions introduce a notion of time, which is more appropriate for the description of incremental processes and for reasoning about the stability of the user intention [3].

3. HYPOTHESES GENERATION BY PARTIAL DEDUCTION

We proposed in [8] the need for systematic knowledge validation, introduced experimentation as a methodology fulfilling this requirement and proposed partial deduction as an approach for hypotheses generation. Despite the problems of partial deduction [9], the proposed partial evaluator suffers from a major impediment : it is uneconomical for incremental knowledge validation.

If a theory is extended and hypotheses are generated, the partial deduction process has to take the whole theory into account. If the theory is extended by just one clause, or if the theory contains a large number of right clauses this approach is especially unsatisfactory. Either a large number or hypotheses is generated (which have already been checked through experiments) or clauses are validated several times. In the background of the complexity of partial deduction useless computations should be avoided.

---

[3] For example the consistency and completeness checker described in [7, 20, 28, 31] or the refinement and debugging methods of [6, 18, 29].

A more economical approach can be developed by distinguishing different types of knowledge in the partial deduction process, thus making partial deduction more knowledge based. On the one hand, we do not like to give up the functionality of certain knowledge, like primitive functions and relations (e.g. "member") or build-in system predicates (e.g. arithmetical computation in Prolog systems). On the other hand new knowledge should be rejectable as long as its correctness has not been shown. We can restrict the number of experimental hypotheses if we can, at certain points of time in the development of a knowledge base , transform the latter type of knowledge into the former type.

Poole et al. [24] introduced with the "Theorist" system a similar distinction of knowledge in the field of "default reasoning". He has shown in [27] that "Theorist" can operate under certain restrictions incrementally. Thus it is worthwhile investigating the "Theorist" approach in more detail to see what we would gain if we were to adopt this approach for incremental functional validation.

3.1 Theorist

Recently Poole [25, 26, 27] and Poole et al. [24] have introduced a new deduction mechanism for default reasoning. The idea behind this mechanism is as simple as it is striking. Instead of introducing non-monotonic operators, Poole's approach stays completely in first-order logic by distinguishing "facts" and "defaults" in a theory[4]. "Facts" are clauses which are true under every interpretation. "Defaults" are clauses that we accept as explanation of an "observation". The set of "defaults" used in a consistent explanation represents "a set of hypotheses which explains the observation". Poole et al. [24] describe an explanation problem as, given

> **Facts** $\mathcal{F}$: consistent formulae, known to be true ;
> **Defaults** Δ : possible hypotheses, that we accept as part of an explanation ;
> **Observations** $\mathcal{G}$: which are to be explained ;

then an observation $g \in \mathcal{G}$ is explainable, if there exists $\mathcal{D} \subseteq \Delta$ such that :

1. $\mathcal{F} \cup \mathcal{D} \models g$ and
2. $\mathcal{F} \cup \mathcal{C} \cup \mathcal{D}$ is consistent.

Poole shows how an interpreter for the explanation of "observations" from "facts" and "defaults" can be built, which returns ground hypotheses (instances of defaults) needed to prove the "observations". As Poole [25, 26] shows, the "Theorist" approach can be extended to incorporate contra-positive inferences and quantified hypotheses for default reasoning in a full first-order

---

[4] in the next subsection we will introduce a different terminology, thus we double quote the terms used by Poole inside quotation marks.

representation language, and by constraints for the reduction of the number of hypotheses.

Let us look at an example taken from [26] to make the "Theorist" approach slightly more clear. In the notation we follow Poole and use the following extended representation language :

fact c, where c is a ground unit clause and means $c \in \mathcal{F}$;

rule c, where c is non-ground clause and means "$\forall c$" $\in \mathcal{F}$;

default n : c, where c is a clause and n is a name[5] with the same free variables as c. The meaning of this is : c is a default with name n, or formally n $\in \Delta$ and "$\forall n \dashrightarrow c$" $\in \mathcal{F}$.

We write clauses in the following in a Prolog-like notation to emphasize the order in which resolutions are performed and assume that clauses are implicitly universally quantified ;

default unemployed_if_student(X) : not employed(X) : - uni_student(X) ;
default employed_if_adult(X)   : employed(X) : - adult(X) ;
default adult_if_student(X)   : adult (X) : - uni_student(X) ;
fact   uni-student(thomas).

Figure 1 : Theory with multiple extensions

Let us assume that the theory shown in figure 1 is given. From this theory we can explain *employed(Thomas)* with *{employed_if_adult(Thomas)}* and *not(employed(Thomas))* from *unemployed_if_student(Thomas)*. If we don't want the "employed_if_adult" default to be applicable, we simply add a further "fact" :

rule not(unemployed_if_student(X)) :- uni_student(X)

which makes the first explanation inconsistent. Thus only the second explanation can be deduced from the theory.

Poole shows in [27] that the "Theorist" approach is flexible enough to allow the construction of an incremental default reasoning system. This can be achieved through the following modifications :

• Compute a description of what is in all extensions. This corresponds to the disjunction of all maximal specific hypotheses, i.e. the disjunctive normal form of a theory.

---

[5] The naming of "defaults" is useful for suppressing their application by the introduction of inconsistencies.

• Reduce this description to the "least presumptive explanations". An explanation $\mathcal{D}_1$ is less presumptive than $\mathcal{D}_2$ if it makes less assumption, i.e. $\mathcal{F} \cup \mathcal{D}_2 \models \mathcal{D}_1$.

If these modifications are introduced then three sets of interesting theorems hold for the "Theorist" approach, which show :

• that the deduction mechanism of "Theorist" can be used to build an incremental default reasoning system, if "least presumptive explanations" are maintained.

• how the "least presumptive explanations" must be modified, if "facts" and "defaults" are added to the theory.

• how we can determine whether a theory still has an extension if a "fact" was added and whether a theory has multiple extensions if a "default" was added.

We have argued in [10] that the "Theorist" approach is a special form of partial deduction. Thus it can be used instead of partial deduction as the hypotheses generation component for validation experiments. This not only makes it possible to construct an incremental functional validation system, it also has some properties which are interesting from the standpoint of knowledge validation :

• The distinction between "facts" and "defaults" is intuitively related to the distinction between "knowledge and belief" [4, 13, 14, 15].

• The number of extensions depends on the "defaults" in a theory. Thus we can reduce the number of hypotheses if we reduce the number of "defaults". This can be achieved by representing validated knowledge, primitive functions and relations, or build-in predicates as "facts".

• In contrast to other approaches to functional knowledge validation which must assume the consistency of the knowledge base, the "Theorist" approach can handle partially inconsistent knowledge bases. Inconsistent hypotheses are not returned as explanation of an observation. We have to ensure only the consistency of "facts".

• A validation component based on the "Theorist" approach extends the applicability range of validation methods to full first-order representation languages and non-monotonic formalisms.

Of course we also have to pay a price for these properties :

• To prove explainability it is in adequate to consider only interpretations in the Herbrand universe [25].

- Explanation construction is undecidable. The construction of explanations is carried out for "defaults" in two steps, where each step uses a first-order theorem prover. So each step is only semi-decidable. The two step approach makes the explanation construction totally undecidable [24].

3.2 Hypotheser

Despite its disadvantages the "Theorist" approach seems useful for incremental functional validation, thus it is worthwhile to adopt the approach for knowledge validation. We will refer to the adopted and modified approach under the term "Hypotheser". On the one hand the following extensions serve the purpose of distinguishing further the different types of knowledge and on the other hand they are needed to adopt the "Theorist" framework for validation by experimentation.

- Poole subsumes under the term "facts" different forms of clauses, which we distinguish into facts and rules :

  Facts $\mathcal{F}$: are consistent ground unit clauses which are logical true or right with respect to the user intention.

  Rules $\mathcal{R}$: are consistent non-ground clauses which are logical true or right with respect to the user intention.

- Instead of using Poole's general term "defaults" we distinguish between defaults and assumptions. Defaults are defaults in the default reasoning sense and cannot be transformed into facts or rules. Assumptions are further distinguished into fact assumptions and rule assumptions, they can be transformed into facts or rules if their rightness has been checked.

  Fact Assumptions $\mathcal{FA}$: unit clauses, not yet shown to be right with respect to the user intention.

  Rule Assumptions $\mathcal{RA}$: non ground clauses, not yet shown to be right with respect to the user intention.

  Defaults $\mathcal{D}$: non-ground clauses.

- The notion of constraints follows references [7, 26, 28]. Test cases are the already mentioned organization of facts. Constraints and test cases are used for debugging respectively validation purposes.

  Constraints C: are restrictions of the actual I/O - behavior.

  Testcases $\mathcal{T}$: are specifications of the expected I/O - behavior.

- Let (I, O) be the I/O - behavior at point of time $t_i \in T$. We say that O is explainable at t_i if

  1. $\mathcal{F} \cup \mathcal{R} \cup \mathcal{FA} \cup \mathcal{RA} \cup \mathcal{D} \cup I \models O$ and
  2. $\mathcal{F} \cup \mathcal{R} \cup \mathcal{FA} \cup \mathcal{RA} \cup \mathcal{D} \cup C \cup I$ is consistent.

We intend to use "Hypotheser" in an incremental knowledge validation setting. Assumptions should be transformed at certain points of time in the development of a theory into facts or rules to reduce the number of hypotheses. This transformation step extends the usual "Theorist" framework, thus we have to investigate whether it influences the deductive behavior of an incremental implementation. In the following section we will discuss this question on the basis of an example.

4. INCREMENTAL KNOWLEDGE VALIDATION

We have argued in the last section that an incremental approach to functional validation can be built. Further, we have seen the properties of such an approach, if it is based on the "Theorist" approach. There are still several questions open. In this section we will address one of these questions and investigate the deductive behavior of "Hypotheser" in a particular incremental validation setting.

The deductive behaviour of "Hypotheser" will not be influenced by the processing order of assumptions if it is applied in the same types of settings and under the same assumptions as "Theorist" . But we intend to apply "Hypotheser" in the following different setting :

> Suppose we have integrated an incremental knowledge acquisition system with an incremental functional validation system. Let the functional validation system be based on "Hypotheser" and let it be incremental under appropriate assumptions. Suppose that the knowledge base built up so far is right with respect to the user's intention. The acquisition component acquires new knowledge. This knowledge is asserted as assumption because it is not yet validated, and is transformed into facts or rules, if its rightness in the background of the theory was shown.

As opposed to the setting in which "Theorist" is applied, we transform in this setting assumptions into facts, or rules. Thus, we should check whether the transformation influences the deductive behavior of an incremental "Hypotheser".

Let us look at two examples of the incremental application of "Hypotheser" to see that the deductive behavior of "Hypotheser" is actually influenced. For both examples we assume the already validated theory shown in figure 2 is given and "Hypotheser" receives incrementally the rule assumptions shown in figure 3.

rule adult(X) :- uni_student(X).
fact uni_student(thomas).

Figure 2 : Initial validated theory

rule_assumption employed_if adult(X)   : employed(X) :- adult(X).
rule_assumption unemployed_if student(X)   : not(employed(X)):- uni_student(X).

Figure 3 : Added rule assumptions

In the first example, when the first rule assumption was asserted, the system can answer the question *employed(thomas)* with the explanation *{employed_if_adult(thomas}*. The question *not(employed(thomas))* cannot be answered. Only after we have asserted the second rule assumption can the answer *{unemployed_if_student(thomas)}* to this question be computed. We see that incremental processing does not influences the I/O - behavior of the resulting theory (compare figure 1).

Let us assume for the second example that after the first rule assumption was asserted, we validate the theory, find that it is right with respect to the user's intention and transform the rule assumption into a rule. The corresponding theory is shown in figure 4.

> **rule** adult(X) :- uni_student(X).
> **fact** uni_student(Thomas).
> **rule** employed_if_adult(X) : employed(X) :- adult(X).

Figure 4 : Example 2 after transforming the rule assumption into a rule

This theory has the same behavior as the theory in example 1 after step 1, the question : *employed(Thomas)*, is explainable with the explanation *{employed_if_adult(Thomas)}* and the question : *not(employed(Thomas))*, is not explainable.

As in step 2 of example 1 we assert the rule assumption *unemployed_if_student(X) : not(employed(X)) :- uni_student(X))*. Again we validate the behavior and find that the question employed(Thomas) is explainable with *{employed_if_adult(Thomas)}*. The question : *not(employed(Thomas))*, to step 2 of example 1, is not explainable. This stems from the fact that *(not(employed(X)) :- uni_student(X))* is inconsistent with the rules *{(employed(X) :- adult(X)), (adult(X) :-uni_student(X)), uni_student(thomas)}* and thus cannot be used in an explanation. We see that the transformation influences the behavior of the system.

4.1. Development history and validated knowledge base states

Let us review the last example in the context of changing user's intention. Because not all adults are necessarily employed, it is reasonable to assume that in validation step 1 the user has either made an error or changes his mind in subsequent acquisition steps.

The first case occurs most frequently in the validation of more complex theories, where hypotheses are larger and the user has more difficulties in the interpretation of questions based on these larger hypotheses. On the other hand we can assume that the user has not taken the implicit universal quantification into account when he interpreted the reasoning chain : *employed(X) :- adult(X), - adult(X) :- uni_student(X)* used by the validation system to explain *employed(thomas)*.

The second case, which also leads to the quantification problem, is more interesting as an example of the behavior of the incremental validation system under construction. Suppose the user has at the moment only "employed adults" in his mind, has extended the initial theory with the rule assumption stating that all adults are employed and has not yet given an example. The corresponding theory is shown in figure 5.

rule adult(X) :- uni_student(X)
rule_assumption employed_if_adult(X) : employed(X) :- adult(X).

Figure 5 : Changing user's intention

After asserting the first rule assumption the validation system discovers that there is not yet a test case for the theory, hence it performs an instantiation experiment with the user. The system asks the user whether he can think of an employed student. The user knows an employed student named Paul, thus he confirms the question with the example *uni_student(paul)*. The validation component has acquired the first test case *(uni_student(paul), employed(paul))* which confirms the theory and thus it can transform the validated rule assumption into a rule. Let us mark this as state 1.

Suppose that in the next acquisition step the user becomes aware, that there are also "unemployed students" needed in the theory. Thus s/he formalizes the rule :

rule_assumption unemployed_if_student(X): not(employed(X): -uni_student(X).

stating that all students are unemployed[6]. This rule is asserted as a rule assumption, because it is not yet validated.

Once more the validation system is triggered to validate the new rule assumption. To avoid unnecessary computations the validation system tries first to validate the rule assumption in isolation. Thus it performs a further instantiation experiment with the user. Suppose the user knows an unemployed student named Thomas and confirms the isolated rule assumption with the example *uni_student(thomas)*. The validation component has acquired a new test case *(uni_student(thomas), not(employed(thomas)))* for the isolated rule assumption.

In a second step the validation system tries to validate the new clause together with the previously acquired background knowledge. It detects that the extended theory still covers the question *employed(paul)* correctly. But, problems occur with the questions *employed(thomas)* and *not(employed(X))*. The first question is wrongly covered and no extension can be determined for the second question, because of the inconsistency shown above.

Although the user has confirmed the rule assumption in isolation, the whole theory is inconsistent. This indicates that the source of the inconsistency must lie in the previously validated facts or rules. In a pure incremental validation system, which started with an empty set of facts or rules, we can only blame a wrong transformation. A transformation can only be wrong if the user has made an error or has changed his mind and we can conclude that the user intention has changed. Thus we have to take back transformations leading to state 1 and have to revalidate the interfering assumptions together.

From the backed-up state we can determine that two extensions of the theory cover the same set of test cases, hence the rule assumptions must be refined. Here a debugging, respectively refinement, tool could be used to try to acquire further knowledge to distinguish both test cases. Let us suppose that this is the case and we have to revalidate the refined rule assumptions before we can transform them again into rules.

This example is interesting, because it points to a new question : What shall we back up? It seems that the answer to this question lies in the introduction of "validated knowledge base states" which record the state of a validated knowledge base and the modifications leading to the next validated state.

Surely we have seen merely an example of a simple back up, where we have to back up only the direct predecessor state. It is reasonable to assume that back ups to earlier points in the "development history" should also be possible. If we define the "development history" of a knowledge the base as the sequence of "validated knowledge base states" then we have on the one hand the possibility of backing up earlier states. On the other hand it seems that the "development history" can guide the automatic revalidation of successor states.

5. SUMMARY

Partial deduction as a hypothesis generation component for functional validation experiments suffers from a major impediment-even for restricted representations it is uneconomical. Incremental functional validation can be used to overcome this problem by distinguishing different types of knowledge and transforming knowledge from one type to another at certain points in the "development history" of a knowledge base.

We have introduced an adaptation of the "Theorist" approach to default reasoning for functional validation, called "Hypotheser". Not only has the "Theorist" approach some interesting properties which are also useful for "Hypotheser" in the validation context, but both approaches can work under appropriate assumptions incrementally.

"Hypotheser" is intended to extend the setting in which "Theorist" is usually applied by transforming assumptions into facts or rules. We have seen in an example that the deductive behavior of "Hypotheser" differs because of the transformation, from the behavior of "Theorist". We reviewed this problem in the context of changing user intentions and proposed as a solution to overcome this problem the introduction of a "development history" of a knowledge base, which keeps track of "validated knowledge base states", thus enabling an incremental validation tool to back-up previously validated knowledge base states.

REFERENCES

1   BACHANT J., Mc DERMOTT J., (1984) : *R1 Revisited : Four Years in the Trenches*, AI Magazine, Fall.

2   BENBASAT I., DHALIWAL J.S., (1989) : *The Validation of Knowledge Acquisition : Methodology and Techniques*, Proceedings of the 3rd European Knowledge Acquisition Workshop.

3   COHEN P.R., LEVESQUE H.J., (1987) : *Intention = Choice + Commitment*, Proceedings of the AAAI-87.

4   FAGIN R., HALPERN J.Y., (1985) : *Belief, Awareness and Limited Reasoning : Preliminary Report*, Proceedings of the 9th IJCAI, Morgan Kaufmann, Los Altos.

5   GENESERETH M.R., NILSSON N., (1987) : *Logical Foundations of Artificial Intelligence*, Morgan Kaufmann.

6   GINSBERG A., (1988) : *Automatic Refinement of Expert System Knowledge Bases*, Pitman Publishing.

7   GINSBERG A., (1988) : *A New Approach to Checking Knowledge Bases for Inconsistency & Redundancy*, Proceedings of the AAAI-88.

8   HOPPE T., (1990) : *Hypotheses Generation for Knowledge Validation*, in : L.C. AIELLO (ed), Proceedings of the 9th European Conference on Artificial Intelligence, Stockholm, Pitman Publishing, London.

9   HOPPE T., (1990) : *Validation of User Intention*, in : B. WIELLINGA, J. BOOSE, B. GAINES, G. SCHREIBER, M.v. SOMEREN (eds), Current Trends in Knowledge Acquisition, Frontiers in Artificial Intelligence and Applications, IOS Press, Amsterdam.

10. HOPPE T., (1990) : *Explanation-based Generalization, Partial Deduction and Non-Monotonic Reasoning*, Technical Report, unpublished.

11 KOMOROWSKI J., (1981) : *A Specification of An Abstract Prolog Machine and Its Application to Partial Evaluation*, Ph.D. thesis, Department of Computer and Information Science, Linköping University, Linköping.

12 KOMOROWSKI J., (1990) : *Towards a Programming Methodology Founded on Partial Deduction*, in : L.C. AIELLO (ed), Proceedings of the 9th European Conference on Artificial Intelligence, Stockholm, Pitman Publishing, London.

13 KONOLIGE K., (1985) : *A Computational Theory of Belief Introspection*, Proceedings of the 9th IJCAI, Morgan Kaufmann, Los Altos.

14 KONOLIGE K., (1986) : *What Awareness Isn't : A Sentential View of Implicit and Explicit Beliefs*, in : J.Y. HALPERN (ed), Proceedings of the 1986 Conference on Theoretical Aspects of Reasoning about Knowledge, Morgan Kaufmann, Los Altos.

15 LEVESQUE H.J., (1984) : *A Logic of Implicit and Explicit Belief*, Proceedings of the AAAI-84.

16 LLOYD J.W., (1987) : *Foundations of Logic Programming*, second extended edition, Springer-Verlag, Berlin, Heidelberg, New York.

17 LOPEZ B., MESEGUER P., PLAZA E., (1990) : *Validation of Knowledge Based Systems : A State of the Art*, Report de Recerca GRIAL 89/9, Centre Estudis Avançats de Blanes, 1989 also in : AI Communications, Vol. 3 no 20.

18 LOPEZ B., (1990) : *CONKRET : Control Knowledge Refinement Tool*, (in this volume).

19 de MANTARAS R.L., KERDILES P.F., LARSEN H., (1989) : *Validation Methods and Tools for Knowledge-Based Systems (VALID)*, in : BRAUER W., FREKSA C., (eds), Wissensbasierte Systeme, Proceedings of the 3rd International GI-Kongress, Informatik-Fachberichte 227, Springer-Verlag.

20 MESEGUER P., (1990) : *A New Method to Checking Rule Bases for Inconsistency : A Petri Net Approach*, in : L.C. AIELLO (ed), Proceedings of the 9th European Conference on Artificial Intelligence, Stockholm, Pitman Publishing, London.

21 MORIK K., (1987) : *Acquiring Domain Models*, International Journal for Man-Machine Studies 26.

22 MORIK K., (1989) : *Sloppy Modeling*, in : Knowledge Representation and Organization in Machine Learning, MORIK K. (ed), Lecture Notes in Artificial Intelligence 347, Springer-Verlag.

23   O'KEEFE R.M., BALCI O., SMITH E.P., (1987) : *Validating Expert System Performance*, IEEE Expert, Winter.

24   POOLE D., GOEBEL R., ALELIUNAS R., (1987) : *Theorist : A Logical Reasoning System for Defaults and Diagnosis*, in : CERCONE N., McCALLA G., (eds), The Knowledge Frontier : Essays in the Representation of Knowledge, Springer-Verlag, New York.

25   POOLE D., (1987) : *Variables in Hypotheses*, Proceedings of the IJCAI.

26   POOLE D., (1988) : *A Logical Framework for Default Reasoning*, Artificial Intelligence 36.

27   POOLE D., (1989) : *Explanation and Prediction : An Achitecture for Default and Abductive reasoning*, Computational Intelligence, Vol. 5 no 20.

28   ROUSSET M.C. (1988) : *On the Consistency of Knowledge Bases : The COVADIS Sytem*, Proceedings of the ECAI-88.

29   SHAPIRO E.Y., (1982) : *Algorithmic Program Debugging*, Research Report 237, Yale University, Department of Computer Science.

30   STERLING L., SHAPIRO E., (1986) : *The Art of Prolog*, MIT - Press, Cambridge, Massachusetts, London, England.

31   SUWA M., SCOTT A.C., SHORTLIFFE E.H., (1985) : *Completeness and Consistency in a Rule-based System*, in : Rule-based Systems, BUCHANAN B.G., SHORTLIFFE E.H., (eds), Addison-Wesley.

PART B

VERIFICATION AND VALIDATION PROCESSES

4

Comparison of Expert System Verification Criteria : Redundancy

Jaak TEPANDI

ABSTRACT

Expert system (ES) verification involves checking the knowledge base for redundancy, inconsistency, incompleteness, circularity, and other errors. Several verification criteria have been proposed. Our study indicates that in order to have a consistent and up-to-date view on ES verification, it is necessary to distinguish between structural (internal) and functional (external) aspects of verification. An error on the structural level may correspond to different error types on the functional level, and vice versa.

We compare several ES redundancy criteria with regard to their strength and the complexity of verification. The results for different typical models of ES indicate that the relationships between some verification criteria vary considerably, while some relationships remain stable. This study also allows us to characterize the strong and weak sides of different verification criteria.

1. INTRODUCTION

Verification, in a broad sense, means checking whether the system is built in the right way, i.e. whether it satisfies the specifications, requirements and constraints, imposed in the earlier stages of development [3, 5-8, 13 16, 21, 22, 26]. In expert system (ES) verification, the errors have been characterised as "redundancy", "circularity in rules", "subsuming rules", "incompleteness", etc. These error descriptions are used interchangeably. Meanwhile, there are at least two different classes of error situations that should not be mixed. The first class includes structural (internal) errors. Among them are syntactical error descriptions, such as "there are two identical rules in the rule base". These errors may be distinguished automatically, based only on the knowledge base (KB) text. Also, there are errors that seem syntactical, but may be interpreted in different ways: "circularity in rules", "subsuming rules", etc. Then, there are errors that require the concept of inference: "This rule cannot be tested."

The second class comprises functional (external) errors. They characterise the situation from the user point of view. They include situations like "redundancy", "incompleteness", etc. In recent literature, these errors are usually given descriptions based only on the properties of the KB. At the same time, it is important that having only a KB text and interpreter, it is often impossible to say whether a particular situation represents redundancy, incompleteness, or contradiction. These situations may be distinguished only with the aid of a specification or a specification oracle. There exists a many-to-many relationship between the structural and functional errors: one and the same error on the structural level may correspond to different errors on the functional level, and vice versa. We give examples of such situations.

Based on the current ES verification research, we also define several different redundancy criteria, compare their strength, and the complexity of verification. This brings to recommendations for the selection of ES verification criteria and methods.

The goals of this study are twofold. At first, it is important to develop a consistent and up-to-date understanding of ES verification, as well as to be able to select between many verification criteria currently available. The second goal concerns ES testing. In our earlier papers we have investigated principles and complexity of ES testing; two verification criteria discussed below have been derived from this study [26]. However, in most cases verification is less expensive than testing because it does not require time-consuming evaluation of test results. Therefore, it is expedient to perform verification before testing, and test only verified (statically correct) ES. This observation, as well as our previous studies indicate that understanding the properties of statically correct ES is vital for developing firmly grounded methods and theory of ES testing.

2. TWO CLASSES OF ES ERROR SITUATIONS

In ES verification, the errors have been characterized as "redundancy", "circularity in rules", "subsuming rules", "incompleteness", etc. These error descriptions are used interchangeably. Meanwhile, there are two different classes of error situations that should not be mixed. The first class includes structural error descriptions, such as "circularity in rules", "subsuming rules", etc. These errors may usually be distinguished automatically, based only on the knowledge base text and the interpreter. The functional errors characterise the situation from the user point of view. They include situations like "redundancy", "incompleteness", etc. In recent literature, these errors are usually given descriptions based only on the properties of the KB. At the same time, it is important that having only a KB text, it is often impossible to say whether a particular situation represents redundancy, incompleteness, or contradiction.

Example 2.1. Let us have a rule base comprising two rules :

(Rule-1) IF   You are interested in computers
         THEN Study computers,

(Rule-2) IF   You read much math and physics
         THEN You are interested in real sciences,
and one conclusion (goal): Study computers.

From the point of view expressed in [16], this rule base is incomplete: the proposition 'You are interested in real sciences' is a dead end. It is not a goal, and it is absent from all antecedent sets. At the same time, from the view point of [8], this rule base is redundant: it contains a rule (Rule-2) which can be view removed without changing the set of conclusions asserted by the knowledge base for any valid input. (End of example.)

These situations may be distinguished only with the aid of a specification or a specification oracle. In the following discussion we concern several criteria from this viewpoint.

2.1 Redundancy

There seems to be at least two different views on redundancy. The first view is given by the following problem. Let us take the knowledge base "as it is" - as a function responding with some output to a given input. Can we simplify this knowledge base (throw out rules, propositions, etc.) so that the function remains the same?

The second view on redundancy deals with another kind of problem. Let K be the knowledge base "as it is", and K' the knowledge base as it should be. Can we simplify K so that it is "nearer" to K'?

Example 2.1 shows that these two different views should not be mixed. There is an interesting problem: Are there any types of redundancies "by definition" - redundancies that must surely be removed - at all? For example, given two identical rules, it seems that this knowledge base is "redundant by definition" : one of these rules must be removed. Nevertheless, there is a possibility that one of the rules misses some extra propositions in the IF or THEN part and is in a sense incomplete.

Example 2.2. Let us consider the rule base :

$$a\&b->c, c->g1, a->g1,$$

with the only goal g1. The first two rules seem to be unnecessary: they are subsumed by the third rule. However, it is possible to complement the rule base in such a way that all these rules are necessary for reaching some conclusion. In this case, the initial rule base should be characterized as incomplete and unredundant. Therefore, already in this simple case the syntactical view is not sufficient to differentiate between redundancy and incompleteness. (End of example.)

2.2 Inconsistency

This term may be and has been interpreted in several different ways. First, it may simply that mean, given some set of input data, the expert system reaches contradictory conclusions, as in the case of a rule base

$$a\text{->}g, a\text{->}not(g).$$

Second, it may mean that the rule base is not correct : it violates some integrity constraints. Such a constraint may state, for example, that an ES should not have a proposition included in a result together with its negation. Note that in the previous case we did not speak about correctness.

Third, it may mean that the rule base is not correct - g and not(g) cannot occur simultaneously. Note that this is no longer an integrity constraint. For some other goal h, it can be possible that h and not(h) occur in the result.

Fourth, it may mean, that given the premise a, two different conclusions may occur: g and not(g). This , again, may mean that the problem is not so simple as it seems, and probably some differentiating proposition is needed - that is, the knowledge base is incomplete.

Fifth, it may mean that one (or both) of the rules given above is unnecessary - the knowledge base is redundant.

Finally, it may mean that life is full of paradoxes - both g and not(g) are simultaneously possible, and the rule base is correct.

The meaning of the first two interpretations represent the structural, the last four the functional view.

2.3 Incompleteness and other properties

As in the previous cases, we may define some "objective" syntactic criteria for incompleteness. However, the previous discussion shows that this criterion may take the form of "inconsistency", or even "redundancy".

The terms such as "circularity", "subsumption", "missing rule", "useless rule", and many others are usually defined on a syntactical level. Therefore, they may be interpreted in a unique way. Nevertheless, it may easily occur that "useless rule" means, in fact, "missing goal". Example 2.2 shows that subsumption may indicate redundancy, as well as incompleteness.

3. A MODEL OF THE EXPERT SYSTEM

There are other problems in ES verification. One of them seems to be the great diversity of the ES methods, formalisms, and shells. Nevertheless, this situation is comparable with the situation in the conventional programming. There is no standard ES shell, just as there is no standard high-level programming language. The syntactical representation of knowledge representation languages varies to a great extent, but it is easy to overcome. It is more important, that each of the following features adds a level of power to an ES shell, and consequently - a level of complexity to an ES testing : weights or probabilities in rules, fuzzy reasoning, hierarchies of rules, frames and inheritance, numerical computations, links to the external programs and databases, graphic interfaces, real-time operation, concurrency, networking, and so on. Nevertheless, similar problems have to be solved for the programs written in conventional programming languages.

At least at this moment, but probably also in the future, it is not possible to investigate verification of ES utilizing all the features listed above. We must begin with the basic structures and combine them after verification of these structures is understood. At the same time, if we are going to study complexity problems, we must be careful to make our concept of ES as exact as possible. We have considered testing of monotonic uncertain rule-based systems without variables in [24, 26]. Below we investigate verification of hybrid ES that utilize rules, frames, and inheritance, but do not make use of procedural code in the knowledge base. Also, we consider only unstructured slot values (for example, the slot value cannot be a frame). The model of such ES include the representation language, the user world (part of the system accessible to the user through queries and responses), and the interpreter.

We define a hybrid ES E as a quintuple E=<K,F,U,G,I>, comprising a knowledge base (a set of rules and frames) K, a set of possible different facts (propositions) F, a set U of propositions accessible to the user through responses, a set of goals G (U and G are subsets of F), and an interpreter I. If there are no frames in K, we may refer to it as a rule base R (E is then a rule-based ES), if there are no rules, - as a frame base.

Sometimes, especially when the ES is implemented in a high-level language such as LISP or PROLOG, it is possible to have separate access to all elements in the knowledge base. For example, one may supply facts that directly activate any rule, or ask slot values for any frame. This can be compared to low-level debugging of conventional programs. Here our concern is with normal execution of the ES. In such a case only some components of the knowledge base are visible to the user. These components form the user world for the given ES. We assume that the user world comprises the set U of user input statements, and the set G of goals. We also assume that U includes propositions that are not defined by any rule, or through any frame. We consider only loop free bases. This is not a serious restriction, since detecting loops is computationally not expensive.

A test t for E is a set of facts from U, that may be used by the interpreter I to achieve some decision about the goals in G (e.g. to select a goal from G). This decision is the result of t over E. A test set is a set of tests.

The rules are statements of the form :

$$\text{(Rule\_id) } a1 \,\&\, ... \,\&\, aK \rightarrow c1 \,\&\, ... \,\&\, cL.$$

Here, Rule_id is a rule identifier, a1,...,aK are antecedents and c1,...,cL - consequents of the rule. In the examples we may omit the rule identifiers, and use the keywords IF and THEN. There may be certainty degrees associated with each rule and proposition. A rule may be activated if all its antecedents are satisfied. We say that a rule base has no rule chains if there are no consequents of rules occurring in the antecedents of other rules. We say that a rule base has separated premises if the sets of antecedents for any two rules from this base do not intersect.

A frame is a statement of the form :

    Frame f_id
    is_instance_of ft,

where f_id is a frame identifier, and ft is a frame type identifier. Frame types are defined as :

    Frame_type ft_id
    is_a f
    has_slots s1,...,sM
    by_default slot1=v1,...,slotK=vK.

Here f is an is_a frame type identifier, s1,...,sM, slot1,...,slotK are slot names, v1,...,vK are slot values. Each frame has only one definition.

We will propose that there exist (1) a computation rule, according to which the rule premises are selected for evaluation (for example, from left to right), and (2) an order relation on the knowledge base, according to which the rules and frames are selected for consideration. In the examples it is assumed that the order relation is defined by the order of the rules and frames in the list. The interpreter I may find the first solution, or all solutions. For interpreter finding all solutions, we accept the usual backward and forward chaining inference procedures [e.g. 4]. An interpreter finding the first solution is defined by similar algorithms, with the exception that the reasoning stops after the first goal g that is found to be satisfied. In the last case the result is {g}. If there are no satisfied goals, then the result is the empty set. If the set V of certainty degrees includes two elements, then we say that the ES is certain. In the case of finite number of elements N (N>2) we will say that the ES is fuzzy, in the case of continuous certainty degree scale that the ES is uncertain.

4. THE EXPERT SYSTEM VERIFICATION CRITERIA

The ES verification criteria may be characterized as based on syntactical and logical properties of the knowledge base, and based on ES testing. Due to the unavailability of the ES specification, all these criteria concern structural reliability: we ask whether the given ES may be made simpler with respect to the function it represents, not with respect to the function it has to represent.

4.1 The verification criteria based on syntactical and logical properties of the knowledge base

Definition 4.1. We shall say that rule **r1 subsumes rule r2**, if one of the following holds: (1) r1 and r2 are identical, (2) ANTECEDENTS(r1) is a subset of ANTECEDENTS(r2), and the consequents of r1 and r2 are identical, (3) CONSEQUENTS(r2) is a subset of CONSEQUENTS(r1) and the antecedents of r1 and r2 are identical, (4) ANTECEDENTS(r1) is a subset of ANTECEDENTS(r2), and CONSEQUENTS(r2) is a subset of CONSEQUENTS(r1). The rules r1 and r2 are subsuming if r1 subsumes r2, or vice versa.

Definition 4.2. Let a rule r' be of the form A1->F1, and rule r'' be of the form F1&A2->F2, where A1, F1, A2, F2 are conjunctions, having no common propositions (A2 may be empty). We say that **rule A1&A2->F2 is a consequence of r' and r''.** Let R be a set of rules and C be a rule chain <r1,...rN>. We say that C is a derivation of rN from R, if every rule rK (K=1,...,N) from C either belongs to R, either is a consequence of rI and rJ, where I<K, J<K.

Definition 4.3. We shall define and compare the following redundancy criteria:

(I). Redundancy in rules: a rule base is **R-redundant** if there is a rule that does not support any goal, or if there exist a pair of subsuming rules in R.

(II). Redundancy in rule chains: a rule has **redundancy in rule chains**, if the situations of R-redundancy occur in rule chains [16]. Here, the notion of "occur in rule chains" may be interpreted in different ways. We will say that a rule base is RC1-redundant, if there is a rule that does not support any goal, or if there exists a derivation C of a rule r1 from R1 (a subset of R), and a rule r2 from R not belonging to R1, such that r1 and r2 are subsuming. We say that a rule base is RC2-redundant if there is a rule that does not support any goal, or if there exist two non-overlapping rule sets R1 and R2, derivations C1 and C2 and two rules r1 and r2 such that C1 is a derivation of r1 from R1, C2 is a derivation of r2 from R2, and r1 and r2 subsume each other.

(III). Redundancy measured by the set of conclusions [8]: a rule base is **S-redundant** if it contains one or more rules which can be removed without changing the set of conclusions asserted by the knowledge base for any valid input. Here also, the notion of "the set of conclusions asserted by the knowledge base" must be made more exact. If we interpret this as "the set of conclusions asserted by the ES", then the concept of S-redundancy is for certain ES identical to the CA-redundancy defined below (however, example 4.1 shows that this definition may be extended to cope with additional forms of redundancy). If we consider this notion as "the set of all conclusions that can be inferred from a given knowledge base" then S- and CA-redundancy may become different. We accept the last possibility, as it gives a useful additional definition of redundancy.

4.2 Verification criteria based on ES testing

By testing, one cannot prove that there are no mistakes in the program, it is only possible to show their existence. Therefore, testing cannot be exhaustive, and one has to decide when to stop it. Several criteria have been developed for this purpose for programs written in conventional languages. For example, according to the adequacy criterion statement, each program statement must be executed at least once. It is possible to reformulate this criterion for production' systems that do not make use of approximate reasoning [9, 20, 24]:

When the ES is executed with the given test data, then each rule must be activated at least once with all its premises satisfied. In addition, it is required that each knowledge base statement must be activated at least once - for example, all goals stated in the knowledge base must be evaluated, all explanatory texts must be displayed, etc.

This criterion is easy to grasp intuitively, especially for a knowledge engineer with the traditional software development background. However, to make this criterion applicable, we must add the important condition, that the activation must not be cancelled through backtracking [25].

The reformulation given above is justified for ES without approximate reasoning: usually, when a rule is activated with all its premises satisfied, then it supports a certain conclusion and takes an active part in of the decision process. On the contrary, in approximate reasoning the decision is often evaluated as the aggregation of all information available. Therefore, a rule may be activated with the given test data, but its contribution to the reasoning process may be negligible. If there are no useless rules (rules that cannot be used for achieving any goal) in the rule base, then the adequacy criterion statement may be fulfilled by evaluating all goals. This is certainly a necessary test, but in no case sufficient. We propose another criterion based on the following idea :

Each component of the rule base should be used effectively, i.e. its contribution should have a crucial impact on the inference process.

More precisely, let D be the set of possible decisions for E=<K, F, U, G, I>; at this moment we need not specify the relationships between E and D. Clearly, not all the decisions are really different from the user's point of view. For example, the conclusions "it is quite possible that John loves Mary" and "it is very possible that John loves Mary" seem almost identical, while the conclusions "John loves Mary" and "John loves Angela" are usually considered different. This motivates the following definitions [25].

Definition 4.4. Let P be a partition of D into disjoint subsets, such that each two different elements of P comprise solutions that are different from the user's point of view. We will say that such solutions are significantly different. Throughout this paper, we consider two results significantly different if they comprise different sets of selected goals.

Definition 4.5. Let EL be a knowledge base element, and K' the result of deleting EL from K. The element EL is effectively tested by a test t, if the result of t over <K, F, U, G, I> and the result of t over <K', F, U, G, I> are significantly different. The adequacy criterion   contribution states that testing of an expert system E may be stopped if each knowledge base element has been effectively tested.

In this definition we have not specified the notions of the "knowledge base element" and "the result of deleting an element from a knowledge base". Example 4.1 shows that different definitions of these concepts will yield different notions of contribution adequacy. Throughout this paper we will assume that the knowledge base elements that can be removed are rules and frames. However, investigation of other possibilities may be of interest in the future.

Example 4.1. Let G={g} and K include the following rules :

(r1) a&d->g   (r2) a&b->d   (r3) c->d.

If we view rules as the basic elements of the rule base, then there exists an adequate contribution test set for K. For example,

t1={a,b} tests r1 and r2, t2={a,c} tests r3. If we accept individual antecedents of the rules as the basic elements, then there is no test for antecedent a of the rule r2. (End of example.)

As Nissen [17] remarks, the idea of subdividing sets of decisions into significantly different subsets from the user's point of view may be seen as one of the first instances of operationalizing the idea by Bateson [2] about "differences which make differences". To make this idea really operational, we must be able to effectively solve several important problems associated with the given contribution adequacy criterion, such as: (P1) Does there exist an effective test for a rule r? (P2) Generate an effective test for r, if one exists. (P3) Does there exists a adequate test contribution set for an ES E? (P4) Generate a contribution adequate test set for E. Similar questions arise for the statement adequacy. The answers depend on the inference method, on the kind of knowledge the system is able to represent, etc.

The adequacy criterion contribution is most useful with respect to the uncertain and fuzzy ES, as considered in [25, 26]. However, these works, as well as other investigations devoted to ES verification, have also demonstrated that it is desirable to have a better understanding about relationships between different correctness criteria for certain ES. We assume that the problems are coded in a standard way, e.g. in the sense of [1].

Testing involves evaluation of correct answers for the test cases. Usually this is very labour-intensive and is therefore expensive. One of the ways to reduce costs is to verify the system before testing. It turns out that the testing criteria proposed above may be used for verification, and vice versa, the verification criteria proposed so far may, at least potentially, be useful for determining whether there exist adequate contribution and statement est sets for a given ES. The contribution and statement adequacy criteria are associated with redundancy. Indeed, if there is no way to generate a test for a given rule, then this rule seems to be unnecessary.

Definition 4.6. A rule base is **SA-redundant** (CA-redundant) if it cannot be tested according to the statement (contribution) adequacy criterion.

5. COMPARISON OF REDUNDANCY CRITERIA FOR CERTAIN ES

We say that a rule base satisfies the R-correctness criterion, if it is not R-redundant, and similarly for other types of redundancy. Let us have a class KL of expert systems, and two correctness criteria: C1 and C2. We say that C1 is strictly stronger than C2 on KL (denoted by C1: ·C2), if every ES from class KL that satisfies C1, also satisfies C2, but not vice versa. Usually, KL is clear from the context, and we shall omit it. In a similar natural way, we shall use the terms "equal to" (=), "not comparable with" (denoted by <> - there exist an ES that satisfies C1 but not C2, and vice versa), and "not equal to" (there exist an ES that satisfies C1 but not C2, or vice versa).

Proposition 5.1. Let KL be the class of certain monotonic rule-based ES E, with I finding all solutions. Then,

(I) CA-correctness = S-correctness > SA-correctness;
(II) CA-correctness <> RC1-correctness;
(III) CA-correctness > R-correctness;
(IV) SA-correctness is not comparable with the RC1- and R-correctness criteria.
(V) RC1-correctness > R-correctness.

Example 5.1. Let the rule base include the following rules with one goal g :

$$(r1)\ a\text{->}d \quad (r2)\ b\text{->}d \quad (r3)\ a\text{->}e \quad (r4)\ c\text{->}e$$
$$(r5)\ d\text{->}g \quad (r6)\ e\text{->}g.$$

This example shows that there exists a rule base that is RC1-correct, but not CA-, S-, or SA-correct. Indeed, no rule from this base is a consequence of other rules, but there is no way to activate rule r3, nor does there exist an effective test for rules r1 and r3. (End of example).

Example 5.2. Let the rule base include the following rules with one goal g :

$$(r1)\ a\&b\text{->}g \quad (r2)\ a\text{->}g.$$

This example shows that there exists a rule base that is SA-correct, but not CA, S-, RC1- or R-correct. Indeed, test {a} tests rule r2 and test {a, b} tests rule r1, so E is SA-correct, but r2 subsumes r1. (End of example.)

The following proposition shows that for ES finding the first solution, the redundancy criteria defined above tend not to be correlated with each other.

Proposition 5.2. Let KL be the class of certain monotonic rule-based ES, finding the first solution. Then,

(I) CA-correctness > SA-correctness;
(II) S-correctness > R-correctness;

(III) RC1-correctness > R-correctness;

(IV) All other pairs of criteria from the set {CA, S, SA, RC1, R} are not comparable with each other.

In hybrid ES, we assume that the propositions are of the form <frame, slot, value>. We also assume, that in all kinds of reasoning, inheritance relations are used after there are no more applicable rules, and that the inheritance direction is only from parent to child.

The implications of subsumption in frames and in rules are different. Rules are usually important only as means for achieving some goals. The names of rules do not represent any reality. Therefore, two subsuming rules are considered to be redundant. In contrast with this, two frames with different names may represent two subsuming concepts, that are both of interest to the user. We have only one definition for each frame, so different frame definitions represent different objects. Therefore, with respect to frames it is difficult to apply analogues of R-, RC1-, or RC2-redundancy. Also, the S-redundancy criterion was based on rules. So we will compare only SA- and CA-correctness criteria. The following proposition demonstrates that the relationships between SA- and CA-correctness are the same for rule-based and hybrid systems.

Proposition 5.3. For certain monotonic hybrid ES, CA-correctness > SA-correctness.

6. THE COMPLEXITY OF CHECKING CA-CORRECTNESS

The results of the previous section indicate that verification based on the adequacy criterion statement may be insufficient, so we shall focus on contribution adequacy. The complexity of checking CA-correctness is determined by the complexity of test generation. We will discuss separately rule-based and frame-based systems and give finally some characterization of test generation complexity for hybrid ES. First, we present a result from [25] characterizing the test generation complexity for rule-based ES.

Proposition 6.1. For certain and fuzzy rule-based ES, the problems P1 P4 are NP-complete. These problems remain NP-complete if we consider classes of R- or RC1-correct ES.

In general, it has been proved that discovering subsumptions through terminological reasoning based on general knowledge representation systems is computationally intractable [18]. However, the frame representation accepted in our paper is much simpler, so the following result holds :

Proposition 6.2. Let E be a frame-based ES. Then the generation of adequate test set an contribution or E has polynomial complexity.

Adding frames to a rule-based ES does not make the test generation simpler.

Proposition 6.3. Let E be a hybrid ES. Then the generation of adequate test set an contribution for E is NP-complete.

NP-completeness is by itself neither extraordinary nor crucial. Many important tasks that are routinely and successfully solved by men and machines, are in their general form NP-complete - or even not solvable (e.g. vision, test generation for programs written in algorithmic languages, etc.). Therefore it is important to find classes of ES, for which one can develop feasible test data generation algorithms.

As the following propositions indicate, the additional complexity introduced by the simple frame and inheritance structures considered here is sufficient to destroy the good properties of some rule-based ES classes with feasible (polynomial) test generation complexity.

Proposition 6.4. For the class of certain rule-based ES E without rule chains, the adequacy test set generation complexity contribution is polynomial. If, in addition, E may include frames, then the problems (P1)-(P4) become NP-complete.

Proposition 6.5. For the class of certain rule-based ES E with separated premises, the adequacy test set generation complexity contribution is polynomial. If, in addition, E may include frames, then the problems (P1)-(P4) become NP-complete.

Therefore we propose a transformation of the hybrid ES into a rule-based ES. In this transformation, all is-a links are replaced by rules with one antecedent and one conclusion. If the transformed ES satisfies the properties required for feasible test generation [24, 25], then the test generation for the original hybrid ES also has polynomial complexity.

7. DISCUSSION

There exist several possibilities of expanding the model of the expert system to be verified. These expansions must be handled carefully. For example, investigations in non-monotonic reasoning have shown that if we take the logical view on inference and accept the deduction theorem, then any non monotonic expert system is inconsistent and, therefore, in some sense redundant.

8. CONCLUSION

This study indicates that the terms used in ES verification often lack clear semantics. We hope that recognizing this situation helps to improve it.

The study shows also that several ES redundancy criteria proposed so far have been inexact and may be interpreted in different ways. We have defined precise criteria and compared them. Due to the fuzziness of some previously defined criteria, we do not claim that our conclusions hold with respect to these criteria : we can rely only on our definitions. It seems that the most useful criteria are R-correctness (due to the computational feasibility) and S-, CA-correctness (due to universality and usefulness). Curiously enough, the intuitively appealing SA-correctness criterion used by several authors seems to be of less value than can be expected - it allows for evident redundancies to remain in the rule base. The logically oriented RC1-correctness criterion also fails to discover some important redundancies. The RC2-correctness criterion may find "redundancies" that are not redundancies in a direct sense. Rather, they indicate a need for restructuring the rule base. There are many ways to perform such restructuring. However, it is not clear yet what undesirable side effects (e.g. inferior comprehensibility) can be the result of this process.

Different inference strategies may seriously affect the relationships between redundancy criteria. We have investigated two possible strategies. The results given above characterize strategies that find all solutions, or the first solution. For ES finding the first solution, the redundancy criteria defined above tend to be less correlated with each other. We have also extended two criteria, CA- and SA-correctness, to cover hybrid ES. This study demonstrated that the relationships between SA- and CA-correctness are the same for rule-based and hybrid systems. Investigation of the adequate test generation complexity contribution has proved that in general this problem is NP-complete for rule-based and hybrid systems, and that the situation does not change if we assume R- or RC1-correctness of ES. The test generation for pure frame-based systems is feasible, but the additional complexity introduced by the simple frame and inheritance structures considered here is sufficient to destroy good properties of rule-based ES classes with polynomial test generation complexity.

REFERENCES

1.   AHO A.V., HOPCROFT J.E., ULLMAN J.E., (1976) : *The Design and Analysis of Computer Algorithms*, Addison-Wesley, London.
2.   BATESON G., (1981) : *Steps to an Ecology of Mind*, Ballantine Books, New York.
3.   BOEHM B.W. (1984) : *Verifying and Validating Software Requirements and Design Specifications*, IEEE Software, 1, No. 1, pp. 75-89.
4.   BUCHANAN B.G., (1983) : *Principles of Rule-based Expert Systems*, Advances in Computers, 22, 163-216.
5.   CRAGUN B.J., STENDEL H.J., (1987) : *A Decision-Table-Based Processor for Checking Completeness and Consistency in Rule-Based Expert Systems*, Int. J. Man-Mach Stud., 26, No. 5, pp.633-648.
6.   EWICS TC7 (1986) : *Techniques for Verification and Validation of Safety-Related Software*, Computers & Standards, 4, No. 2, pp. 101-112.
7.   GASCHNIG J., KLAHR P., POPLE H., SHORTLIFFE E., TERRY A., (1983) : *Evaluation of Expert Systems: Issues and Case Studies*. In F. Hayes-Roth, D. A. Waterman, and D. B. Lenat (Eds.), Building Expert Systems. Addison-Wesley, Reading, MA.

62   References

8.   GINSBERG A., (1987) : *A New Approach to Checking Knowledge Bases for Inconsistency and Redundancy*. In Proc. Third Annual Expert System Gov. Conf. Washington, DC, pp. 102-111.
9.   GREEN C.J.R., KEYES M.M., (1987) : *Verification and Validation of Expert Systems*, In Proc. Western Conf. on Expert Systems. IEEE Computer Society Press, pp. 38-43.
10.   INCE D.G. (1987) : *The Automatic Generation of Test Data*, The Computer J., 30, pp. 63-69.
11.   O`KEEFE R.M., BALCI O., SMITH E.P., (1987) : *Validating Expert System Performance*, IEEE Expert, 2, No. 4, pp. 81-90.
12   LEUNG, K. S., LAM,W. (1988) : *Fuzzy Concepts* . In Expert Systems. Computer, 21, No.9, pp. 43-56.
13.   LAURENT J.P., AYEL M., (1990) : *Coherence Checking for Knowledge Bases*, 8th Int. Congress on Cybernetics and Systems, June 1990, New York.
14.   MEISTER D., (1987) : *Behvioral Test and Evaluation of Expert Systems*. In G. Salvendy (Ed.), Cognitive Engineering in the Design of Human-Computer Interaction and Expert Systems. Elsevier Science Publishers, Amsterdam, pp. 539-549.
15.   MYERS G.J., (1979) : *The Art of Software Testing*, New York, Wiley.
16.   NAZARETH D.L., (1989) : *Issues in the Verification of Knowledge in Rule-Based Systems*, Int. J. Man-Machine Studies, 30, No. 3, pp. 255-271.
17.   NISSEN H.E., (1990) : Private Communication.
18.   NEBEL B., (1988) : *Computational Complexity of Terminological Reasoning in BACK*, Artificial Intelligence, 34, pp. 371-383.
19.   RAMAMOORTHY C.V., SHEKHAR S., GARG V., (1987) : *Software Development Support for AI Programs*, Computer, 20, pp. 30-37.
20.   REINKENSMEYER E., (1989) : *Designing ASICs in a Knowledge-Based Environment*, Design Automation Guide, pp. 14-18.
21.   ROUSSET M.C., (1990) : *Detection of "Deep" Inconsistencies in Rule-Based Systems: The COVADIS System*, 8th Int. Congress on Cybernetics and Systems, June 1990, New York.
22.   SUWA M., SCOTT A.C., SHORTLIFFE E.H., (1984) : *Completeness and Consistency in a Rule-Based System*, In B. G. Buchanan and E. H. Shortliffe (Eds.), Rule-Based Expert Systems. Addison-Wesley, London, pp. 159-170.
23.   TEPANDI J., (1988) : *A Knowledge-Based Approach to the Specification-Based Program Testing* Computers and Artificial Intelligence, 7, pp. 39-48.
24.   TEPANDI J., (1989a) : *The Generation of Test Data for Rule-Based Expert Systems*, In Proc. 10th Int. Symp. Algorithms '89, April 17-21, 1989, Vysoke Tatry, Bratislava, pp. 310-312.
25.   TEPANDI J., (1989b) : *Test Generation for Expert Systems with Fuzzy Truth Values*, Bulletin for Studies and Exchanges on Fuzziness and its Applications, 39, pp. 83-92.
26.   TEPANDI J., (1990) : *Verification, Testing, and Validation of Rule-Based Expert Systems*. In Proc. 11th IFAC World Congress, Vol. 7, pp. 162-167.

5

SACCO-SYCOJET:
Two Different Ways of Verifying
Knowledge-Based Systems

Marc AYEL
Jean-Pierre LAURENT

1. INTRODUCTION :
THE TWO APPROACHES TO THE VERIFICATION PROCESS

As in Figure 1, two approaches can be distinguished : with the first approach, the KBS is considered as a whole, while with the second one, the KBS is seen as a set of components which have to be verified separately.

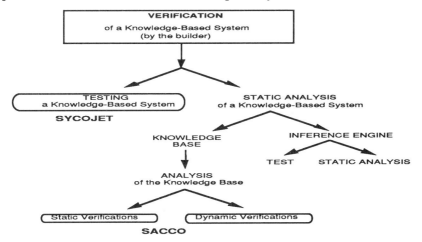

Figure 1 : The two approaches of the verification process

The second approach seems stricter than the first one. In fact the two approaches require very different tools and they can be considered as complementary. In addition to this, the first approach is well suited to studying the good working order of the KBS while the second one is preferable for local studies of the components of the KBS.

We will present these two approaches by the way of two systems: SACCO and SYCOJET. These systems are specific for KBS.

2. SACCO AND KB VERIFICATION

2.1 Introduction

The analysis of a KBS requires the analysis of its Inference Engine and the analysis of its KB.

The SACCO system [1-4] is concerned with the analysis of the KB only. The knowledge base is composed of facts describing the application domain and of rules describing the know-how of the domain. In addition the Inference Engine, regarded as classical software, can be verified with classical methods.

SACCO uses a strict definition of the notion of coherence by way of a conceptual model of a KB adapted to the application domain, noted C-Model. This model groups all the properties that sets of facts or sets of rules must verify to be classed as coherent.

Example of facts properties :

- coherence constraints : if X is_a rectangle
    andif X width > X length
    then incoherence
- arity of attributes : the number of parents is always less than or equal to 2
- contradictory values : big and small are contradictory values for the attribute "size" (they are not necessary complementary values)
- etc . . .

Example of rules properties :

- internal coherence of a rule
- redundancy rules
- conflict rules
- circular rules
- etc .

The rules properties are syntactic properties of the set of rules and the deductive power of the rule base is not really taken into account. So the rule properties may be considered as warnings for the builder : he has to interpret these warnings and perhaps to modify the KB.

When a fact property is not satisfied on a set of facts, it must be changed and when a set of deduced facts is incoherent, then either the rules or the facts must be changed.

We will note FC (resp. RC) the predicate which controls the fact (resp. rule) properties of a set of facts (resp. rules). A set of facts (resp. rules) is coherent if and only if FC (resp. RC) is true on it.

The definition of this model is well suited to studying the "static coherence" of the KB, that is the coherence of the set of rules and the coherence of the set of facts. But it is not enough to guarantee the "dynamic coherence"of the KB, that is the coherence of all the sets of facts which can be deduced by using the KB.

If KB = FBdom U RB, where FBdom is the set of facts describing the domain and RB the set of rules, KB is statically coherent when FC(FBdom) and RC(RB) are true.

If [KB] is the set of all the deducible sets of facts, KB is dynamically coherent when for all FB owing to [KB] then FC(FB) is true. Notice that the size of [KB] depends on the unknown set of initial coherent fact bases and depends also on the complexity of RB.

To solve this essential problem the SACCO system has a clear objective : to keep under control the combinatorial explosion which is potentially associated with the Expert System approach.

So the system has the behaviour of an expert verifying a KB :

- it checks for incoherence (it does not try to prove coherence exhaustively),
- it does not check all the potential incoherences, but selects a small set of "pertinent" incoherences,
- it does not check all the proof paths for incoherences but checks only some of them.

To do this the SACCO system requires specific expert knowledge to select the pertinent incoherences and to focus their proof.

Therefore particular knowledge is associated with a process of incoherence detection. This knowledge is the specification of a "protocol" for one incoherence study.

Protocols may be defined throughout the life cycle of the KB, from the acquisition phase to the maintenance phase and through the acceptance phase.

This set of protocols is built gradually and offers the builder ways of studying the dynamic coherence of the KB.

2.2 Label calculus

In a first step we will make the following assumptions :

1. There is no risk of combinatorial explosion during Label calculus [7, 10].
2. The Conceptual Model for Coherence can be transformed into a set of coherence constraints.

The first assumption is verified when the size and the complexity of the rule base is small. The second assumption is not well - founded when the C-model contains arity properties or properties concerning the sets of legal values for attributes.

Under these assumptions, each set of coherence constraints can be integrated into the Rule Base : the left-hand associated rule is the set of coherence constraints and the right-hand rule is a specific fact, named "incoherence fact." To each of these incoherence rules is associated a specific incoherence fact, IFi.

Now, it is possible to build the label of each "incoherence fact." Each element of the label is a description of the potential initial fact bases from which the fact "incoherence" can be deduced. We name this description a specification of initial fact bases, SIFB.

To simplify the presentation, we will assume that the fact bases describing a problem are always instantiation of specifications of initial fact bases.

These specifications are built from a "incoherence fact", IFi, by using rules in a backward-chaining manner, until no rules can be used. The intermediate results are also specifications of fact bases, SFB.

SIFB = SFBn -->   . . .   --> SFBo --> IFi

SFBo is a coherence constraint from which the incoherence fact IFi can be deduced. SFBo is an implicit description of an initial fact base.

SFBi is also an implicit description but this description is more explicit than SFBj when i<j.

SIFB = SFBn is the most explicit description of an initial fact base from which the incoherence IFi can be deduced.

If, for each IFi, the label of IFi is empty then the KB cannot produce a incoherent set of facts, and the KB has the property of dynamic coherence.

If a label of IFi is not empty, it is possible to build a counter-example of initial fact bases from which can be deduced the incoherent fact IFi.

2.3 SACCO: an heuristic approach

In general the previous assumptions cannot be made. So it is necessary first to focus the label calculus on a small group of coherence constraints, named pertinent conjectures of incoherence, and second to limit the label calculus.

2.4 The definition of pertinent conjectures of incoherence

The definition of the conjectures of incoherence comes from the definition of the C-Model. Each property of this model can be transformed, easily or not, into one or several coherence constraints, also named conjectures of incoherence.

With the arity property a large number of coherent constraints can be defined. So in some cases the expert neglects this property for the definition of the conjectures: in this case the builder first makes a restriction of the C-Model. In other cases, the violations of this property are explicitly viewed: in this case the builder has to define specializations of the C-Model.

The property of legal values of an attribute is the intensive or extensive definition of the set of values which can be associated in a fact with this attribute and a particular class of objects. To express the violations of this property a specialization of the C-Model can be also envisaged: it is the notion of singular values of an attribute.

These two possibilities are offered to the builder and, in this way, he defines the specific knowledge for detecting incoherences, named CKc.

This first knowledge makes it possible to restrict the set of potential conjectures which have to be built and also to control the combinatorial explosion.

The second knowledge, named CKs which can be used by the builder, concerns the selection of a small number of conjectures: the pertinent conjectures from which the label calculus can be tried. The builder can use sensitivity coefficients attached to the entities to represent the links between these entities and the "risk" of incoherence.

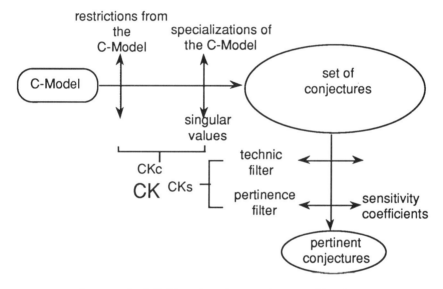

Figure 2: The definition of pertinent conjectures of incoherence

2.5 CKc : knowledge to build conjectures of incoherence

This knowledge allows the C-Model to be transformed into a set of conjectures. As we have previously seen, this transformation is easy for coherence constraints. Furthermore, one coherence constraint is associated with one conjecture.

With the arity property of a multi-valued attribute, the number of the associated conjectures is very large. Very often this property is not taken into account in building the conjectures and some specific sets of values are used to build only some specific conjectures.

The violations of the legal value property are not well characterized and the number of non legal values can be very large. The definition of a small number of singular values (figure 3) offers to the builder the possibility of focusing the construction of conjectures in accordance with the general objective of SACCO, that is, to be able to pinpoint incoherencies.

The singular values defined in this way are named external singular values because they are not-legal values of the attribute. In a symmetrical manner between the attribute and its opposite attribute we can also define internal singular values.

The singularity of a value depends on the distance from the value to the border of the set of legal values. The proximity of the border is a semantic notion and the builder can define several kinds of semantic proximity : historic proximity, geographic proximity, temporal proximity.

Set of conjectures = function (C-Model, CKc)

Example : the attribute "name" of the class " EEC Countries"

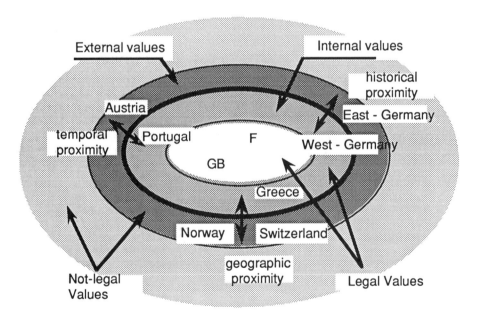

Figure 3 : Singular values

2.6 CKs : a knowledge to select pertinent conjectures

When the number of generated conjectures of incoherence is not reasonable, SACCO uses the knowledge CKs to select a subset of "pertinent incoherence conjectures". CKs groups the knowledge of the builder concerning :
- the "risk" of having an incoherence because poor use of such and such an entity (class, object, value or rule),
- the "interest" of detecting an incoherence linked to specific entities.

For the builder, this knowledge cannot be expressed in terms of specific coherence constraints. This knowledge is founded on the experience of the builder in the application domain and upon his experience in the acquisition process.

So this knowledge can form sensitivity coefficients for pertinence of entities. They are an implicit representation of a set of potential incoherences.

Some functions make it possible to integrate the pertinence of each entity in the pertinence of one conjecture, after which the most pertinent conjectures are selected.

For example, in a NATO-KB the expert may judge that it is more important ("interest") to search for possible incoherencies about EAST-Countries than about WEST-Countries. Also he may judge that possible incoherences about the USSR should be more important ("interest") than about ALBANY, that incoherencies about SS20 missiles should be more likely ("risk" : what is the information supplied by the spies worth) than incoherences about guns. For each of these entities the builder may define weights which will be used for calculating the pertinence of each conjecture which concerns them.

Thus the possibilities of eventual false deductions about the SS20 missiles of the USSR will be better explored by SACCO than the possibilities of errors about the guns of ALBANY, which is only natural !

The set of pertinent conjectures = function (conjectures, CKs)

CKs = {technical filter, pertinence filter = (sensitivity coefficients, pertinence threshold)}

2.7 Heuristic proof of the pertinent conjectures

The label of the pertinent conjectures could be computed but the risk of combinatorial explosion is present again and only some elements of the label of each pertinent conjecture must be computed.

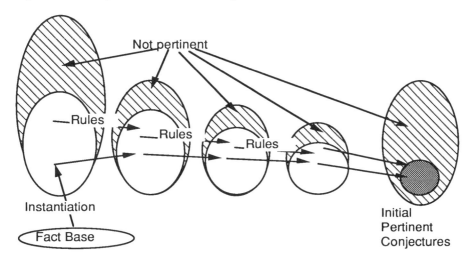

Figure 4: The proof of pertinent conjectures

The labels are computed with rules in a backward chaining manner (figure 4).

At each step a part of the label is gone over because the pertinence of this part is not sufficient.

The pertinence of an SFB is a new kind of pertinence concept when the fact base specification is strictly deduced from pertinent conjectures. To compute this new pertinence concept it is necessary to take into account the pertinence of the initial pertinent conjecture, the pertinence of the rules required to obtain SFB, and the sensitivity coefficients of SFB itself.

when   SFB --ri-->   . . . --rj--> SFBo ----> IFp
pertinence (SFB)
= function (pertinence (SFBo), sensitivity (ri, . . ., rj), sensitivity of elements of SFB).

This function is a heuristic function defined by the builder for a particular detection of incoherence.

With SACCO we make the assumption that the knowledge CKs used to select the pertinent conjectures is the same as the knowledge used to select the part of the label of a pertinent conjecture which is required to be computed. In fact it is not easy to distinguish these two kinds of knowledge especially when the label calculus is just beginning.

At each step the elements of a label are filtered with technical filters and with the pertinence filter. The rejected elements of the labels are specifications of initial fact bases from which an incoherence fact can be deduced. These specifications may or may not be proposed to the builder.

A KB can contain, in addition to a rule base, a fact base describing the application domain and sometimes some common facts to a particular set of problems.

When a rejected element of a label can be partially instantiated on the fact base included in the KB, it is possible that this new specification will satisfy the technical filters and the pertinence filter, in which case this specification is added to the part of the label from which the label calculus is carried our. Otherwise this new specification may be proposed to the builder.

A time limit for the label calculus can be defined by the builder. At the end of the process the calculated elements of the labels of pertinent conjectures are proposed to the builder. The builder has to judge whether or not these specifications are a counter-example for the KB coherence.

2.8 Protocols for incoherence detection

We have previously seen that incoherence detection depends on several kinds of knowledge or heuristics and depends, in fact, on the objective of the builder when he wants to have incoherence detection. So it is necessary to create and to manage a set of incoherence detection processes that we have named "incoherence detection protocols". Let SP be a set of such protocols.

These protocols contain knowledge and heuristics required for incoherence detection such as :

- CKc : the restrictions of the C-Model, the singular values taken into account;
- CKs : the technical filters, the sensitivity coefficients, the pertinence threshold;
- the pertinence calculus functions;
- the limit time for label calculus.

SP allows the dynamic coherence of KB to be guaranteed. When the builder make a modification ΔKB of KB, he can check if this modification has modified the dynamic coherence of KB in a previous sense. Thus he uses SP to check the coherence of KB+ΔKB. But he can also build specific protocols which better characterizes the incoherence detection due to ΔKB. He builds ΔSP and finally he uses SP+ΔSP to check the dynamic coherence of KB+ΔKB. Thus, the management of a set of protocols is required.

2.9 SACCO and the verification or validation process

The set of protocols can be defined partly by the builder to check the acquisition process, the maintenance process and consequently the verification process and partly by the customer who has to check if the KB cannot provide incoherences in accordance with the problems treated by the KBS (figure 5).

The customer protocols can be defined early, before the beginning of the acquisition process, in the contract between the builder and the customer. So the builder can, during the acquisition process, verify and validate his KB at the same time. Furthermore the builder can integrate the protocols for the verification process in the validation process and thus reinforce it.

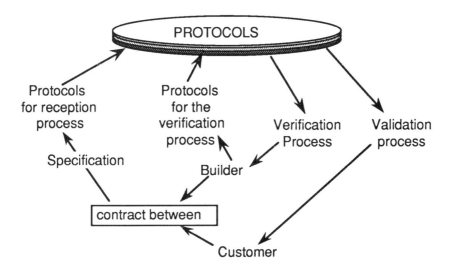

Figure 5: Using protocols

2.9.1 Conclusion

This method of validation or verification is only suited for coherence checking of knowledge bases and especially for heuristic checkings.

3. SYCOJET and KBS TESTING

This method reveals three difficulties (figure 6).

The first one is concerned with the definition, the selection and the building of an ad hoc set of test cases, that is a specific set of test cases for studying as fully as possible the good working order of the system. To solve this problem the builder - or an automatic system - has to take into account all the components of the KBS to optimize the building of this set of test - cases. Let us note that the test cases are not necessarily realistic problems.

The second difficulty is concerned, for each test case, with the acceptance or the rejection of the results obtained by the KBS. It must be borne in mind that the test cases are not realistic problems and perhaps the builder will have some difficulties in judging these results.

The last difficulty concerns the quality measurement of a set of test cases and the definition of a quality threshold beyond which the test of the system can be stopped.

For each of these three problems a specific solution has to be found when the system is a KBS. Usually the quality threshold is expressed in terms of the number of rules fired, the number of initial facts used or the number of goals obtained.

The SYCOJET system [5, 12,14] deals with these three problems and particularly with the problem of automatic building of sets of test cases adapted to KBSs.

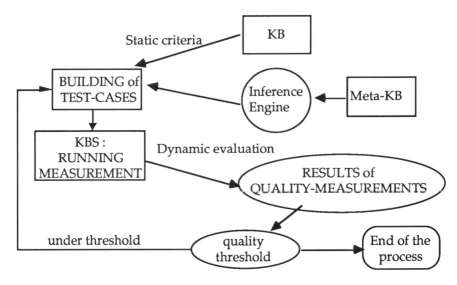

Figure 6: Testing process

3.1 The automatic building of a set of test cases

In the present version of SYCOJET, the selection of test cases is founded on static criteria. These static criteria take into account the entities of the KB which would potentially be used when the KBS is running, that is, initial facts, rules, deducible facts, goals. The features of the Inference Engine and the Meta-Knowledge are not used for building test cases. Great differences may appear between the aims of the static criteria used for building test cases and the evaluation of the set of entities really used when the KBS is running. The automatic building of a set of test cases is an incremental process: new test cases are built since the dynamic evaluation of the KBS is over the quality threshold.

For building a new test case it is required to take into account the test cases which are known (and the evaluation level obtained in terms of fired rules, deduced facts, initial facts) and the objectives of the evaluation. These differences allow static criteria for building a new test case to be defined (figure 7).

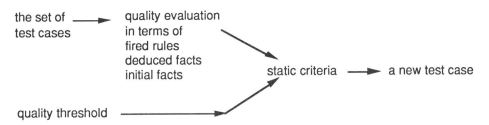

Figure 7: Automatic building of test cases

The static criteria use the same items as the quality evaluation, but a static criteria cannot guarantee the level of the quality evaluation because of the behaviour of the Inference Engine.

For using static criteria in test case building, it is necessary to have an appropriate representation of the set of rules, the set of paths and the set of deduced facts: to do this the SYCOJET system builds extended labels of each deducible fact.

An extended label of a fact F is a set of c-couples where a c-couple contains a specification of an Initial Fact Base, SIBF, and a deduction path, DP, from which F can be deduced.

    label (F) = [c-couple (F)]
    c-couple (F) = (SIFB, DP)
    SIFB   ---DP---> F, where DP is an ordered set of rules.

If these labels are restricted to the first part of the c-couple, they become De Kleer labels. The second part allows rule criteria to be obtained for selecting the test cases.

So the building process starts with two steps :

Step 1 : the choice of a deduced fact F among all the rule conclusions.

Often the set of rule conclusions is limited to those which cannot be instantiated in a premise of another rule. If the static criteria are concerned with the choice of a rule, the conclusion of the chosen rule becomes the deduced fact F.

Step 2 : the choice of a c-couple in the label of F.

If the chosen c-couple is (SIFB, DP), then all the initial fact bases which satisfy the specification SIFB allow F to be deduced, in particular by using the deduction path DP.

But the behaviour of the Inference Engine may differ in these different initial fact bases. So we have introduced the concept of equivalence classes of initial fact bases: they are initial fact bases satisfying the same specification SIFB for which the expert expects the same behaviour of the Inference Engine.

Step 3 : the choice of an equivalence class EqFB according to the SIFB description.

Now it is necessary to choose an Initial Fact Base in an equivalence class, that is to choose values for the variables. This step depends on the kind of test required. The choice is not the same for a "semantic boundary test "or for a "robustness boundary test". For these two tests it is necessary to define the internal or external singular values of an attribute. This definition of singular values appears similar to the definition of singular values in SACCO. Nevertheless there are differences: in SACCO the values are singular because the expert expects the detection of incoherences on using them; with the building of test cases the values are singular because the expert is afraid of a false behaviour of the KBS, not necessarily an incoherent result.

Also, the attributes considered are not the same: in SACCO the attribute concerned allows incoherences to be described (that are possible results of the KBS), in SYCOJET the attribute with singular values allows an initial fact base to be described. These two kinds of attribute are at both ends of the deduction paths.

Step 4 : the choice of values to obtain a test case

Step 5 : checking the validity of the test case obtained.

This step is required to be sure that the expert will be able to judge the results of the KBS on the test case. If the expert does not accept them, the test case will not be taken into account in the quality evaluation of the set of test case.

We can put together all this knowledge required for building a test case from criteria previously defined. We name this set a T-Model, that is, knowledge for building test cases.

The T-Model contains the definition of equivalence classes, the set of singular values for the attributes used in Initial Fact Bases, and the concepts of validity of test cases.

The T-Model may also contain some more specific properties, such as the obligatory presence of some attributes in all the test cases or such as the dependency links between attributes in a test case.

An example of the first property may use the attribute temperature for a KBS in medicine.

In the same domain an example of the second property is: when the fact "a laboratory analysis is present" is inside a test case, the test case must contain a fact concerning the result of this laboratory analysis.

3.1.1 Conclusion

The automatic building of test cases is solved by the SYCOJET system by way of a computation of extended labels. After that, the definition of the quality threshold for a set of test cases and the evaluation results of the known test cases allows static criteria to be defined (in terms of rules and facts) for building a new test case.

This construction uses specific knowledge, the T-Model, that is a set of different criteria required with the static criteria for building a new test case.

4. CONCLUSION

These two methods seem to have the same goal, that is, verification, and to use the same knowledge, but in fact the goals are different and different kinds of knowledge are used. Goals and knowledge are appropriate for the two kinds of verification that have to be performed.

This raises some questions :

Is SYCOJET well suited to make coherence studies ?

Are the different kinds of knowledge (the C-Model, the T-Model, the knowledge KC) really different and what is the common knowledge ?

The main difference between the T-Model and KC is that these two kinds of knowledge are at the two ends of the deduction paths. So it is not easy to characterize and to focus on such or such incoherence in terms of properties of Initial Fact Bases, because incoherence appears only after many deductions from an Initial Fact Base.

Another difference is that testing of a KBS is concerned with the whole behaviour of the KBS, not only with the incoherent behaviour.
We have seen that the T-Model and KC are two different kinds of knowledge. The C-model can be used to define the validity of the test case, but perhaps this is not enough because the C-Model makes it possible to check only the coherence validity of a test case.

So these two verification processes are complementary. The systems SACCO and SYCOJET are implemented in KOOL, an environment for Expert Systems, and SACCO is completely integrated in an extended environment named SACKOOL.

REFERENCES

1.   AYEL M., (1987) : *Détection d'incohérences dans les bases de connaissances : SACCO,* Thèse d'Etat, Chambéry, September, 217pp.

2.   AYEL M., (1988) : *Protocols for Coherence Checking in Expert System Knowledge Bases,* Proc. of ECAI-88, Munich, August, pp. 220-225.

3.   AYEL M., LAURENT J.P., (1989) : *Coherence testing of knowledge Bases,* Congress Applications of Artificial Intelligence VII, March 1989, Orlando.

4.   AYEL M., LAURENT J.P., (1989) : *Off-line Coherence Checking for Knowledge Based Systems,* 2nd Workshop on Validation, Verification & Test, IJCAI, Detroit, August.

5.   AYEL M., VIGNOLLET L., (1990) : *A specific knowledge for testing Knowledge Bases,* 2nd International Conference on Software Engineering and Knowledge Engineering, Skokie (ILLINOIS), 21-23 June.

6.   AYEL M., VIGNOLLET L., : *A Conceptual Model for Construction of Sets of Test Samples for Knowledge Bases,* ECAI 90, Stockholm, August.

7.   DE KLEER J., (1986) : *An assumption-based TMS,* AI Journal, vol. 28, n° 2, March 1986, pp. 127-162.

8.   GINSBERG A., (1988) : *Knowledge-Base Reduction : A new Approach to Checking Knowledge Bases for Inconsistency and Redundancy,* Proc. of AAAI-88, St Paul, August.

9.   NGUYEN T.A., PERKINS W.A., LAFFAY T.J., PECORA D., (1987) : *Knowledge base verification,* AI Magazine, summer 1987, pp. 67-75.

10.   ROUSSET M.C., (1988) : *About the Coherence of a Knowledge Base : the COVADIS System,* Proc. of ECAI-88, Munich, August 1988, pp.79-84.

11.   STACHOWITZ R.A., CHANG C.L., (1989) : *Research on Validation of Knowledge-Based Systems,* 2nd Workshop VV&T, IJCAI, Detroit, August.

12.   VIGNOLLET L., AYEL M., (1989) : *Automatic Building of Test-samples for Validating Knowledge Based Systems,* 2nd Workshop on Validation, Verification & Test, IJCAI, Detroit August.

13.   VIGNOLLET L., AYEL M., (1989) : *SYCOJET : A tool for building automatically sets of test for knowledge bases,* VIIIème Conf. SPIE on Applications of Artificial Intelligence, Orlando April.

14.   VIGNOLLET L., AYEL M., (1989) : *Generating test sets for knowledge bases,* Proc. of Ninth International Workshop, Expert Systems & Their Applications, Avignon, June 1989, pp.247-260.

6

The Use of Object-Oriented Process Specification for the Validation and Verification of Decision Support Systems

Paul J. KRAUSE
Paddy BYERS
Saki HAJNAL
John FOX

ABSTRACT

Much of the current development work on the validation, verification and test of Knowledge-based Systems has concentrated on checking the integrity of the rule set and the knowledge base itself. It is also important to ensure that the behaviour of the software which implements any operations on the knowledge base is well understood. In the Biomedical Computing Unit of the Imperial Cancer Research Fund, we have been developing a number of decision support applications involving large knowledge bases. As part of our programme of work to provide a formal basis for the symbolic decision procedure, we have been investigating the use of Formal Specification Languages in the validation of the software which implements this decision procedure.

We present here a discussion of the benefits gained from formally specifying a truth maintenance system (TMS). A short introduction to the Specification Language used is given. There then follows an analysis of the intended properties of the TMS in order to give the rationale behind the specification which is presented here. This paper is intended as a tutorial guide to the benefits that may be gained from the use of Formal Methods, and so we present the specification in a restricted form (allowing the use of a propositional, rather than first order, rule set) to avoid too much technical detail.

1. INTRODUCTION

The validation and verification of knowledge-based systems may at the coarsest level be divided into two sub-problems :

    i. checking the integrity of the Knowledge Base itself,
    ii. validating the software which controls the manipulation and accessing of the Knowledge Base.

Although the work described here has some bearing on the first, this paper will concentrate on the second sub-problem. With KBS's as with any other well-engineered software product, it is increasingly important to have a clear unambiguous statement of the intended behaviour and properties of the software. In addition, an assurance that the software as implemented will behave correctly with respect to the specification will be required.

Many of the more recent high level programming languages free the implementer to a certain extent from thinking about the details of the control of flow and assignments in an algorithm. Using a declarative programming language such as Prolog or ML, for example, allows the development of a program which contains a much clearer statement of the logic underlying the implementation. Declarative programming languages are increasingly being used in the development of Expert Systems. However, one potential difficulty is that the expressiveness of a programming language may encourage the use of the program itself as a specification of the intended behaviour of a piece of computer software. This is not in itself sufficient. A Prolog rule, for example, may capture clearly the programmer's intuition about the intended functionality in a simple demonstration, but behave quite counter-intuitively if used in a different environment or under a different modality [2]. Although some of the very high-level programming environments now on the market enable professionals with little formal training in computing science to produce applications for their own field of expertise, there is an increasing danger that the behaviour of such applications under extreme conditions will not be defined or predictable [5]. There is, at present, no substitute for thinking hard and deeply about the intended behaviour of a computer application.

The Biomedical Computing Unit of the Imperial Cancer Research Fund (ICRF) is working on a variety of applications of Artificial Intelligence to biology and medicine. To support these applications a number of Prolog-based inference tools have been developed, and a general symbolic decision procedure has been developed using these tools. Although these techniques are now quite mature and seem to be robust, their theoretical basis requires more rigorous development. Bearing in mind that many biomedical applications can be considered to be "safety critical" it is now highly desirable to address questions of formal specification and soundness of the decision procedure, and to produce software suitable for routine use which correctly implements this procedure.

As a preliminary to this programme of work, we have been investigating the possible role Formal Methods in Software Specification may play in the specification and validation of decision support software. The term "Formal Methods" is perhaps ill defined, and covers a wide range of techniques [11]. In our usage of the term, we are interested in the use of formal languages in the specification and analysis of the properties and behaviour of software systems. The formal specification languages that are currently available fall into two classes. In model- or state based approaches, the aim is to build a (mathematical) model of the program state, and the operations to which it may be subjected. Z and VDM are increasingly widely used examples of this approach. In algebraic, or property-based techniques, theories are developed which describe the intended behaviour of the software. Clear, ACT ONE, Larch and OBJ are examples of algebraic specification languages. In the case of a complex software system it may be necessary to use both model-based and algebraic approaches, as appropriate, to specify different aspects of the complete system. In this paper, we will concentrate on discussing the use of a model-based approach to specify one particular aspect of a knowledge-based system. The particular formal language we have used is an object-oriented variant of the language Z [9, 10].

We will first present a brief introduction to the object-oriented specification language. A formal specification will then be given of a database in which information is explicitly maintained on the forward closure of the rule set, grounded in the set of facts asserted into the database. After a brief discussion of the properties of this specification, a revised version will be presented which overcomes some of the weaknesses of the first version. The actual final version of the specification is more complex than the version which will be presented here. The aim of this paper is to provide a discussion of the benefits which may be gained from the use of Formal Methods, rather than concentrate on the technicalities of one completed specification. A full version of the specification may be found in [6].

2. THE ROLE OF TRUTH MAINTENANCE IN DECISION SUPPORT SYSTEMS

A number of experimental applications under development at the Biomedical Computing Unit of the Imperial Cancer Research Fund use a simple version of a Justification-based Truth Maintenance System (JTMS). The JTMS is used to manipulate object rules which express the symbolic decision procedure under development here. Classical decision theory can be very restrictive when formulating decision models for practical situations. The principal group of restrictions, inherent in numerical decision theories, is that they make no provision for reasoning about the decision process itself [3]. Classical procedures cannot reflect on what the decision is, what the options are, what methods may be used in making a decision, what knowledge may be relevant, and so forth. The Biomedical Computing Unit is developing an approach which accommodates classical decision theory within a framework of first-order logic with non monotonic extensions [4]. Among the benefits offered by the approach are the potential to: express qualitative arguments about the desirability of decision options in the absence of probability or utility parameters; automate techniques for generating decision options; initiate, control and terminate a decision process autonomously. A truth maintenance system is used to enable a logical extension of the known facts to be maintained in such a way that the "beliefs" of the system may be revised in the light of new information. A particular benefit of implementing decision procedures in a non-monotonic logic is that decision systems can adapt automatically as beliefs change, contradictions are encountered or new knowledge is acquired.

One aspect of the current work at the Biomedical Computing Unit[1] is to develop a formal framework for the symbolic decision procedure. If the object rules expressing the decision procedure are to be manipulated by a JTMS, then we need to have a clear understanding of the intended behaviour of the JTMS.

3. INFORMAL STATEMENT OF BEHAVIOUR OF THE JTMS

Typically, an implementation of this JTMS uses concepts *logically assert* and *logically retract*. The intended function is that upon logically asserting a fact into the database, that fact and all logical consequences of that fact (inferred using the rule set) are stored. Upon logically retracting a fact, that fact is removed from the database together with all consequences dependent on the truth of that fact.

The following is an operational statement of the JTMS, which has been derived from a declarative implementation.

To **logically assert** a fact X :

> Check X is not already known.
> If it is not, then
> > - assert the fact X into the database.
> > - and derive all consequences of X being true.

To derive all consequences of X being true :

> Identify all object rules for which the truth of X is a condition of the antecedents being satisfied.
> > For each such rule, check that all the antecedents of the rule are satisfied.
> > For the rules where they are satisfied, **logically assert** each consequent of the rule, and also assert the **justification** for the truth of each consequent.
> > In addition, for each fact C whose justification includes the negation of X logically retract C provided there is no other justification for C being true.

[1]. In particular, the SERC funded project : "A Formal Basis for Decision Support Systems : Theory Tools and Applications".

To **logically retract** a fact X that was previously believed to be true :
    Retract X from the database, and then withdraw all consequences of X being true.
To withdraw all consequences of X being true :

    For all facts C whose justification includes the truth of X, withdraw that justification and retract C if there is no other justification for C.
    In addition, for all object rules for which the falsehood of X is a condition of the antecedents being satisfied, check if the antecedents are now satisfied.
    For those rules which are now satisfied, logically assert each consequent of the rule, and also assert the justification for the truth of each consequent.
Inference rules used are of the form
$A_1, \dots, A_n \Rightarrow C_1, \dots, C_n$
Where A_i, i=1 ...n, n ≥ 1 are the **antecedents** of the rule (may be negated terms),
    C_i, i=1 ... n, n ≥ 1 are the **consequents** of the rule.
The only inference mechanism used is *modus ponens*.
If a consequent C_i is inferred from such an inference rule, the list of antecedents of the rule is a **justification** for this inference.
Negation is negation by failure using the closed world assumption.

4. OBJECT-ORIENTED PROCESS SPECIFICATION

Behavioural Object-Oriented Process Specification [7, 8] is a variant of the specification language Z [9, 10]. As the name suggests, the most obvious difference between the Schuman-Pitt notation and Z is in the former's commitment to the "object-oriented" paradigm for structuring and decomposing complex systems. This notation provides a framework for formally specifying and reasoning about the behaviour of user-defined "classes" of abstract objects. As with Z, data types are specified using simple set-theoretic constructs, with constraints on their values specified using first-order predicate calculus. A simple syntactic structure using "schemas" provides a framework for the specification. A "state-schema" is used to introduce a specific class of abstract objects. Contained within this schema is a characterization of the internal state for each instance of the class (state components together with state invariants), together with the conditions which must hold in any initial state. A state schema has the following generic form:

$\Gamma(\pi_1, \dots, \pi_k)$		
X	*Component Declarations*	
Y	*Invariant Predicates*	
Z	*Initialization Predicates*	

The header of a state schema provides an identifier for the class in question (Γ), as well as naming any formal parameters for that class ($\pi_1, \ldots, \pi_k$).

The associated "event -schemas" specify the operations which may be carried out on instances of the corresponding classes. The event schema headers include the identifier for the class with which the event is associated (Γ), together with the name of the operation (ϕ_i) and the names of any input (α_i) and/or output parameters (ρ_i) figuring in its signature. Contained within the event schema are the type declarations for the parameters, and statements of the preconditions and post-conditions which must be satisfied by the state before and after the event respectively:

$$\Gamma.\phi_i(\alpha_1, \ldots, \alpha_k \rightarrow \rho_1, \ldots, \rho_n)$$

P	*Parameter Declarations*
Q	*Precondition Predicates*
R	*Postcondition Predicates*

Primed variable names in the post-conditions refer to state components after the application of the event. The state invariant introduced in the state schema must continue to be satisfied after any operation on the database is carried out. Consequently, a succinct statement of the explicit changes made by the operation is all that is necessary. A significant departure from Z or VDM is the use of a special rule of historical inference in the Schuman-Pitt notation, whereby only the minimal effect (change of state) need be specified for each event associated with a given class. That is, any elements of the program state which are not explicitly referred to in the event specification are assumed to remain unchanged by the event. This "rest-unchanged" semantics has particularly important implications for the specification of concurrent systems, although this is not a major concern for the present work. It does, however, make for a more succinct specification than that obtained using Z or VDM.

5. PRELIMINARY SPECIFICATION OF DATABASE EXTENSION MANAGEMENT SYSTEM

As a simple example of the use of the specification language, we give here a naive specification of a truth maintained database, which is composed of a set of facts, a rule set and the set of consequences deducible from those facts and rules. The state invariant ensures that any consequences which cease to be supported by at least one applicable rule (as a result of some operation being carried out on the database) are removed from the consequence set. Equally, any consequences which become supported by a valid rule are added to the consequence set. Initially, no facts are contained in the database. A brief glossary of the notation used in the declarations and predicates may be found in Appendix 1.

Two given sets provide the basic building blocks from which all data types are constructed :

Given Types: **DATA**   (Positive literals)
                ANTECEDENT   (Positive or negative literals)

Derived Type: **RULE**: (Set(**ANTECEDENT**),Set(**DATA**))

The class "DB" is then defined by the following state schema:

DB _____

    Facts   : Set(**DATA**)
    RuleSet : Set(**DATA**)   *STATE COMPONENTS*
    ConsSet : Set(**DATA**)

_____

$\forall C : \textbf{DATA} \bullet$ *STATE INVARIANTS*

$\quad (\exists (\text{Antes},\text{Conses}) : \textbf{RULE} \bullet$

$\quad ((\text{Antes},\text{Conses}) \in \text{RuleSet} \wedge \text{statisfiable}(\text{Antes}) \wedge C \in \text{Conses}))$

$\qquad\qquad\qquad\qquad\qquad\qquad\qquad\qquad \Leftrightarrow C \in \text{ConsSet}$

_____

$\quad \text{Facts}' = \varnothing$ *INITIALIZATION*

The nature of the relation "satisfiable" is left undefined at this stage. The state invariant may be given the following gloss. For any rule such that the antecedents are in some sense "satisfiable", then the consequences of that rule will be contained in ConsSet. All such consequences will be present in ConsSet, and these are the only members of this set.

The definition of "satisfiable" is actually the difficult part of this specification. The discussion in the next section will provide some insight into the requirements of its definition.

"Event-schemas" specify the operations which may be carried out on instances of the corresponding classes. As mentioned already, a succinct statement of the explicit changes made by the operation is all that is necessary. For example, we may define the operation of "asserting" an element into the database DB with the following event schema (there are no preconditions, other than that the element j to be inserted must be of type **DATA**):

DB.Assert(φ)
φ : **DATA**

$\varphi \in$ Facts'	*POSTCONDITIONS*

All that need be specified is that the element φ be contained in the set Facts' after the event has occurred. The "rest-unchanged" semantics ensures that all other elements that were present in the set Facts before the operation are present in Facts' after the operation. The state invariant ensures that the elements of ConsSet are modified accordingly.

An operation to remove facts from the database may be similarly defined.

6. DISCUSSION OF FIRST VERSION OF THE SPECIFICATION

Because of the lack of definition of the relation "satisfiable", the state invariant in the previous example is not completely specified. The following simple examples can be used to demonstrate some of the constraints which must be imposed on the possible final states by this invariant. Some intuitively undesirable behaviours are consistent with this specification. Not all of them are demonstrated by the present implementations of the JTMS, but it is worth mentioning each one to give some insight into the reasoning behind the next definition of the TMS specification.

It should be a fairly natural thought that a specification for a JTMS should have some reference to the justifications. The following example demonstrates that this is indeed a requirement. Consider the following rule :

$$a \wedge \neg b \wedge \neg c \Rightarrow d$$

Implicit in this particular specification language is the concept of "minimal change". As a result of any operation, it is intended that the minimal change to the database occurs that is consistent with the specification. If fact "a" is asserted into a database containing the above rule, with facts "b", "c" and "d" absent, then the following minimal changes to the database are consistent with the above specification: any one of the three sets of facts {a, b}, {a, c} or {a, d} is added to the database. What is actually intended is that only those facts are added to the database which have a justification; in this case, the set {a, d} (we may give "user" as a justification).

This is still not quite a strong enough statement. The unintended behaviours of the previous paragraph are not demonstrated by any of the current implementations of the JTMS, but the following is. Consider now the pair of rules:

$$a \wedge \neg b \quad \Rightarrow c \quad \text{-----------------------------------} \quad \text{(i)}$$
$$c \wedge \neg d \quad \Rightarrow b \quad \text{-----------------------------------} \quad \text{(ii)}$$

Initially, none of the facts "a", "b", "c" and "d" are known. The user asserts "a". "c" is concluded using rule (i), then "b" concluded using rule (ii). After concluding "b", the justification for "c" {a $\wedge$ ¬b} is no longer valid. The current implementation of the JTMS will add the set {a,b,c} to the database. However, the simultaneous conclusion of "b" and "c" is invalid. We need to explicitly state that in the invariant concerning justifications each fact must have a currently valid justification.

The next problem gives an abbreviated version of a form of self supporting circular reasoning which may quite legitimately be present in a knowledge base. The error here is that once triggered, the mutual supports may continue to justify conclusions even after the triggering fact has been withdrawn. The example rule set is :

$$c \quad \Rightarrow d \quad \text{-----------------------------------} \quad \text{(iii)}$$
$$d \quad \Rightarrow e \quad \text{-----------------------------------} \quad \text{(iv)}$$
$$e \quad \Rightarrow d \quad \text{-----------------------------------} \quad \text{(v)}$$

Again, initially the facts "c", "d" and "e" are not present in the database. The user then asserts "c". "d" and "e" are then both concluded, "d" having support {c,e} and "e" having one justification {d}. The user now retracts "c". Only the justification {c} for "d" is withdrawn, but justification {e} remains. So "d" remains in the database. Once triggered, the conclusions of rules (iv) and (v) will never be withdrawn. If this is regarded as undesirable behaviour, then a further constraint must be placed on the set of justifications: the justification set should be well - founded. That is, any conclusion must be derivable in an ordered sequence of inference steps from asserted facts.

A final insight into the behaviour of the JTMS may be gained from the pair of rules :

$$d \wedge \neg a \quad \Rightarrow b \quad \text{-----------------------------------} \quad \text{(vi)}$$
$$d \wedge \neg b \quad \Rightarrow a \quad \text{-----------------------------------} \quad \text{(vii)}$$

Even with the above invariants, we still have two possible models on asserting "d"; viz. {d, b} and {d, a}. So in a hypothetical medical expert system :

$$\text{has\_child}(A,C) \wedge \neg\text{adopted}(C) \quad \Rightarrow \text{fertile}(A)$$
$$\text{has\_child}(A,C) \wedge \neg\text{fertile}(A) \quad \Rightarrow \text{adopted}(C)$$

given no knowledge as to whether a child **carla** has been adopted, or whether her parent **alexandra** is fertile, the present system will conclude **adopted(carla)**, and **fertile(alexandra)** will be blocked. However, if the rule order is reversed, the system will conclude **fertile(alexandra)**. This is just an artefact of this particular implementation. As the system is intended, there should be no way it can give a preference for **adopted(carla)** or **fertile(alexandra)**, and in the circumstances it should either conclude **adopted(carla)** ∨ **fertile(alexandra)**, or we may take an approach from modal logic. That is to say, with these rules there is one possible world in which **adopted(carla)** is true, and one in which **fertile(alexandra)** is true, but neither is true in all possible worlds. Thus conclude ◊**adopted(carla)** and ◊**fertile(alexandra)**, i.e. both states are possible. Were, for example, **adopted(carla)** true in all possible worlds (through some other constraint), then conclude □**adopted(carla)** - it is necessary that **adopted(carla)**.

In summary, we also require in the specification statements to the effect that:

1. Justifications for all consequences added to the database must be currently valid.
2. All chains of justifications generated by application of the rule set should be grounded in user asserted facts.
3. Account must be taken of possible indeterminacy in the applicability of rules in the rule set.

In order to fulfil these requirements, we have produced the following formal specification. The system specified differs significantly from the classical JTMS of Doyle so we prefer to use the name "Database Extension Management System".

7. FORMAL SPECIFICATION OF THE DATABASE EXTENSION MANAGEMENT SYSTEM

This is a specification of a database extended by the deductive closure of the rule set contained in the database. The database contains a set of facts asserted by the user, and a rule set. Information about all possible extensions generated by the rule set, grounded in the fact set, is maintained in the database. Facts are positive ground literals, and conclusions are also positive literals. The use of negation by failure is implicit in this specification.

Rules may contain positive or negative literals as antecedents. In the form presented here, we evade the problem of specifying the instantiation of variables by assuming the rule set consists of ground rules where all possible instantiations of variables are present. The instantiation of variables in first-order rules is covered in the specification as documented in [6]. Each rule is specified as a triple (positive antecedents, negative antecedents, consequent). A rule is satisfiable if all of the positive antecedents, and none of the negative antecedents, are present in the database. Note there is only one consequent. With the use of ground rules, there is no loss of generality with this as rules with multiple consequents can be rewritten as multiple rules with single consequents.

We first define a class **DB** with four components; *Facts, RuleSet, PossibleC* and *NecessaryC*. The user may assert facts into, or retract facts from the set *Facts*. The RuleSet is as discussed above. Initially the set of Facts is empty.The last two state components contain information on the deductive closure of the rule set, grounded in the set of asserted facts. As discussed in the previous section, there may be some non-determinacy in the applicability of the rules, so we define two additional state components: *PossibleC* and *NecessaryC*. *PossibleC* contains all those items of data for which there exists at least one viable extension of the fact set containing that item. *NecessaryC* contains those items of data which are contained in all viable extensions of the fact set.

The use of the term viable is intended to capture an intuition, but it does need a precise definition. An extension is *viable* if it contains all the user asserted facts and *all*, *and* *only*, consequences of those facts which may be derived by a finite sequence of rule applications. In addition, the formal definition of a viable extension given below captures the notions of well-foundedness and validity of the supports for the consequence set (the appendix contains a glossary of the Z notation used here).

Given Types: **DATA**   (Positive ground literals)
Derived Types: **GROUND_RULE** : (Set(**DATA**),Set(**DATA**),**DATA**)

DB_____

Facts   : Set(**DATA**)
RuleSet   : Set(**GROUND_RULE**)
PossibleC   : Set(**DATA**)
NecessaryC   : Set(**DATA**)

PossibleC = {φ:**DATA**| $\exists$S $\subseteq$ **DATA** • viable(Facts,S,RuleSet) $\wedge$ φ $\in$ S}

NecessaryC = {φ:**DATA**| $\forall$S $\subseteq$ **DATA** • viable(Facts,S,RuleSet) $\Rightarrow$ φ $\in$ S}

Facts' = $\varnothing$ *Initialization*

Where:

viable(Facts,Consequences,RuleSet) $\equiv$
  ($\exists$ J : seq Set(**DATA**) •
    head J = Facts
    $\wedge$ last J = Consequences
    $\wedge$ $\forall$ i < #J • $\exists$C : **DATA** •
        J(i+1) = J(i) $\cup$ {C}
      $\wedge$ $\exists$ (P,N,C) $\in$ RuleSet •
            P $\subseteq$ J(i)
          $\wedge$ N $\cap$ Consequences = $\varnothing$)
  $\wedge$
    ($\forall$ (P,N,C) $\in$ RuleSet •
      P $\subseteq$ Consequences
      $\wedge$ N $\cap$ Consequences = $\varnothing$
      $\Rightarrow$ C $\in$ Consequences)

The first condition for a consequence set to be *viable* ensures that all consequences are grounded in the set *Facts*. A consequent is only added to the conclusion set if it could be derived from the fact set in a finite sequence of inferences, and if the derivation will not be invalidated by the later addition of further consequences to the database.

The second condition ensures that any consequence which could be legitimately added to the consequence set is added.

These are the only data which are added to the consequence set in deriving it from the set *Facts*.

As before, *assert* and *retract* are simple to specify in this notation. *Assert* remains unchanged; we only need specify that the data item of interest, φ, is present in the set *Facts'* after the operation:

DB.assert(φ)_____

$\varphi : \textbf{DATA}$

$\varphi \in \text{Facts'}$

Retract just removes an item of data from the fact set. The datum is not necessarily removed from the database. It may be present in either of *PossibleC* or *NecessaryC* if it is derivable from the remaining facts.

DB.retract(φ)_____

$\varphi : \textbf{DATA}$

$\varphi \notin \text{Facts'}$

Having now captured the notions of "possible" and "necessary" in terms of *viable* extensions, we can specify two query operations. The first succeeds if the specified element is a member of all possible extensions of the fact set :

DB.nq(φ)_____

$\varphi : \textbf{DATA}$

$\varphi \in \text{NecessaryC}$

The second succeeds if the specified element is a member of at least one of the possible extensions :

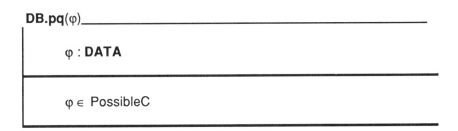

8. PROOF OBLIGATIONS

In many engineering disciplines it is common for a model to be constructed as part of the process of specifying and designing a system. This enables predictions to be made about the properties of the end product, and a full analysis of its behaviour under extreme conditions to be carried out before construction is initiated. The model may be a physical scale model or it may be a mathematical model. Both permit the design to be evaluated in terms of some known underlying theory. Formal specification languages are intended to enable software engineers to produce a mathematical model of the software they wish to build before committing themselves to coding it. As well as providing an unambiguous statement of the program's intended behaviour, the formal specification may be subject to mathematical proofs and formal analysis of its properties. In addition, once the formal specification has been finalized, a process of "stepwise refinement" may be used for generating software which correctly implements the specification [12].

A demonstration of the fulfilment of the static proof obligations for the Extension Management System is given in [6]. These are the minimum set of proofs which need to be undertaken in the validation of a formal specification. A complete statement of the requirements can be found in [8], but essentially, for the static validation of a schema defined class Γ, it is necessary to show that :

- the subsystem class Γ is *consistent*
- the initialization is always *effective*

In addition, for each event $\Gamma.\phi_i$ associated with the class Γ, we must demonstrate that

- the event is *applicable*
- the event is *effective*

A specification is *consistent* if there exists at least one model. This can be demonstrated by exhibiting a particular model. An event is applicable if there exists an instantiation of the state components such that the preconditions of the event are satisfiable. An event is *effective* if in all circumstances when it may occur, it can indeed occur. That is, whenever a state exists which satisfies the preconditions for the event, there will always exist a state satisfying the postconditions.

The fulfilment of these obligations is in fact very straightforward for this particular specification.

The next step is to consider the dynamic behaviour of the complete system as specified. A significant benefit accruing from a commitment to the object-oriented paradigm in the specification language we have been using is that it becomes plausible to speak about the behaviour of individual instances of a given class. That is, to consider how the state of such objects may evolve from initialization over time. A full discussion of these aspects does, unfortunately, become quite technical. It is, for example, necessary to augment the event schemas with predicates embodying an explicit statement of the "rest-unchanged" semantics before an analysis of the behaviour can be undertaken. For a description of the nature of these predicates and the sort of proofs of behaviour that may be undertaken see [8, 1]. The point to emphasize here is that the behaviour of the specified system *can* be subject to mathematical analysis.

9. DISCUSSION

We have presented here a very abstract specification of a database extension management system. At this level of refinement there is little guidance as to how such a system may be implemented, or even whether it is feasible to implement such an idealized system at all. One particularly computationally demanding requirement is the proposal to maintain information about all possible extensions of the database. It may be that in the context of a particular application this requirement can be relaxed, on the assumption, say, that there will be no indeterminacy present in the rule set. A refinement of this specification may then be produced in which information concerning the one necessary extension is all that is required. The domain of application of the system will be circumscribed, but a clear statement of the restrictions on the allowable properties of the rule set will also be generated.

Although declarative programming languages can be a great aid to productivity and clarity in programming style, they may be responsible for lulling the programmer into a false sense of security as to the soundness of an implementation. In situations where confidence in the correct behaviour of a software system is critical, a deeper analysis of the intended properties of the system is required. The development, as described here, of a mathematical model of an important component of a software system has provided us with valuable insights into the behaviour of the current implementation. We have

i. a clear statement of the properties of the rule set to which the current implementation of the JTMS may be applied.
ii. design criteria for a system which may be used with a less constrained rule set, should future applications require it.

We believe that the use of Formal Methods of Software Specification has a valuable role to play in producing clear statements of the properties of software used in knowledge based systems. The tool support for such methods which is at present under development will enable the formal validation of the properties of such a specification. In addition, there are clearly defined procedures for refining such a specification into a software system which correctly implements the specification. The more widespread use of such methods will be a major step towards the production of soundly engineered and reliable knowledge based systems.

REFERENCES

1. COZENS J., BYERS P.J., (1990) : Computing Science Technical Report, University of Surrey, in preparation.
2. DEVILLE I., (1990) : *Logic Programming: Systematic Formal Development*, Addison-Wesley.
3. FOX J., (1986) : *Three arguments for extending the framework of probability*, in L.N. Kanal & J.F. Lemmer (eds), Uncertainty in Artificial Intelligence, Amsterdam: North Holland.
4. FOX J., CLARK D.A., GLOWINSKI A.J., O'NEIL M.J., (1990) : *Using predicate logic to integrate qualitative reasoning and classical decision theory*, IEEE Trans. on Systems Man. and Cybernetics, 20, no. 2, pp. 347-357.
5. INCE D., (1988) : *Return of the Hacker*, in Software Development. Fashioning the Baroque, O. U. P., pp. 20-24.
6. KRAUSE P.J., BYERS P.J., HAJNAL S.J., COZENS J., (1990) : *The Formal Specification of a Database Extension Management System*, Biomedical Computing Unit Technical Report, Imperial Cancer Research Fund.
7. SCHUMAN S.A., PITT D.H., (1987) : *Object-Oriented Subsystem Specification*, in Meertens (ed.), Program Specification and Transformation, North-Holland, pp. 313-342.
8. SCHUMAN S.A., PITT D.H., BYERS P.J., (1989) : *Object-Oriented Process Specification*, Computing Science Technical Report, University of Surrey.
9. SPIVEY J.M., (1988a) : *Understanding Z: a Specification Language and its Formal Semantics*, Cambridge Univ. Press.
10. SPIVEY J.M., (1988b): *The Z Notation. A Reference Manual*, Prentice -Hall International
11. WING J. M., (1989) : *What is a Formal Method ?*, Computer Science Technical Report CMU-CS-89-200, Carnegie- Mellon University.
12. WORDSWORTH J.B., (1988) : *Specification and Refinement Using Z and the Guarded Command Language: a Compendium*. Technical Report, IBM United Kingdom Laboratories.

Appendix 1: Glossary.

We assume the reader is familiar with the usual logical connectives ($\land$, $\lor$, $\neg$, $\Rightarrow$), and the set theoretic constructs ($\cap$, $\cup$, $\subseteq$, $\in$). Some additional notation is used in the specifications which follows that of the Z language. Spivey [10] includes a complete glossary of the Z notation; the following are informal definitions of the additional constructs used here.

S : Set(T)	$\hat{=}$ S is a set of elements of type T.
S : seq(T)	$\hat{=}$ S is a sequence of elements of type T.
head S	$\hat{=}$ the first element in the sequence S.
last S	$\hat{=}$ the last element in the sequence S.
S(i)	$\hat{=}$ the 'i'th element of the sequence S.
#S	$\hat{=}$ the number of elements in the sequence S.
$\emptyset$	$\hat{=}$ the empty set.

PART C

COHERENCE CHECKING

7

MELODIA : Logical Methods for Checking Knowledge Bases

Evelyne CHARLES
Olivier DUBOIS

ABSTRACT :

We present MELODIA, a general system using boolean techniques for checking knowledge bases. We describe the methods used in MELODIA for detecting inconsistencies, redundancies and hidden theorems in knowledge bases written in an extension of propositional logic. These methods have been applied to bases used in the maintenance of nuclear power plants at Electricité de France (EDF).

1. INTRODUCTION

MELODIA analyses a knowledge base in order to find inconsistencies, redundancies, and other anomalies in the rules. For us, a knowledge base consists of a set of production rules (denoted rule base) plus a set of semantic constraints. Rules are written in an extension of propositional logic. Semantic constraints are constraints on the working memory the rule base manages when running.

Guaranteeing a "correct" utilization of the knowledge base means for us that, when the user submits an initial database to the Knowledge Base System (KBS), the KBS provides him with a consistent result.

Let us consider the following example:

R1: A > O and B < 0 --> C = 3

R2: A = 5 --> C = 2

When running the system {R1,R2} with D = {(A = 5), (B < 0)} as initial database, two conflicting facts (C = 3) and (C = 2) are inferred. For us, this is a case of inconsistency.

The study of consistency of a knowledge base is part of the VV&T problem. This study is the main objective of MELODIA. In the framework of KBSs, the notion of consistency is stronger than consistency in propositional logic.

In propositional logic, a theory T is consistent iff p and *not* p are not both deducible from T, for any p of T. A knowledge base KB can be seen as a set of clauses in propositional logic, which describes a theory denoted T_{KB}. In this framework, we give the following definitions:

KB is *intrinsically consistent* iff T_{KB} is consistent.

KB is *consistent* iff T_{KB} is consistent, and if T_{KB} is consistent with each consistent database D submitted by a user.

In the example above, the theory $T_{R1,R2}$ is consistent but $D \cup T_{R1,R2}$ is inconsistent. So, KB = {R1, R2} is intrinsically consistent but is not consistent.

We have defined a transformation for solving problems considered, i.e. inconsistencies, redundancies, and hidden theorems, in propositional logic. This transformation is described in the section 2. In sections 3, 4 and 5, we present the methods used by MELODIA for detecting such anomalies.

2. CLAUSAL FORM

In this section we describe the syntax of the knowledge bases MELODIA studies. Then we present the transformation of a knowledge base into clausal form, and we give a simple example of this transformation.

2.1 Syntax of knowledge bases

The *rule base* is made up of production rules A --> B, where A and B are conjunctions of disjunctions of elementary expressions. An elementary expression has the form a R b where a and b are either an attribute or a value, and where R is a comparator among =, <=, <, >, >=, <>. In this syntax, attributes are single-valued.

A *semantic constraint* is a rule A --> , where A is a conjunction of incompatible elementary expressions. The right-hand side of a semantic rule is empty, which means that a contradiction occurs if the rule can be fired.

A *database* is a set of elementary expressions. All the comparators may be used in a database.

2.2 Transformation into clausal form

Rules are translated into clausal form by replacing each distinct elementary expression of the form $a = b$ or $a < b$ by the positive form of a logical variable x, i.e. the literal x. The opposite expressions of such forms, respectively $a <> b$ or $b >= a$, are replaced by the complemented literal $-x$. Each rule A --> B is translated into clauses resulting from the equivalent formula -A ∨ B. The sets of clauses resulting from the conversion of a rule base RB and of a set of semantic constraint SC are respectively denoted S_{RB} and S_{SC}.

We must also express the dependencies between the elementary expressions by generating logical exclusion clauses. For example, the incompatibility of the three expressions a < b, b = c, c <= a is expressed by the exclusion clause -l1 V -l2 V -l3 where l1, l2, l3 are the literals respectively associated with the expressions. We just mention here that MELODIA generates all the minimal logical exclusion clauses from the following graph: the vertices are the attributes and the values appearing in KB, and the arcs are the relations between attributes and/or values corresponding to the elementary expressions of KB. The exclusion clauses are given by some well-defined types of circuits in this graph (or reference, see [2]).

The set of clauses resulting from the generation of the whole exclusion clauses concerning the elementary expressions of KB, is denoted S_{LE}.

2.3 A simple example

Let us consider the following rule base RB:

R1: A1 = TRUE and A2 < 0 --> A3 = 9 and A4 = BLUE
R2: A1 = TRUE and A2 = 4 --> A3 = 20
R3: A1 = TRUE and A5 = 1 --> A3 < 1

MELODIA creates logical variables associated with the following elementary expressions:

1 : (A1 = TRUE)	5 : (A2 = 4)	7 : (A5 = 1)
2 : (A2 < 0)	6 : (A3 = 20)	8 : (A3 < 1)
3 : (A3 = 9)		
4 : (A4 = BLUE)		

With these associations, rules are rewritten:

R1: 1 and 2 --> 3 and 4
R2: 1 and 5 --> 6
R3: 1 and 7 --> 8

Rule R1 is equivalent to the formula -(1 & 2) ∨ (3 & 4). This formula can be rewritten (-1 ∨ -2 ∨ 3) & (-1 ∨ -2 ∨ 4). For convenience, we shall denote the two clauses -1 -2 3 and -1 -2 4 (connectives ∨ are omitted).
The resulting set of clauses S_{RB} is:

S_{RB} = {-1 -2 3, -1 -2 4, -1 -5 6, -1 -7 8}

The generated logical exclusion clauses of S_{LE} are:

-2 -5 (exclusion for attribute A2, since A2 = 4 and A2 < 0 are incompatible) and
-3 -6, -3 -8, -6 -8 (exclusion for attribute A3)

Finally, {S$_{RB}$, S$_{LE}$} is the set of clauses resulting from the translation of the knowledge base RB into clausal form.

2.4 Fundamental justification of our approach

In the following, we denote S$_{KB}$ the set of clauses {S$_{RB}$, S$_{SC}$, S$_{LE}$}.

It can be shown that to any logical interpretation satisfying S$_{KB}$ corresponds to an interpretation which satisfies the original base KB, and conversely. This property justifies that we can transpose to S$_{KB}$ the checking problem concerning KB. Therefore, MELODIA studies S$_{KB}$ for checking KB.

3. THE CONSISTENCY PROBLEM

In this section we present the major aspect of our work: how to discover inconsistencies. If we can guarantee that for each initial consistent database given to the KBS the inferred database is consistent, then we can be sure that the knowledge base is consistent: no contradiction can appear in the utilization of the KBS as long as it is not modified.

3.1 What is an initial database made up of ?

Very often, it turns out that the designer of KB knows that only part of the attributes mentioned in KB can be mentioned in any initial database. This information can be given to MELODIA by considering this subset of attributes we call *initial attributes*. Moreover, whether the user omit to define the set of initial attributes, MELODIA makes the default assumption that initial attributes are only those attributes which are mentioned in no right-hand side of the rules.

In the previous example (2.3), the default initial attributes are A1, A2 and A5.

So, we assume that *initial databases* which are used for running KB only mention only initial attributes and values.

3.2 What is a consistent database ?

The expert expresses the incompatibilities among attributes through semantic constraints. These constraints are used to specify consistent databases.

Example. The expert gives the semantic constraint:

CS: A = 5 and B < 0 —> .

This means that a database containing both facts (A = 5) and (B < 0) or instances of them is prohibited: this database is not meaningful in the expertise of the domain. For example, database D = {(A = 5), (B = -1)} is inconsistent according to the previous constraint, since the semantic rule CS can be fired from D.

A database must also verify *the single-valuation constraint,* i.e. that each attribute must be single-valued. For example, databases D1 = {(C=2), (C=3)} and D2 = {(A<=0), (A=5)} are both inconsistent.

Definition: *A database D is consistent iff D satisfies the semantic constraints and the single-valuation constraint.*

The principle used to transform rule bases can also be applied to represent databases into clausal form. Each elementary expression of the database is replaced by the corresponding literal (according to the associations already made for rules). If new variables are created, MELODIA will add to S_{LE} the necessary logical exclusion clauses.

Let D be a database, and S_D its representation into clausal form. By definition, the database D is consistent iff {S_D, S_{LE}, S_{CS}} is logically consistent, i.e. satisfiable.

3.3 Detection of inconsistencies

3.3.1 Principle

MELODIA studies the clausal form S_{KB} of the knowledge base KB. By definition, a knowledge base KB is consistent, iff KB is intrinsically consistent, and if KB is consistent with each consistent database submitted by a user. This may be expressed within propositional logic:

Definition: *KB is consistent iff S_{KB} is satisfiable, and if for each consistent initial database D, {S_D, S_{KB}} is satisfiable*

First, MELODIA determines whether S_{KB} is satisfiable by applying an improved version of the Davis and Putnam procedure, denoted IDPP (see [2], [3], [4]). If KB is intrinsically inconsistent, KB will be inconsistent with any initial database submitted by a user. Therefore rules must be modified. In a practical sense, this never happens.

After KB has been proved intrinsically consistent, MELODIA theoretically has to study the satisfiability of each set {S_D, S_{KB}}. However, it is impossible to generate all the initial databases D for an attribute-value type of syntax.

In MELODIA, the basic idea is to generate from S_{KB} all the consistent initial databases which lead to a contradiction during inference. These initial databases are said to be inconsistent with KB. In order to find these databases, MELODIA looks for subsets of initial literals inconsistent with S_{KB}. An initial literal is a literal associated with an initial elementary expression.

In doing this, MELODIA eliminates non-initial literals between clauses of S_{KB} according to the following operations:

Elimination of pure non-initial literals.
    If a literal l of S_{KB} is such that -l does not occur in S_{KB}, l is said to be pure ([3]). All the clauses containing l can be removed from S_{KB}, without changing the satisfiability of S_{KB}. All the pure non-initial literals are

eliminated from S_{KB} in this way.

Elimination of a non-initial variable.

Let x and -x be two opposite literals having to be eliminated. $S_{KB} = P$ & N & R, where P (respectively N) is the conjunction of clauses containing x (respectively   -x), and where R is the conjunction of clauses containing neither x nor -x. The elimination of x is achieved by replacing P & N by P * N, where P * N is the set of clauses obtained by combining each clause p of P with each clause n of N. The clause p*n obtained by this combination is the disjunction of the literals of p and of n, except variable x.

Elimination of tautologies and subsumed clauses.

The **tautologies** (clauses containing both 1 and -1), and the **subsumed clauses** (clause C is subsumed by clause D if all literals of D are in C) can be removed from S_{KB} without changing the satisfiability of S_{KB}. This procedure is used to decrease the number of clauses in S_{KB}.

These 3 operations are applied to S_{KB} while non-initial literals remain in S_{KB}.

3.3.2 The inconsistencies

After achieving elimination, the final set of clauses, denoted S_F, only contains initial literals.

We can prove that, for any consistent initial database D, the set of clauses {S_D, S_{KB}} is satisfiable if and only if {S_D, S_F} is satisfiable.

Hence, if S_F is empty or contains only exclusion clauses, then any consistent initial database is consistent with KB, and KB is proved consistent. Otherwise, S_F provides all the potential inconsistencies of KB. Each clause of S_F which is not an exclusion clause is called an *initial constraint*. The database corresponding to this constraint consists of the expressions associated with the literals opposite to those of the clause. This database is said to be inconsistent with KB because it will provide a contradiction during the inference.

The designer must now examine each initial constraint to determine whether or not the contradiction might occur. For each constraint:

If the corresponding database is not semantically valid (expressions are incompatible), the contradiction will not occur. So, the constraint given by MELODIA is added to the set of semantic constraints. Otherwise, this database is semantically valid, and will provide a contradiction. There is a real inconsistency in the rules. The designer must modify the rule base, so as to eliminate this inconsistency.

3.4 Example

Let us consider the previous set of 8 clauses (see 2.3) :

S_{KB} = {-1 -2 3 (c1), -1 -2 4 (c2), -1 -5 6 (c3), -1 -7 8 (c4), -2 -5 (c5), -3 -6 (c6), -3 -8 (c7), -6 -8 (c8)}

The default initial literals are: 1, 2, 5 and 7.

First step: S = S$_{KB}$
Elimination of pure non-initial literals:

Literal 4 is pure, the clause c2 : -1 -2 4 is removed.

Elimination of a non-initial variable.
Variable 3 is selected to be eliminated (all the non-initial variables have the same number of occurrences in S$_{KB}$. So, we choose the first one).
parent clauses:

   P = {-1 -2 3 (c1)} and N = {-3 -6 (c6), -3 -8 (c7)}

resulting clauses:

   P * N = {-1 -2 -6 (c9=c1*c6), -1 -2 -8 (c10=c1*c7)}

There is no tautology and no subsumed clause.

Now, S = {-1 -5 6 (c3), -1 -7 8 (c4), -2 -5 (c5), -6 -8 (c8), -1 -2 -6 (c9), -1 -2 -8 (c10)}

Second step:
No pure non-initial literals in S.
Variable 6 is selected for elimination:
parent clauses:

   P = {-1 -5 6 (c3)} and N = {-6 -8 (c8), -1 -2 -6(c9)}

resulting clauses:

   P * N = {-1 -5 -8 (c11=c3*c8), -1 -5 -2 (c12=c3*c9)}

Clause c12 is subsumed by c5, c12 is removed.

Now, S = {-1 -7 8 (c4), -2 -5 (c5), -1 -2 -8 (c10), -1 -5 -8 (c11)}

Third step:
The last variable 8 is selected for elimination:
parent clauses:
   P = {-1 -7 8 (c4)} and N = {-1 -2 -8 (c10), -1 -5 -8 (c11)}

resulting clauses:

   P * N = {-1 -7 -2 (c13), -1 -7 -5 (c14)}

Finally, S = {-2 -5 (c5), -1 -7 -2 (c13), -1 -7 -5 (c14)}. S contains only initial literals, so S$_F$ = S.

Clause c5 is an exclusion clause, always satisfied by consistent initial databases. The initial constraints generated by the rules are c13 and c14. These two clauses give all the potential inconsistencies of KB.

Clause c13 is equivalent to the constraint:
IC1: A1 = TRUE and A5 = 1 and A2 < 0 --> .

With initial database D1 = {(A1 = TRUE), (A5 = 1), (A2 < 0)}, rules R1 and R3 are fired, hence the conflicting facts (A3 = 9) and (A3 < 1) are deduced. Constraint IC1 prevents this contradiction about A3.

Clause c14 is equivalent to the constraint:
IC2: A1 = TRUE and A5 = 1 and A2 = 4 --> .

This constraint prevents another contradiction about A3, provided by rules R2 and R3.

If the corresponding databases D1 and D2 are semantically valid, the expert must correct the rules.

4. DETECTION OF REDUNDANCIES

In this section we describe the methods used by MELODIA for checking redundancies in KB, by studying S_{KB}.

By definition, a rule R is *redundant* in KB iff {KB - R} is equivalent to KB. The suppression of redundant rules can improve the use of the base.

Example. Let us consider the following rules:

R1: A --> B and E
R2: A or C --> B
R3: A and D --> E
Rule R3 is redundant because E can be deduced just from A by R1.

MELODIA detects redundancies by eliminating *redundant literals* in each clause, and also by eliminating *tautologies* and *subsumed clauses* in S_{KB}. If the whole clauses derived from a rule R are eliminated, then R is redundant. If only some clauses derived from R are eliminated, then R has just redundant premises or conclusions.

In the example above, the clause -A -D E produced by R3 is subsumed by the clause -A E produced by R1. Thus, R3 is redundant and can be removed. A clause -A B is produced by R1, and the same clause is produced by R2. Eliminating this redundant clause boils down either to removing B in R1, or to removing A in R2.

5. DETECTION OF HIDDEN THEOREMS

We call *hidden theorems* elementary expressions which are theorems of KB.

Such theorems can reveal anomalies in KB, such as inconsistencies or literals which are always deduced.

MELODIA detects them by looking for the literals l such that $\{S_{KB}, -l\}$ is inconsistent. This is done by applying the procedure IDPP.

Example. Let us consider the following rules:

R1: E1 > 3 --> E2 = TRUE
R2: E1 < 4 --> E2 = TRUE

With the associations 1 : (E1 <= 3), 2 : (E2 = TRUE), 3 : (E1 < 4), the equivalent set of clauses is S = {(1 2), (-3 2), (-1 3)}. Literal 2 is a theorem in S, because {S, (-2)} is unsatisfiable. This results from an anomaly in the rules: E2 = TRUE is always deduced, whatever the value of E1.

6. RESULTS

We experimented with MELODIA on 8 knowledge bases. Bases B1 and B2 make a psychological analysis of a human personality. The other bases are prototypes of bases used in the maintenance of nuclear power plants. Some features of these bases are described in the below table.

MELODIA is written in Pascal and runs on an IBM 3090. It takes from 3 seconds to 6 minutes for checking each of the eight bases. This shows that MELODIA can efficiently process large real-word knowledge bases.

bases	B1	B2	B3	B4	B5	B6	B7	B8
rules	85	74	272	312	546	990	615	10562
semantic constraints	0	0	124	0	0	0	0	0
clauses in S_{KB}	1826	1795	1413	736	1595	2145	1458	8194
redundancies								
tautologies	0	0	0	1	74	8	0	0
subsumed clauses	5	0	0	5	147	26	0	100
eliminated rules[1]	0	0	0	2	51	16	0	98
hidden theorems	21	0	0	0	1	0	0	0
inconsistencies								
initial constraints[2]	49	0	1764	0	0	0	0	27874
real inconsistencies[3]	9	0	32	0	0	0	0	0

[1] The number of rules which can be eliminated from KB.
Some rules are redundant because they appear twice in KB, under different rule names (for example the 98 redundant rules of B8). The other redundancies stem from redundant premises or conclusions which can also be eliminated (for example 54 conclusions in B5).

[2] The number of initial constraints generated by MELODIA.
Three bases are potentially inconsistent.

[3] Indeed, only two bases are inconsistent, B1 and B3.
For B1, the 49 constraints found stem from 9 inconsistencies, i.e. from 9 couples of rules which can be fired simultaneously with conflicting conclusions.
For B3, some of the initial constraints were added to the set of semantic constraints. 626 constraints remained,

7. RELATED WORK

Early work [9, 13] consisted of checking the consistency of each rule individually, or of pairs of rules. Recent work [1, 6, 10, 11] goes further, and checks the global consistency of the knowledge base, independently of any test cases, as MELODIA does. These tools differ from MELODIA either by the syntax of the rules they study [10], by the definition of consistency they adopt [1], or by the method they use. Some of them are compared with MELODIA in [2].

8. CONCLUSION

MELODIA is an efficient tool for guaranteeing the "correctness" of a knowledge base. Once the consistency of KB is proved by MELODIA, we are sure that, for any consistent input data given by the user, no inconsistency can be generated by the KBS. If KB is proved consistent, the initial constraints generated by MELODIA are used to improve the set of semantic constraints, and then to specify the consistent initial databases.

In the future, the methods presented here could also be applied to check the completeness of KB, or to reduce the knowledge base by replacing some rules by equivalent ones containing less expressions [5].

REFERENCES

1.   BEAUVIEUX A. (1988) : *Interactive checking of knowledge base consistency*, International Computer Science Conference, Hong Kong.
2.   CHARLES E. (1990) : *Méthodes logiques pour la détection d'incohérences et autres anomalies dans les bases de connaissances : le système MELODIA*, Ph.D. Thesis, Université Paris 6.
3.   DAVIS M., PUTNAM H. (1960) : *A computing procedure for quantification theory*, Journal of the A.C.M., Vol 7, no 3.
4.   DUBOIS O. (1985) : *Résolution du problème de satisfiabilité, et application aux Systèmes Experts*, Rapport de stage de DEA. Université Paris 6.
5.   DUBOIS O., CHARLES E., ANDRE P. (1990) : *Méthodes de diagnostic et d'utilisation des bases de connaissances*, Comptes Rendus de l'Académie des Sciences de Paris, t. 311, Série I, no 6, pp. 383-388.
6.   GINSBERG A. (1988) : *Knowledge-base reduction: a new approach to checking knowledge bases for inconsistency and redundancy*, Proceeding of AAAI 88, St Paul.
7.   KOWALSKI R. (1979) : *Logic for Problem Solving*, North-Holland, New - York.
8.   LYNDON R.C. (1966) : *Notes on Logic*, Van Nostrand Mathematical Studies, New - York.

---

thus revealing *32 inconsistencies* in the rules. This base was at development stage.

Base B8 is supposed by its designers to be consistent by construction, because it is automatically synthesized from a deep model of the plant. So, no valid initial database can provide a contradiction. As initial databases are provided by instrumentation, the 27874 constraints may be used to invalidate unrealistic initial databases given by an erroneous instrumentation.

The other bases are proved consistent.

9.   NGUYEN T.A., PERKINS W.A., LAFFEY T.J., PECORA D. (1985) : *Checking an expert system's knowledge base for consistency and completeness*, Proceedings of IJCAI 85, Menlo Park.

10.   PIPARD E. (1988) : *Détection d'incohérences et d'incomplétudes dans les bases de règles : le système INDE*, Journées Internationales sur les Systèmes Experts, Avignon.

11.   ROUSSET M.C. (1988) : *On the consistency of knowledge bases: the COVADIS system*, Proceedings of ECAI 88, Munich.

12.   SIMON J.C., DUBOIS O. (1989) : *Number of solutions of satisfiability instances. Applications to knowledge-bases*, Int. Journal of P.R. & A.I., Vol 3, no 1, pp. 53-65.

13.   SUWA M., SCOTT A., SHORTLIFFE E. (1982) : *An approach to verifying completeness and consistency in a rule-based expert system*, The AI Magazine, 3(3), Fall.

PART D

TESTING

8

Consistency, Soundness and Completeness of a Diagnosis System

Vincent GUIBERT
Alain BEAUVIEUX
Marc HAZIZA

ABSTRACT

This paper presents a software program which is currently developing in order to validate DIAMS, an expert system shell for troubleshooting and controlling a satellite. Several checkings for consistency are made, including the soundness and completeness of the DIAMS, which are presented in detail. In addition, a set of syntactic consistency rules has been defined in order to check the DIAMS knowledge base statically.

1. INTRODUCTION

When developing a software program as part of a space project, an essential requirement is that the program should meet very high standards of reliability. In particular, the designing of an expert system for such an application must incorporate checking and validation procedures. Engineers from Matra Espace and

IBM Paris Scientific Centre are currently working on a software program to validat
DIAMS, which is a prototype of an expert system shell for the troubleshooting an
fault isolation of the attitude and orbit control sub - system (SCAO) of the satellit
Telecom 1. The purpose of the study is thus the verification, at different levels, of a
operational expert system.

2. THE DIAMS SYSTEM

2.1 Overview

DIAMS belongs to the class of second generation expert systems based on mode:
("model-based expert systems"); however, it allows the application of diagnos:
heuristics which have been acquired during the orbit of the satellite. The first orde
generic expert system is made up of classes of objects necessary for the representatio
of the models, methods and daemons associated with those classes. In addition, a se
of generic rules allows these models to be used and the expected diagnosis to be buil
In this way, the generic inference mechanism can be separated from th
representation of the system. Although the reasoning is sound with respect to th
models, the latter may not be complete.

The knowledge base (KB) is based on fault propagation models for each class c
electronic component. In particular, the functional model uses influence rules t
describe the different ways the components of the system interact functionally wit
each other, especially the remote controls and telemetric data which provide th
only information that is transmitted between the satellite and ground contro
DIAMS applies these influence rules to each class of components and thus builds
graph, called the influence graph, which connects the causes and symptoms of fault
Each path of the graph shows the propagation of faults between the components c
the system. The problem is to determine for each type of elementary componei
how it propagates the anomalies between its inputs and its outputs and to establis
in this way the set of generic rules, while at the same time distinguishing betwee
different types of anomalies. The system can then, by an analysis of the models an
with the aid of the generic rules, establish the causality links between the modes e
anomaly and the observables of the system.

The diagnosis of failures makes use of models, including the functional mod
which contains the functional TM-RC (telemetry and remote controls) schemes. Th
propagation modes of anomalies (or influence rules that are used to define th
context in which the influences are propagated) are extracted from the function
schemes. In addition, the system is structured in functional subsystems calle
knowledge islands. Our goal is to check the functional model for soundnes
consistency and completeness.

2.2 Initial data

The following information is available:

- During the conception phase of the satellite, the reliability engineers (in charge of reliability checks) gather all information concerning a given set of failures in a special table, called Failure Mode Effects and Criticality Analyses (FMECA). This information is made up of the causes associated with each piece of equipment, row basis data for the acquisition of knowledge, and the optimization of the diagnosis strategy (criticism of the running of the satellite, fault rate and finally observable effects).

- AIT experiments (Assembly, Integration and Tests phases) before launching.
- Orbital operational experiments.

Definition

Using this information, for each cause of failure C, the reliability engineers have drawn up a table T(C) which indicates the effects (or symptoms) and the critical nature of failure C on the working of the satellite.

Table T represents a "reference" that the DIAMS system must respect when making deductions. This table, which can be considered as one of the "conceptual models" of the SACCO system developed by Marc Ayel, contains items of information that are both concise and independent of each other, but not necessarily complete as far as the failure is concerned.

We can run the DIAMS prototype ourselves on the same cause of failure C. It produces two influence trees using the functional model: the effect(s) tree of C, ETr(C), and the cause(s) tree CTr(Sid) for each symptom presents in ETr.(C).

Definition

Let C be a fault cause of T; DIAMS(C) is the set of symptoms of ETr(C), deduced from C, using the functional scheme.

Note: There may be cases where some specifications of T do not correspond to reality. This is why, when a fault is detected, the expert is asked to confirm the validity of T *a posteriori*.

Using the above data, the following checking operations are performed.

3. CHECKING DIAMS STATICALLY

3.1 Static consistency: definition

Using the static description of each basic component of the satellite we must verify
that the functional scheme, which gathers and links these components, is consistent
syntactically speaking. Their static descriptions must also be verified to make sure
they respect certain rules. A set of conditions has therefore been defined that has to
be satisfied by the inputs and outputs of the components.

In addition, the functional model can be broken down into a hierarchy of
subsystems and general blocks, starting from the satellite and ending up at the non
decomposable elements, where each unit has a specific function. We verify that the
decomposition and the structure of these units respect a certain number of rules,
embedding rules in particular.

So, we get a set SSc. of *syntactic consistency rules*. Some rules are general whereas
others are specific to the components. This leads us to the following definition:

Definition

The knowledge base of the DIAMS system is *syntactically consistent* if the set of
rules SSc is satisfied by the knowledge base.

General consistency rules specify the constraints that must be verified by each class
and each component.

RCS0: Every object of the KB is either a class belonging to the predefined list of
the model, or an instance of a class.
RCS1: A component belongs to one and only one knowledge island.
RCS2: Concerning the "inherits" relation in the decomposition of the
functional model, there cannot be any multiple inheritance between
particular element of a scheme and the different classes of components of the
functional model, with a few clearly predefined exceptions. For example,
component cannot be both a relay and a register.

Specific consistency rules specify the constraints that must be verified by a specific
component. For instance, the following rule must be verified by components of the
class "relay1_1":

*A component of the class "relay1_1" has one and only one input, one and
only one output, at least one default position, at least one remote control
that sets the relay to "on" and one that sets the relay to "off".*

3.2 Proof method

We possess the entire list of all the static descriptions (in internal form) of all the components of the TM-RC scheme and the functional decomposition of the satellite. For each object of the KB, RCS0 is applied. If this object is an instance, the static description of the component is completely checked in order to verify that the syntactic consistency rules, first general then specific, of the set SSc are satisfied.

Note: If one of the previous rules is not respected, the expert is asked by the system to provide the required correction.

4. CHECKING DIAMS DYNAMICALLY

4.1 General definitions

An *observable* is an entity (telemetry, remote control or link) which can have a special value. These values belong to a finite set and are called *qualifications* here. When such an entity is qualified, it is called a *symptom*. In the next section, we are going to study the relation between T(C) and DIAMS(C). There are two possible cases:

- There exist fault symptoms associated in T by the reliability engineer with a cause C that is deduced by DIAMS from C. In this case, the KB of DIAMS is said to be *incomplete* with respect to T.

-There exist fault symptoms that are deduced by DIAMS from a cause C but that do not belong to T(C). An error can be suspected since this symptom, deduced by DIAMS, was not foreseen by the reliability engineer. But, as the table T(C) is not necessarily complete, the expert must validate this new deduction Si in order to verify that Si is sound with respect to T(C). Otherwise, DIAMS is said to be *unsound*.

On the other hand, if neither of the previous problems arise, *DIAMS is said to be sound and complete with respect to T.*

4.2 Checking the soundness of DIAMS

First, the expert must check the soundness of T(C). For a given cause C, each deduction leading to a symptom of T(C) must be correct. After having checked and made the necessary corrections, the system searches for the symptoms of DIAMS(C) that are not in T(C), by simply going through the effects graph and comparing it with

For each symptom S associated with C which cannot be found in T(C) the expert must validate this deduction. Since table T is not necessarily complete, a symptom of C, that is absent from T(C), does not always mean an incorrect deduction. This absence can be the result of a mistake when building T, and the deduction can be validated by the expert who determines whether or not to add the causality link (C,S) to T(C) and why it had not been done beforehand. If the expert assumes that, given the experiments carried out on the satellite and the analysis of T, this deduction is not valid then DIAMS should not have made this deduction which is incorrect here. The fact that the deduction was not in T(C) was justified. We must try to find out in the effects graph the reasons for this incorrect deduction.

-First, we accurately determine the causality links between C and S produced by DIAMS, to give us the effects path leading from C to S:
(C = C0, C1, C2.,...,Cj.,...,Cn.,S).
-Once we know that all the links connecting C to other elements of T(C) are correct, we can search for causality links i.e. paths between C and symptoms Si of T(C) such that a subpath (which is necessarily correct) of the path (C, Si) is a subpath of the path leading from C to S. The system studies the paths between C and Si and provides the distinct and maximal subpaths included in (C, S).
-Therefore, we will obtain two sets: the first one is made up of subpaths which are correct since they belong to T(C), and the second is made up of subpaths which are suspected of being incorrect. In the second case, the expert decides which subpaths must be removed from the knowledge base.
The above is performed by the *Soundness* procedure.

4.3 Checking the completeness of DIAMS

If DIAMS is not complete (according to our definition, see 4.1), a new graph, called *connection graph* is built.

4.3.1 The connection graph

Definition:

1. The graph that provides the set of potential paths between two observables C and S is called a connection graph, denoted $\Gamma(C, S)$. More precisely, it is made up of a list of "connection(X, Y)" predicates such that X is a neighbour of Y and the edge between X and Y is an edge included in a potential path linking C to S.
2. There exists a potential path (C, C1, C2,..., Cn, S) between C and S, if there exists a relation of functional dependency between C and C1, Ci and Ci+1, for all values of i belonging to (1,...,n-1), and Cn and S.

In this way, the graph models the connections between the telemetry, the remote controls and their electronic "links" viewed as components. Each graph is built a oon as needed, from the static instantiated description of the functional model, ising the *Build_connect_graph* procedure.

4.3.2 Application of the connection graph to the search for incompleteness

The influence graph E(C), where symptom S is missing, is built from the onnection graph of the potential paths CG(C, S): it is thus possible to localize one or nore cuts in E(C) and to highlight the edges that must be added to the influence graph in order to make it complete. We assume that the elements contained in T(C) re always reliable and correct. By a simple study of the graph, C can easily be linked vith any one of its effects. We also assume that the observables along a path from a ause to a symptom all possess the same qualification. Then, the connection graph is natched to the effect graph. From C, the algorithm verifies all the paths leading to S, lepth first, and compares them edge by edge and node by node, with those of E(C). It vill thus provide the missing edge(s) of E(C). These calculations are performed by he *Incomplete* procedure.

.4 Checking the consistency of the deductions

Three types of checking are carried out in order to detect inconsistent subsets in)IAMS(C), with respect to particular consistency specifications defined by the expert.

4.4.1 The "monoqualification" of the observables

During any given session, the observables can have only one qualification. This roperty is called "monoqualification".

For each set DIAMS(C) this property is checked by the system using the *Ionoqualification(Si, Sj, C)* procedure where Si and Sj represent the same bservables but with two different qualifications. Note that Si and Sj cannot both be imultaneously in T(C) since the monoqualification of T is checked first.

If Si and Sj are not in T(C) at least one of these two elements can be considered as abnormal".

Finally, if Si belongs to T(C) and Sj does not belong to T(C) (or vice versa) then the xpert must suspect Sj because, since the soundness of all the deductions of T(C) has ready been verified, then Si is necessarily sound.

4.4.2 Heuristics for consistency checking

xperience has led us to generate heuristics on the qualifications of a cause C and its ssociated symptoms Si.

During a session, *every* symptom associated with a given cause must have the same qualification. If not, a failure can be suspected. Our system verifies that these heuristics are respected for all DIAMS(C) sets, using the *Verif_heuristic* procedure.

4.4.3 Consistency rules specific to the components

Certain specific features of components, in particular concerning their action and influence on other components, allow us to define "consistency rules" which are specific of the application domain to the component. For instance, we have the following rule:

> *Action of a component on other components:* the application of a "tc_relay" or a "command" to a relay, or of a "tc_authorization" to a "reg_authorization" can only modify this component with respect to its position or its value in two ways: "on" or "off".

All these rules are checked using the *Specific_rules* procedure.

5. GENERAL ALGORITHM

5.1 Presentation

We start first by verifying static consistency since it is independent of all causes C; is therefore not necessary to know the symptoms deduced from C by DIAMS or to have already run DIAMS. The other verifications are carried out afterwards for each cause C present in table T.

I. SYNTACTIC_CONSISTENCY(satellite).
II. For every C in T, Do
  1. DIAMS(C) -> (SiD) deduced from C.
  2. MONOQUALIFICATION(T(C)) .
  3. For all (Si, Sj) member of DIAMS(C) such that
  Si = (O, qi) and Sj = (O, qj) Do
   - If qi =/= qj then Do
    * MONOQUALIFICATION(Si, Sj, C).
  4. VERIF_HEURISTIC(T(C)) .
  5. For all (Si, Sj) member of DIAMS(C) such that
  Si = (Oi, qi) and Sj = (Oj, qj)
  Do
   - If qi =/= qj then Do
    * VERIF_HEURISTIC(Si,Sj,C).
  6. SPECIFIC_RULES(T(C)).
  7. SPECIFIC_RULES(DIAMS(C)).
  8. For all Si member of T(C) Do

- If Si not member of DIAMS(C) then Do
      * BUILD_CONNECT_GRAPH(Si,C).
      * UNCOMPLETE(Si,C).
9. SOUNDNESS(T(C)).
10. For all Si member of DIAMS(C) Do
   - If Si not member of T(C) then Do
      * SOUNDNESS(Si,DIAMS(C),T(C)).

2 Software implementation

e have chosen to apply all the algorithms described in the above sections to the mplete example of a "clock" (a functional unit that is a knowledge island) in order make up a demonstrator. We are currently building a set of programs in Prolog, d applying all the verifications described above to the sub - system "clock".

CONCLUSIONS

e four checking procedures described above and their implementation in Prolog rrespond to the first stage in the building of a consistency and completeness ecking system, and can be compared to the work described in [1]. But it is clear that e problem that we have dealt with is not closed. Several possible lines of research uld be developed to extend and improve our system and to optimize our code. rther work will be done on the following:

-Table T represents a finite set of specifications that have to be checked. Since this t is not necessarily complete (have all failures been foreseen?) it would be desirable devise an exhaustive checking procedure from the knowledge base itself, dependent of any table. This approach is similar to those described in [2, 4].
-Each time a model is modified after a fault has been detected by one of the four evious checking procedures, new problems may arise. It may therefore be better t to consider DIAMS as an indissociable entity and, instead, try and build an cremental proof mechanism which would show whether or not the modification ads to new problems without having to recompute the sets DIAMS(C) for all the uses C [2].
-Problems of soundness between the different knowledge islands will have to be ken into account although, so far, we have only considered the problem of one nowledge island at a time. All the islands will have to be taken into account cluding global elements situated at the border of any two islands.
-We may consider applying our system and developing it in other languages pecially object oriented languages. Replacing Prolog facts by objects would allow us use the structure and inheritance tools of these languages and thus optimize the de.

REFERENCES

1.   AYEL M., (1988) : *Protocols for Consistency Checking in an Expert System Knowledge Base*, ECAI 88, Munich.
2.   BEAUVIEUX A., DAGUE P., (1990) : *A General Consistency (Checking and Restoring) Engine fo Knowledge Bases*, ECAI 90, Stockholm.
3.   GINSBERG A., (1988) : *Knowledge Base Reduction: A New Approach to Checking Knowledge Bases for Inconsistency and Redundancy*, National Conference of American Association for Artificial Intelligence, St Paul (USA), August.
4.   ROUSSET M.C., (1988) : *On the Consistency of a Knowledge Base: COVADIS System*, ECAI 88, Munich.

9

Design Knowledge Validation Through Experimentation: The SYSIFE System

Philippe MAZAS

ABSTRACT

The work presented here concerns the issue of knowledge base validation in the context of design domains.

The paper comprises three main sections. The first one is dedicated to assessing the general principles of validation which emerge from the analysis of the specific features of design knowledge. It shows that validation criteria which are generally taken into account by the present validation approaches are weakly relevant in the context of Design and that the election of more adequate criteria leads to adopting a dynamic approach. The specifications of a dynamic validation process, called **experimentation**, are then presented, defining the structural expression of the selected criteria and the task allocation between man and machine within the validation process.

The second section describes the outline of **SYSIFE**, a validation support system based on this analysis. The presentation focuses on the functional architecture of the system which comprises three cooperating agents: the Examiner, the Student and the Jury. This architecture is responsible for the autonomy which SYSIFE needs to fulfil its role within the experimentation process. Also outlined is the qualitative modelling of the knowledge which supports both the Student's and the Examiner's problem-solving methods.

The last section is an attempt to assess the scope of the proposed approach by relating it to other alternative or complementary approaches and by analysing the results of a first experimentation which was carried out on an operational design Knowledge Base.

1. INTRODUCTION

The past years have seen a significant increase in the interest in Knowledge Acquisition and Validation issues within the AI community. However, for different reasons, very little research has been focused on these issues in the domain of constructive   problems and particularly in Design [3]. The work presented here concerns the problem of Knowledge Validation for simple design tasks.

The first four sections of this paper describe the specific features of the validation issue that we have identified through the analysis of simple design domains. They can be summarized as follows:

(1) Validation criteria which are generally taken into account by structural validation systems are weakly relevant when the KB comprises **constraints**. In particular, consistency has been the major concern of most previous research, whereas this characteristic does not apply to design knowledge, as constraints are very often found to be contradictory during the design process. *KB consistency should thus be replaced by the notion of KB **robustness***, which means that the KB may produce contradictions but that it is then able to solve them itself.

(2) Static analysis is able to detect major flaws in a design KB (particularly concerning completeness). We will show, however, that it is of little use as regards to robustness and that *a design knowledge validation support system should therefore encompass a **testing** facility* to deal with this latter criterion.

(3) Testing a KB means: building test - cases, attempting to solve them by application of the KB, evaluating the results and modifying the KB when these results prove unsatisfactory. We believe that, in design domains, the best man-machine cooperation scheme consists of assigning the tasks of test case generation and resolution to the machine while letting man be responsible for results evaluation and KB modification. This process of iteratively generating and solving test cases is called **experimentation**.

(4) Test - case coverage is one of the main issues of experimentation as it is of all other types of testing approaches. This has led us to propose two hypotheses, presented in section 5, under which only one test - case per constraint (called **exercise**) must be solved satisfactorily to give strong presumptions of the robustness of the KB. This presumption relies on the ability of the system to choose the *most difficult exercise*, defined as *the set of input values which causes the greatest difficulties in satisfying the constraint under study*.

Based on these ideas, an experimentation support system was integrated in a validation support system for design knowledge called SYSIFE. Its functional architecture is comprised of three main components: the **Student**, the **Examiner** and the **Jury**.The Student must try to solve the exercise while the Examiner attempts to come up with reasonable exercises that the Student cannot solve. Both the Student and the Examiner refer to the Jury when they fail to achieve their goal. When this occurs, the Jury may conclude that there is a malfunction of the KB which is worth presenting to the Expert.

The problem solving methods of both the Student and the Examiner are based on a qualitative representation of the knowledge to be tested which represents statically its dynamic behaviour. This special purpose representation is interpreted in the same way by the two modules but with opposite goals. The Student uses it to meet the constraints while the Examiner relies on it to generate exercises where they are difficult to meet.

Section 6 describes the functional architecture and global behaviour of SYSIFE's experimentation module. Section 7 focuses on the tasks of the Student and the Examiner, showing how they can rely on the qualitative representation of the design knowledge. The last two sections attempt to assess the scope and relevance of experimentation by relating it to other alternative or complementary approaches and by analysing the results of a first experimentation which was carried out on an operational design KB.

2. STRUCTURAL VALIDATION OF A DESIGN KB

Whereas Knowledge Acquisition has reached a point where one can speak of Second-generation Knowledge Acquisition Systems [8], Knowledge Validation Verification and Testing is still an emerging field within the domain of Knowledge-based Systems design. As with all emerging fields, authors are temporarily faced with terminology problems, such as defining the precise range of the field itself (e.g.: what is the difference between Verification and Validation?).

It seems, however, that a certain form of consensus is being reached concerning the distinction between structural verification and functional verification. As stated in [12], structural verification means checking a certain set of properties on the KB components whereas functional verification consists of checking the KBS behaviour with respect to the problem to be solved. As with more traditional types of software, structural verification (or testing) is based on the inner structure of the program while functional verification is based on its specifications [22].

Functional validation is a wide and still ill-defined issue. It comprises topics such as specification expression, metrics definition and quality management, topics which have been poorly investigated in the past. On the contrary, much research has been focused on the structural validation issues, producing interesting results in the verification of KB consistency and completeness [1, 16, 17, 20, 21]. The work presented here is also concerned with structural verification but its application to design problems has major implications on the KB structure and therefore on the validation criteria to be used.

The two following paragraphs describe the nature of the expertise to be validated and its implication in the choice of validation criteria.

2.1 What is the knowledge to be validated ?

The knowledge we want to validate can be defined as the knowledge involved in the solution of those *Routine Design* problems where the artefact is designed on the basis of a pre - determined model. This class of problems is roughly equivalent to what is often referred to as the *class III* design problems [4, 6].

2.1.1 The domain model

For these problems, the specifications of the artefact to be designed are directly expressed in terms of the pre-defined **domain model**. The model defines the structure of the artefact (or, possibly, different alternative structures), the attributes of its components and the range of possible values for each of these attributes. It also establishes the distinction between two classes of non-computable attributes: the **input attributes**, the value of which should be given in the specifications, and those, called **degrees of freedom**, which are to be tuned by the designer to meet the requirements of the specifications.

With the help of this model, **formulae** are used to compute intermediate or output attributes, and simple **constraints** express the limitations of the technology[1] and the requirements of the specifications.

Attributes

Input Attributes
• Habitation-V
• N-bedrs

Degrees of liberty
• Bedr-average-A [10,16]
• Livingr-A [15,100]

Computable Attributes :
• Ceiling-H

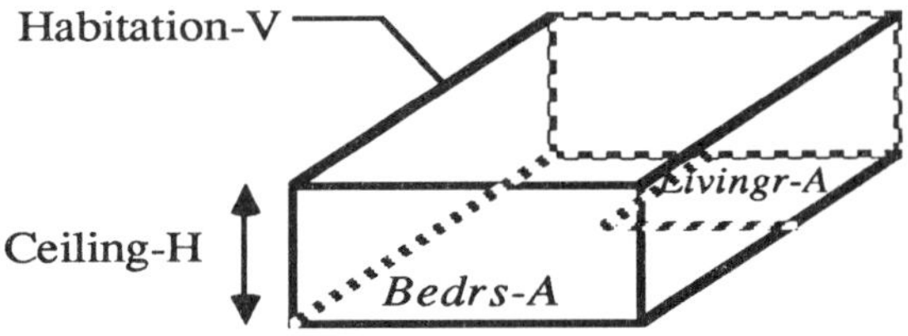

Constraints

Ceiling-H = $\dfrac{\text{Habitation-V}}{\text{Livingr-A} + \text{Bedr-average-A} \times \text{N-bedrs}}$

Ceiling-H ≥ Min-ceiling-H
Min-ceiling-H = 2.2 m

Figure 1: The knowledge to be validated : a simple example

An example of this kind of domain model is given in figure 1. In this toy problem, the artefact to be designed is an apartment which is composed of a single component defined by its *volume*, its *number of bedrooms, the average area of the bedrooms, the area of the living-room* and *the height of the ceiling.* The *habitation volume* and the *number of bedrooms* are input attributes; their values are part of the specifications. *The average area of the bedrooms* and the *area of the living-room* are degrees of freedom; they must be chosen by the designer so that the *ceiling height,* computed through its formula, meet the only

---

[1] The range of possible values for the attributes can be understood as technology related constraints. They are nonetheless integrated in the model, as part of the features of the artefact which are predefined and, therefore, independent of each different specification.

requirement of the specifications which states that it should be greater than a minimum value.

2.1.2 Laws vs heuristics

Solving this problem involves a *synthesis task* (as defined in [5], which means that the solution should be constructed rather than chosen within a set of pre - defined solutions. Indeed, the problem, although very simple, will often prove to accept an infinite number of solutions which cannot be enumerated and saved in the KB.

The solution must therefore be constructed, which means: choosing the values of the degrees of freedom, developing the solution through application of the formulae, testing the constraints as they are encountered and, if these are not met, backtracking to make alternative and hopefully more adequate choices.

For example, in the apartment problem, the designer chooses plausible values for the areas of the living-room and the bedrooms; from these values, he computes the ceiling height and checks the minimum ceiling height constraint. If this is not satisfied, the designer backtracks to choose less constraining (i.e. smaller) values for the areas.

This problem - solving process can be described as a form of Heuristic Search and indeed the use of this metaphor for design problem solving helps in formalizing the knowledge it requires; thus two classes of knowledge can be distinguished : the **laws**, which define the limits of the solution space, and the **heuristics** which guide the search of this space.

The laws are comprised of the formulae and the constraints. They define the set of legal solutions, i.e. those which will meet the requirements of the specifications while keeping within the technological limitations.

The heuristics take various forms. They establish preferences between alternative choices throughout the design process thus promoting quality criteria or performance considerations.

In the apartment example, the set of laws is comprised of the *ceiling height* formula and the *minimum ceiling - height* constraint. Heuristics can be included such as comfort criteria (e.g. if necessary, decrease the *average bedroom area* rather than the *living-room area*) or advice for a quicker resolution (e.g. If several attributes are candidates for modification, choose the less constrained one).

2.2 What are the validation criteria ?

We have shown that a subclass of design problems can be defined as those which can be solved by heuristic search, and that solving these problems requires two types of knowledge: laws and heuristics. Each of these has a specific function within the design process and from these two different functions, two distinct sets of validation criteria are derived.

2.2.1 Criteria for laws and criteria for heuristics

Laws, on one hand, are responsible for defining the set of legal solutions. From a functional point of view, they can be considered valid if they ensure the ability of the KB to find a legal solution to any problem which deserves it.

Heuristics, on the other hand, are no. involved in deciding whether or not a solution is legal (i.e. acceptable). They help in choosing the best among alternative solutions or in reaching these solutions more quickly, but they have no influence on their actual existence. Their correctness may be valued on the grounds of validation criteria, such as solution quality or problem solving efficiency, which are fundamentally different from those which derive from the ability to find a legal solution.

In other words, *each type of knowledge must show specific abilities and each defines a validation problem of its own.*

The automatic acquisition of heuristics is an attractive direction of research and much work has been devoted to it [11, 15, 19]. Most of the approaches however, presume the existence of a theory defining the frame, inside which learning can occur. This hypothesis holds in a number of well - formalized domains but does not apply to industrial design applications where theory may have its role in some local subproblems but never covers the whole design process. Automatic acquisition and/or validation of heuristics can take place, however in such ill-defined domains, if the laws of the domain are sound enough to be considered as a theory. In other words, *the validity of heuristics can only be studied once the validity of laws has been established.*

This analysis has led us to consider the validation of laws in the first place, and the work presented here is entirely devoted to this issue. In the rest of this paper our concern is focused on the part of the Knowledge Base containing the constraints and formulae which will be called the **Law Base** (LB).

2.2.2 Validating the Law Base : Robustness

The validity of a Law Base has been functionally stated as *the ability to find a legal solution to any problem which deserves it.* To support automatic validation, this somewhat fuzzy definition must be translated into more definite structural terms.

Five main validation criteria have emerged from studying various examples of LBs :

- completeness of the formulae set,
- soundness of the formulae,
- completeness of the constraints set,
- soundness of the constraints, and
- robustness of the LB.

All these criteria should be fulfilled to ensure a proper behaviour of the LB. Some may be checked, at least partially, using static verifications (completeness of the formulae set, see [13]). Others can be handled by the expert himself without too much difficulty (soundness of the formulae). One of these criteria, the robustness of the LB, should further retain our attention as it can hardly be guaranteed through static or manual verifications. We have already mentioned that this criterion plays a central role in the validation of design knowledge; it is now time to define it in more detail and show how it leads to the necessity of providing the validation support system with a testing facility.

3. FROM STATIC ANALYSIS TO TESTING : ANALYSING THE NATURE OF VALIDATION CRITERIA

As stated above, validation support systems can be grouped according to the goals they are pursuing, i.e. structural vs functional validation. An orthogonal classification is sometimes proposed, based on the method used rather than the goal pursued. Indeed, it seems that all validation methods may be separated between static analysis methods and testing methods. In **static analysis** methods, flaws are detected through observation of the KB whereas, in **testing** methods, flaws are detected in the KB through its actual use in the resolution of test cases.

The most adequate type of method mainly depends on the goal of the validation, in other words, on the validation criteria. If applicable, static analysis methods are usually preferred to testing methods as the latter give rise to serious difficulties, namely the generation of test cases and the evaluation of results which make them much less systematic and reliable. In the following section we show that this is not possible for robustness since static analysis is unable to tackle this kind of criterion.

Robustness has been defined as the ability of the KBS to solve any conflict[2] which might appear in the problem - solving process. This property can be illustrated in the apartment example.

If we assume very constraining input values, such as 4 bedrooms and a *habitation volume* of 110 m^3, an initial choice of standard areas for the degrees of liberty, 25 m^2 for the living room and 10 m^2 for each bedroom, then the resulting *ceiling height* will not meet the *minimum ceiling height* constraint. Here the ability to find a legal solution means the ability to solve the conflict, i.e. the robustness of the LB as regards to the *ceiling height* constraint.

The question is, therefore can the LB solve the conflict ? The answer depends on several factors. The first is the level of dissatisfaction with the constraint: does the solution require a major modification or will a fine tuning do the job ? The dual factor is the space left for modification: what are the remaining domains for the degrees of liberty ? Finally, other related constraints may appear unsatisfied after modification of the solution. They must therefore be taken into account when planning the conflict resolution.

---

[2] The word "conflict" strictly means the appearance of one or more unsatisfied constraints. This meaning should not be confused with the one it has in the expression: conflict set.

Trying to answer these questions in the example of the apartment shows that *conflict resolution is a dynamic and global process.* Dynamic, since it involves the specific values given in the terms of the problem: each session comprises a particular set of input values, so that each one is liable to give rise to an original type of conflict. Therefore, for most LBs, the ability to solve all potential conflicts cannot be ensured beforehand but must be sought dynamically for each session. Furthermore, conflict resolution is also a global problem since it simultaneously involves pieces of knowledge which have been introduced independently in the LB : constraints, formulae and domain of possible values are fed to the LB by the expert in a piecemeal way so that all potential conflicts between them cannot be foreseen.

In short, conflict resolution is a dynamic and global process, and the ability to achieve it in all circumstances cannot be checked statically. This does not mean that static analysis is of no use for design knowledge validation. Indeed, in the SYSIFE system, the LB is first submitted to a static analysis which is able to detect a variety of major flaws (particularly concerning completeness). However, the validation of robustness, which is the main concern of this paper, cannot be carried out in this preliminary phase; it is the goal of a testing phase, called experimentation, which we will now proceed to describe.

4. FROM TESTING TO EXPERIMENTATION : ALLOCATING THE TESTING TASKS

Software testing procedures are made up of four main tasks: test case generation, test case resolution, results evaluation and software refinement. Various combinations of these are possible, according to the adopted control scheme. Figure 2 displays a simplified version of the testing procedure implemented in SYSIFE: in the first phase, a test case is generated, later we will show how test cases are constructe rather than chosen in a predefined set. The test is then transmitted to the performance module which attempts to solve it. The resulting solution is then evaluated and, if found to be incorrect, motivates the repair of the faulty knowledge item. If the solution proves satisfactory, another test is generated, if possible.

As well as different control schemes, different task allocations can take place within the testing framework. The resolution task, of course, is attributed to the machine. The allocation of the three other tasks, however may differ, according to what appears to be the most suitable man-machine cooperation in the context of the domain where the knowledge to be tested belongs. In SYSIFE the commitment is to trust the machine with the test generation task and leave the expert with the results evaluation and LB refinement tasks. In the following sections we explain why results evaluation can only be achieved by the expert and why, in design domains, the best man-machine cooperation scheme consists of assigning the tasks of test case generation to the machine while letting man be responsible for results evaluation.

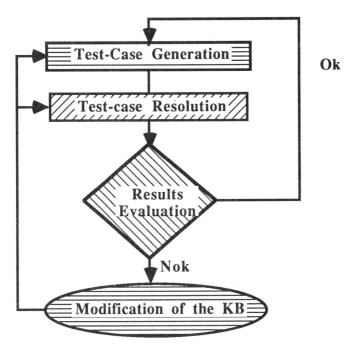

: Necessarily computerized

: Necessarily manual

: Can be assigned to man or machine according to the domain requirements

Figure 2 : SYSIFE's testing procedure

4.1 Results evaluation

The validity of a design KBS has been broadly defined as *the ability to find a legal solution to any problem which deserves it*. The word "deserve" refers here to the general issue of test case validity which is shared by all testing approaches. Indeed, the evaluation task not only consists of validating the outputs but also the inputs of the resolution.

Consistency (as regards integrity constraints [20], or a conceptual model of the KB [1]) has been used in the past to model validity. Similarly, constraints are introduced in the LB to define satisfactory solutions, and may also be used to restrict the set of syntactically possible problems to those which are reasonable. Thus, **legality**, i.e. : constraints satisfaction, can be adopted as a formalization of **validity**. In this context, the system would be able to perform evaluation through simple constraint checking.

However, in our context, where contraints belong to the LB to be validated, legality cannot be identified with validity, since a solution, or a test case, may be legal, i.e. may satisfy all the constraints, and still be invalid as constraints may happen to be missing or incorrect. The completeness of the constraints set and the soundness of each of its elements have been previously pointed out as validation criteria. They cannot be ensured by the machine itself for lack of external reference. If, for example, the minimum ceiling - height constraint was missing in the habitation design LB, nothing could lead the program to detect it; the only effect would be that the design would be easier to achieve than it should be.

In conclusion, test case and solution validity can be grouped under the issue of results evaluation: each test produces a solution together with the given test - case and gives rise to an evaluation phase which incriminates one of them, or validates both. In the case of design knowledge, *the machine itself can verify the legality of both the test - case and the solution, but the expert alone can ensure their actual validity*. The evaluation task is therefore the responsibility of the expert.

4.2 Test case generation and LB refinement

Previous works have shown that machines can prove very useful in achieving both test case generation and LB refinement.

Test-case generation has been the mainspring of several researches on KB consistency. Systems like COVADIS [20] or SACCO [1] are able to build sets of input facts, called *inconsistency contexts*, which lead to an inconsistent fact base through application of the KB. These inconsistency contexts can be viewed as particularly relevant test - cases since they demonstrate a flaw in the KB.

KB refinement has generated much interest in recent years within the Knowledge Acquisition community. The first example of a KB refinement support system is TEIRESIAS [7]. It has shown that the pre-existence of a KB helps the process of knowledge acquisition in two ways: firstly, it supports acquisition *in context* where the refinement process is triggered, and therefore focused, by a failure of the KB; secondly, the system can construct a model of the KB which will help in understanding the failure and in devising the adequate refinement. More recently, A. Ginsberg [9] has further explored the area of KB refinement, showing how the use of a meta-language can help in defining specific concepts and heuristics, and thus adapt the refinement strategies to the domain. Although these approaches were developed on diagnostic applications, it is very likely that interesting results would evolve by adapting them to design domains.

Few researches however, have aimed to support both test case generation and KB refinement; the general option being to focus on the task which appears the most difficult for the expert.

In the context of a Law Base, the refinement task can be carried out without much difficulty by the expert himself. Formulae and constraints are simple numerical expressions which can easily be modified or updated when necessary. They are expressed in a purely declarative way without any control consideration.

Test-case generation, on the contrary, is known to be a complex task. Collecting standard test cases is common practice, but constructing a complete and adequate set of test cases is still an open issue in the design of knowledge-based systems as well as of more conventional software. This is particularly significant in the case of a design Law Base, where the behaviour to be tested, especially conflict resolution, is chiefly dynamic, global and therefore difficult to anticipate and circumscribe (see § 3).

In conclusion, representing the laws piecemeal and declaratively makes it easier for the expert to complete or modify them. On the other hand, it also conceals potential interactions between pieces of knowledge. It thus increases the difficulty of generating adequate test - cases for the solving process, this being strongly affected by the concealed interactions. Analysing the relative complexity of the testing tasks gives grounds for focusing the role of the testing support system on the test case generation task while making the LB refinement task the responsibility of the expert. The system should therefore be able to test its own knowledge through building test - cases and submitting them to itself. This self-testing activity will be referred to as **experimentation**.

5. FROM TEST CASES TO EXERCISES

The previous sections have shown that robustness appears as a key validation criterion in the context of design knowledge, that it can only be checked dynamically, and that experimentation seems the most adequate man-machine cooperation scheme within the testing framework. Now that the tasks of the machine have been defined (test case generation and resolution), it is time to describe the goal of these tasks more precisely, in other words, the nature of test cases.

5.1 Functional definition of an exercise

From a syntactic point of view, a test - case can be defined as a set of input values, i.e. of values for input attributes (as defined in § 2.1.1). From a functional point of view, a test - case is meant to reveal a flaw in the LB. The choice of relevant test -cases among all syntactically possible ones is therefore driven by the type of flaws that we are looking for.

We have seen above that the main validation criterion which makes experimentation necessary is robustness, i.e. the ability to solve conflicts in as much as they appear during the resolution. A test - case should therefore *create the conditions so that a conflict may appear*. As conflicts are due to unsatisfied constraints, this means that a test - case is the statement of a design problem which will be difficult to solve as regards to one or more constraints. While attempting to solve the problem the system should encounter conflicts on these constraints - otherwese the problem is not sufficiently difficult. If it fails to solve the conflicts, this may be the symptom of a flaw[3]; if it succeeds, there is definite evidence that the LB is robust towards this specific conflict and strong presumption that it is also robust as regards similar conflicts. However, the range of this generalization, from the conflict actually solved to those which are *similar*, necessitates a more precise definition as it is the basis of test coverage assessment.

5.2 Test coverage

After test case generation and results evaluation, test coverage estimation is the last of the three difficulties of KBS testing, as recorded in [2]. Last but not least, this issue must be taken into account at the very early stages of the design of the testing procedure since test case definition, which underlies test case generation and thence results evaluation, also forms the foundation for test coverage assessment. Indeed, in our case, the specification of the test case set mainly derives from the objective that the system should guarantee the robustness of the LB after the experimentation has been completed, i.e. after all test - cases have been proven to be solved by the LB.

So the question is: how many test - cases should the LB accomplish in order to be considered robust? Or, in other words: *how many conflicts should the LB have to solve to convince the expert that it is capable of solving all conflicts* ? The answer proposed here is: *one per constraint*. It is based on two hypotheses: the first will be called the world cup hypothesis and the other will be referred to as the goal - posts hypothesis.

5.2.1 The World Cup hypothesis

Each test case should aim to test the behaviour of the LB as regards a conflict, and the test - case generation should come up with those test cases which induce the most difficult conflicts. As stated above, a conflict appears each time a constraint proves to be unsatisfied but, since constraints are sometimes antagonistic, it may happen that two or more constraints are alternatively violated during the problem - solving process and that this should be regarded as one *multi-constraint* conflict resolution. The World Cup hypothesis, however, is only concerned with building the most difficult *mono-constraint* conflict. These test cases, which are focused on a single constraint, will henceforth be referred to as **exercises** devoted to this constraint. The multi-constraint conflicts will be dealt with in the next section as they require the commitment to the goal posts hypothesis.

Whereas exercises devoted to different constraints involve different pieces of knowledge, conflicts motivated by the same constraint, though with different levels of gravity, involve the same type of problem - solving. The world cup hypothesis is based on a total order relationship between conflicts on the same constraint which derives from an estimate of the gravity of a conflict.

---

[3] As we saw earlier, it may also be that the problem is unreasonable because it is impossible to solve and that it is therefore invalid as a test - case.

This estimate is called the **response** of the conflicting constraint and can easily be computed as the distance between the current value of the attribute and the value limit imposed by the constraint. As different types of constraints can be encountered (i.e. with different comparators), the computation of the response is normalised so that it is positive as long as the constraint is unsatisfied.

For example, the response of the minimum ceiling height constraint is given by the following formula :
$$R\ (Ceiling\text{-}H \geq Min\text{-}ceiling\text{-}H) = (Min\text{-}ceiling\text{-}H - Ceiling\text{-}H)$$
its value remains positive as long as the ceiling height remains lower than its minimum value.

The World Cup hypothesis can then be stated as follows: *the higher the response of the conflicting constraint, the more difficult the conflict*; the rationale being that the higher the response of the constraint, the further the attribute current value is from the value it should have and, hence, the more difficult it will be to bring it back to its minimal or maximal acceptable value. It follows that one can speak of *the most difficult exercise for a given constraint* as the one which maximises the response of the constraint.

Thus, in the example of appartment design, the most difficult exercise is the one which maximises *(Min-ceiling-H - Ceiling-H)*. Since the *minimum ceiling height* is constant, it is equivalent to minimizing the *ceiling height*. This attribute depends on two input attributes : the *habitation volume* and the *number of rooms*. According to the ceiling height formula, it increases with the *habitation volume* and decreases with the *number of bedrooms*; its minimum value will therefore be reached for the smallest *habitation volume* and the highest *number of bedrooms*. In short, the most difficult exercise is obtained when the habitation is the smallest possible and the number of bedrooms is the highest possible; which corroborates the intuition that this is actually the case where keeping a minimum ceiling height is most difficult.

In conclusion, the World Cup hypothesis gives support for drastically reducing the number of test - cases to be constructed. It may be stated as follows: the most difficult exercise for a given constraint is the set of input values which maximizes the response of the constraint.

Thus, only one exercise per constraint should be solved satisfactorily to ensure the robustness of the LB as regards *mono-constraint* conflicts. We will now show that this also results in strong presumptions of robustness concerning multi-constraint conflicts.

5.2.2 The goal-posts hypothesis

One will reasonably assume that a conflict involving several constraints simultaneously is more difficult to solve than any conflict involving only one of them. It follows that multi-constraint test - cases, which will be called **problems** (as opposed to **exercises)**, should be carried out in the assessment of the global robustness of the LB. This would greatly increase the total number of test - cases, as each combination of two, or even more, constraints would give rise to a problem.

The goal posts hypothesis however, allows this combinatorial difficulty to be ignored and focuses the experimentation on the exercises alone. It is revealed in two steps: firstly, a given set of constraints deserves that a problem be specifically devoted to it only if its elements are mutually antagonistic. Secondly, a difficult exercise devoted to one constraint is very likely to come out as a difficult problem on its antagonistic constraints. It follows from these two assertions that a complete set of exercises will test the LB on all its sets of antagonistic constraints, and that it is therefore adequate to assess its global robustness. However we must first justify these assertions, beginning by defining more precisely the concepts they are based upon.

Only **antagonistic** *constraints deserve that a problem be specifically devoted to them.* Two constraints are antagonistic if they depend on at least one common attribute and if this dependency has opposite effects on them: any variation of the attribute value relaxing one constraint will, simultaneously, tighten up the other.

Let us suppose, for example, that the habitation design LB comprises the following constraint: *Living-room-area* ≥ *Min-Living-room-area*. This constraint is antagonistic with *the minimum ceiling height* constraint as an increase, for example, of the same attribute: *the living-room-area* will relax the former and, at the same time, tighten up the latter. Thus, one cannot solve a conflict motivated by any of these two constraints without taking the other into account.

Conversely, conflict resolution for two *non - antagonistic* constraints are two *independent* problems. They can therefore be studied separately and, ensuring that the LB can solve each one in a different exercise, guarantees that it can solve both simultaneously in the same problem.

The first part of the goal - posts hypothesis has defined the goal posts : as antagonistic constraints. The second part means that if the right - hand post is shifted markedly to the left, the player, if he has noticed it, is very likely to come across difficulties with the left hand - post.

The **most difficult** exercise for a given constraint is very likely to result in a **difficult** problem as regards to its antagonistic constraints. The notion of *most difficult exercise* is defined in the previous section. An exercise is difficult if it creates the conditions for a conflict to appear on the constraint to be studied. Similarly, a problem is difficult if conflicts are actually encountered on all the constraints to be studied. The second part of the goal posts hypothesis states that, in the process of solving the conflict on the constraint associated with the exercise, the system is very likely to encounter conflicts on its antagonistic constraints.

If, for example, the *minimum ceiling - height* constraint is far from being satisfied, the designer will be compelled to drastically decrease the areas of the living-room and the bedrooms. If he does not anticipate the *minimum-living-room* constraint, he is very likely to encounter a conflict on this constraint. If he does, for example, after the first trial of conflict resolution, he will be looking for a compromise to solve the problem of two antagonistic constraints rather than a simple exercise on a single constraint.

Thus the goal-posts hypothesis leads to the conclusion that an exercise centred on a single constraint is in fact a problem devoted to all its antagonistic constraints. However, it only gives good presumptions concerning the robustness of the LB towards these constraints since it cannot ensure that the most difficult exercise is also the most difficult problem.

In conclusion, test coverage is a difficult issue in experimentation on robustness as it is in all other types of testing approaches. This has led us to propose two hypotheses under which only one test - case per constraint, called **exercise**, must be solved satisfactorily to ensure the robustness of the LB as regards **mono-constraint** conflicts and to give strong presumptions concerning **multi-constraint** conflicts. This holds if, for each constraint, the experimentation support system is able to generate the *most difficult exercise* , i.e. the set of input values which maximises the **response** of the constraint.

6. FUNCTIONAL ARCHITECTURE

The ideas presented above have led to the implementation of a validation support system, called SYSIFE, which encompasses a static analysis facility, which will not be presented here, and an experimentation module devoted to supporting the validation of dynamic criteria. The functional architecture of this module, see figure 3, reflects the tasks allocation proposed in section 4 and the goals of these tasks deriving from the definition of an exercise, as presented in the previous section.

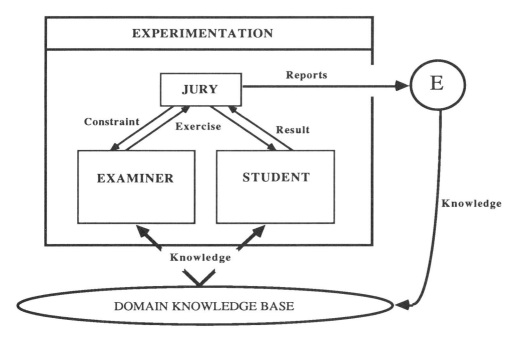

Figure 3: Functional architecture of the experimentation module

The experimentation facility is thus comprised of three modules : the Examiner, the Student and the Jury. The **Examiner** is responsible for constructing the exercises and the **Student** attempts to solve them; the **Jury** controls the experimentation and leads the interaction with the expert.

Based on this architecture, the experimentation proceeds as a succession of examinations. For each **examination**, the Jury chooses the constraint to be studied. He submits this theme to the Examiner, who tries to construct the most difficult exercise on it. The exercise is then passed on to the Student via the Jury. When the Student has found the best solution that can be reached, he returns this to the Jury who evaluates the *difficulty* of the exercise and the legality of the solution (see §§5.2.1 and 4.1 resp.) and from this decides whether it is sufficiently relevant to invoke the expert. Three main situations can occur: the exercise is difficult and the solution is legal; there is no legal solution; and the exercise is not difficult.

(1) - *If the exercise is difficult and the solution is legal,* the solution must be displayed to the expert for evaluation. If its validity is confirmed, the LB can be regarded as robust towards the constraint which motivated the exercise.

(2) - *There is no legal solution.* This is the most interesting case since it reveals a fault of the LB. Exercise and solution are passed on to the expert for diagnosis and, hopefully, LB refinement.

(3) - *The exercise is not difficult.* The exercise generation is a heuristic process, such that the Examiner may not produce the most difficult exercise at the first trial. In that case, the Jury asks him to attempt to make a more difficult one.

In conclusion, SYSIFE's functional architecture is composed of three agents, the Student, the Examiner and the Jury, whose interactions are centred on the concept of exercise which supports the dialectics of the experimentation process. The Student must try to solve the exercise while the Examiner attempts to come up with reasonable exercises that the Student cannot solve. Both the Student and the Examiner refer to the Jury when they fail in achieving their goal. In this case the Jury may conclude that there is a malfunction of the KB worth presenting to the Expert.

This architecture is largely responsible for the ability of SYSIFE to carry out autonomously his tasks within the experimentation process.

7. QUALITATIVE KR FOR EXPERIMENTATION

The role of the Jury is complex. It relies on control knowledge, the representation of which is based on a task-oriented model of the experimentation process. It is beyond the scope of this paper to describe it fully, as this requires the presentation of the task model [14]. This section focuses on the tasks of the Examiner and the Student, in particular showing how these tasks can rely on a qualitative representation of the objects they have to manipulate : the laws.

7.1 The tasks of the student

The tasks of the Student consist in   solving design exercises. The involved
problem-solving method is the regular design method which will be applied by
the ES after validation (see §2.1.2):   it includes two alternative phases, the
construction phase and the **revision** phase.

In the construction phase the solution is obtained in a data driven manner.
When no formula is applicable, the value of a non-computable attribute (degree
of freedom) may be chosen within its set of possible values.

For instance, the resolution of an exercise on the minimum ceiling - height
constraint starts with a construction phase comprised of the following steps:

Exercise : *number of bedrooms = 4*
    habitation volume   = 110 m³
Step 1 : Choice -> *average area of the bedrooms = 16 m²*
Step 2 : Choice -> *area of the living-room = 25 m²*
Step 3 : Application of a formula :
Ceiling-H = Habitation-V / (Livingr-A + N-bedrs x Bedr-average-A)
-> *Ceiling-H = 1.23 m*
   Conflict : The constraint
Ceiling-H < Min-ceiling-H is not satisfied
-> *Response = 0.4*

During this construction phase the constraints are checked inasmuch as they
are encountered. In our example, the computation of the ceiling - height triggers
the checking of the minimum ceiling - height constraint which is not satisfied.

The appearance of such a conflict switches the problem solving into a
backtracking phase[4].

The object of the revision phase is to define the characteristics of the backtrack
which would solve the conflict encountered, namely the degree of liberty which
should be modified and the variation which should be applied to its value. To do
this, the Student must (1) establish the links between the degrees of liberty and
the conflict, in order to identify those which are relevant, and (2) characterize the
nature of these links to determine the way they may be modified to solve the
conflict.

These links derive from the knowledge of the formule: as they led the student,
during the construction phase, from the choices he made to the conflict he
encountered, they should also lead him, during the revision phase, from the
conflict encountered to better alternative choices. However, while the objects
involved, i.e. the formulae, are clearly the same in both the construction and the
revision, the way they should be represented varies according to the specific
needs of each phase. The construction phase is straightforward and does not
involve any original representation; the revision phase, on the other hand,
requires that the dependencies deriving from the formulae be explicitly
represented and that the nature of these dependencies be modeled. The model of

---

[4] This would not happen immediately in the case of a multi-constraint conflict as it is often
preferable to evaluate all the involved constraints before starting the revision.

dependencies we propose is simple and easy - to - use: it is referred to as the qualitative dependencies model and is the subject of the next section.

7.2 Representing knowledge qualitatively

The qualitative dependency model is no more than a representation of the laws, mainly the formulae, which are specifically devoted to facilitate the tasks of the experimentation modules. We introduced it through the requirements of the Student, but the next section will show that it is also very useful to the Examiner.

7.2.1 The qualitative dependancy model

A qualitative dependency represents the link that ties two attributes when one can be computed from the other through a formula.

For instance, the following formula of the ceiling height :
ceiling-height = habitation-volume / habitation-area   establishes   two dependencies involving the *ceiling-height* : one with the *habitation-volume* and the other with the *habitation-area*..

The nature, or behaviour, of a dependency between two attributes is the effect that the variation of one would have on the value of the other. In the previous example, an *increase* in the habitation volume would result in a *increase* in the ceiling height, while an *increase* in the habitation area would result in an *decrease* of the ceiling height. This behaviour is represented qualitatively, i.e. : in differential terms. Under certain conditions[5], the expression of the formula can be derived qualitatively towards each of its variables, so that each of the corresponding dependencies is provided with its qualitative derivative, in other words, with its direction of variation.

For example, the qualitative derivation of the ceiling height formula yields the following derivatives :
Qd (*ceiling-height % habitation-volume*) : +
Qd (*ceiling-height % habitation-area*) : -
The explicit representation of a dependency between two attributes, together with its qualitative derivative is called a **qualitative dependency** (noted Q-dependency).

7.2.2 The qualitative dependancy graph

The implementation of the Q-dependency model results in a graph which is built in four steps (see figures 4.1 - 4.4): (1) building the dependency graph, (2) compiling the dependencies, (3) Q-deriving the dependencies and (4) composing the Q-dependencies.

---

[5] Namely that the expression of the formula be uniformly monotonous towards all its variables. If this condition is not satisfied the qualitative derivative of the expression is unknown.

(1) - Building the dependency graph

As shown in figure 4.1, each formula yields a number of dependencies equalling the number of arguments of its right-hand side expression. All these dependencies are integrated in a graph.

FORMULAE :

A44 : Ceiling-H = Habitation-V / Habitation-A
A5   : Habitation-S = Livingr-A + Bedrs-A
A7   : N-bedrs   = N-rooms - 1
A6   : Bedrs-A = N-bedrs x Bedr-average-A
A73 : Min-ceiling-H = 2.2
...

CONSTRAINTS :
I5 : Ceiling-H ≥ Min-ceiling-H
...

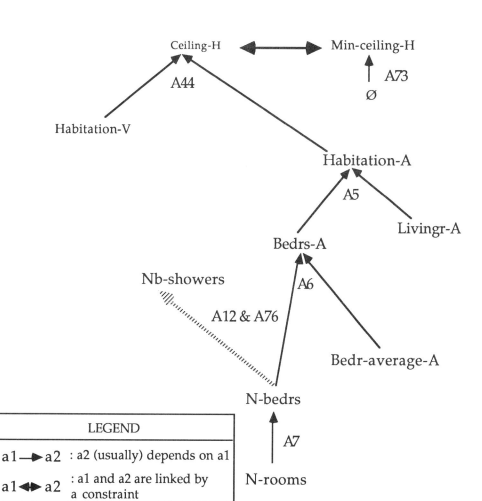

Figure 4.1. : Building the dependency graph

(2) - Compiling the dependancies

Once the graph is completed, the non computable attributes, including the **degrees of freedom** and the **input attributes** (see § 2.1.1), can be identified as those which depend on no other attribute.

I5 : Ceiling-H ≥ Min-ceiling-H

J = { Bedr-average-A, Livingr-A, N-rooms, Habitation-V }

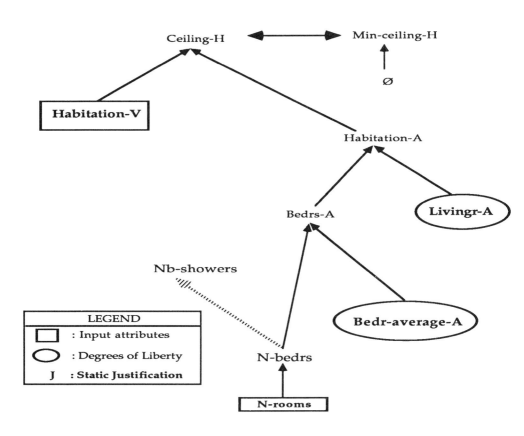

Figure 4.2 : Compiling the dependencies

A restricted form of transitive closure of the dependency relation is then built so that each attribute knows its **static justification**, i.e. the set of all the non-computable attributes it depends upon. A static justification can also be attached to each constraint as the set-union of the static justifications of the attributes involved in the constraint (see figure 4.2).

The static justification provides the student with the necessary information concerning the *existence* of dependencies between degrees of liberty and constraints: while attempting to solve a conflict, the degrees of liberty he should take into consideration are those which belong to the static justification of the unsatisfied constraint. This, however, does not help him in deciding how the relevant degrees of liberty can be modified to solve the constraint. This level of information, regarding the *behaviour* of dependancies - and not merely their existence -, is provided by the integration of the qualitative derivatives in the dependency graph.

(3) - Q-deriving the dependencies
Inasmuch as they are integrated into the graph, the formulae are Q-derived and the resulting Q-derivatives are attached to the corresponding dependencies (see figure 4.3)

FORMULAE :
A44 : Ceiling-H = Habitation-V / Habitation-A
...

    I5 : Ceiling-H ≥ Min-ceiling-H

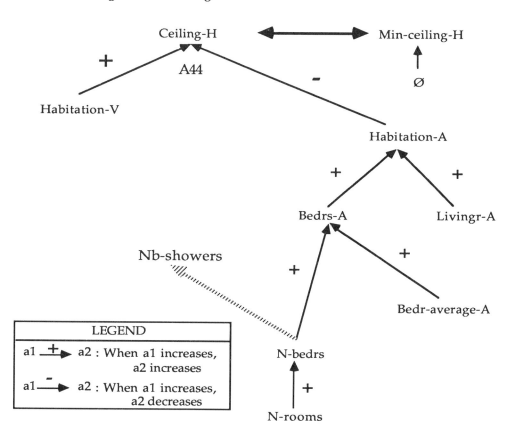

Figure 4.3 : Q-deriving the dependencies

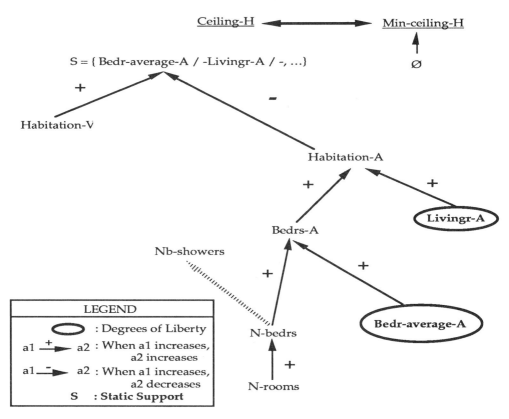

I5 : Min-ceiling-H - Ceiling-H ≤ 0

S = { Bedr-average-A / + Livingr-A / +, ...

Ceiling-H

Min-ceiling-H

S = { Bedr-average-A / -Livingr-A / -, ...}

Habitation-V

Habitation-A

Bedrs-A

Nb-showers

Livingr-A

Bedr-average-A

N-bedrs

N-rooms

LEGEND

◯ : Degrees of Liberty

a1 —+→ a2 : When a1 increases, a2 increases

a1 —-→ a2 : When a1 increases, a2 decreases

S : Static Support

Figure 4.4: Composing the Q-dependencies

(4) - Composing the Q-dependencies

The Q-dependencies can be composed using the laws of Qualitative Algebra (see figure 5) so that each attribute knows its Q-derivative towards each degree of freedom it depends upon[7]. These "global" Q-derivatives can be merged with the static justification to yield what is called the **static support** of an attribute.

For example, the static support of the *ceiling height* is :

S = { *average area of the bedrooms* / - ; *area of the living-room* / - }, which means that its value decreases when any of these two degrees of liberty are increased.

+	o	?	+	-
o	o	?	+	-
?	?	?	?	?
+	+	?	+	?
-	-	?	?	-

ADDITION

×	o	?	+	-
o	o	o	o	o
?	o	?	?	?
+	o	?	+	-
-	o	?	-	+

MULTIPLICATION

Figure 5: Tables of the laws of qualitative algebra

A static support can also be associated with a constraint. We have seen that solving a conflict can be formalized as decreasing the response of the unsatisfied constraint until it becomes no greater than zero (see § 5.2.1). Knowing the degrees of liberty upon which the response depends, and knowing the corresponding Q-derivatives, the Student can easily determine the alternative possible ways of solving the conflict.

For example, it is straightforward to deduce from the knowledge of its supports that a conflict on the *minimum ceiling height* constraint can be solved through decreasing either the *average area of the bedrooms* or *the area of the living-room* (see fig.ure 4.4).

7.3 The tasks of the examiner

The goal of the Examiner is to provide the Student with the most difficult exercise on the constraint submitted by the Jury. In other words, the Examiner should find input values such that the Student will have the greatest difficulty in meeting the constraint under study.

The principle of the generation is therefore to anticipate the way the Student will solve the exercise in order to lead him towards the desired event : the encounter of a conflict on the constraint under study. The generation process consists of a form of backward simulation of the Student's constructing process, where the Examiner, starting from the conflict he wishes to incite, applies the formulae in reverse until he reaches input attributes, the value of which can be chosen to maximize the chance of provoking a conflict.

This process can also be understood as finding a maximum for the response of the constraint while being restricted to the influence of the input attributes. It is comparable to the revision process where the Student attempts to decrease the response of the constraint while being restricted to the influence of the degrees of freedom (the other type of non-computable attribute).

The mainspring of exercise generation is therefore very similar in principle to the revision of a solution. It is based on the interpretation of the static support of the constraint as demonstrated in the following example.

The most difficult exercise on *the minimum ceiling height* constraint has been evoked previously (see § 5.2.1.). It is obtained with the highest possible *number of bedrooms* and the smallest possible *habitation volume*. This can easily be worked out by the Examiner, knowing the support of the *minimum ceiling height* constraint, i.e. knowing that *number of bedrooms* and *habitation volume* are the two input attributes the constraint depends upon and that its response increases with the former and decreases with the latter (see figure 6).

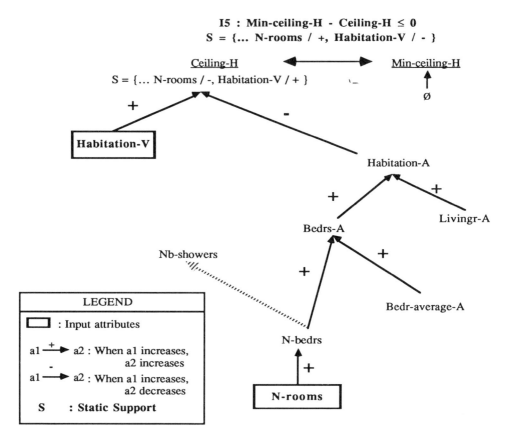

Figure 6: The examiner's use of qualitative dependencies

In conclusion, qualitative representation of knowledge is well suited to experimentation purposes. The qualitative dependencies represent statically the dynamic effects of formulae and, therefore, help both the Student and the Examiner in estimating the topology of the search space. They are interpreted in the same way by the two modules but with opposite goals. The Student uses them to reach a legal solution as quickly as possible while the Examiner follows them to explore those areas of the search space where few or no solutions can be found.

8. SCOPE AND RELATED WORK

SYSIFE is a structural validation support system for design knowledge. It assists the verification of several structural properties of the Law Base such as completeness, soundness or robustness. In its goals, it can be compared to other systems like COVADIS [20] or SACCO [1] where dynamic flaws are detected through searching the contexts in which they can occur. SYSIFE helps in testing the robustness of a Law Base as these systems help in verifying the consistency (resp. coherence) of a Rule Base. There is a great similarity of function between SYSIFE's exercises and COVADIS' counter-examples or SACCO's inconsistency contexts. Many differences are found, however, regarding their building methods as these strongly depend on the type of knowledge to be validated : COVADIS' and SACCO's methods for detecting inconsistency contexts are based on logic (resp. propositional and first order) while SYSIFE's method for generating exercise is mainly based on qualitative reasoning.

SYSIFE also has a functional flavour as its main functioning mode takes the form of an experimentation where the expert is asked to evaluate the results obtained by application of the LB. Indeed the experimentation procedure is very close to the refinement cycle followed by systems like TEIRESIAS [7] or SEEK2 [9]. We have seen, however, that, within this common cycle, the task distribution between man and machine strongly differs and that this can be explained by the fact that SYSIFE is devoted to design domains while TEIRESIAS and SEEK2 both apply to diagnostic domains.

We have briefly evoked SYSIFE's static analysis facility. This can be compared to validation support systems like ONCOCIN [21] or CHECK [16] but the greatest similarities are found with the SALT system [13]. SALT is a knowledge acquisition system which assists the expert in introducing its knowledge piecemeal and interactively, then verifies that the different pieces of knowledge are mutually compatible and will fulfil the role they are assigned within the problem solving method. SALT applies to the same domain as SYSIFE and, indeed, SYSIFE's static verifications are a subset of those performed by SALT. Most of the additional verifications carried out by SALT aim at foreseeing the robustness faults which are detected by SYSIFE through experimentation.

9. CONCLUSION :
EXPERIMENTING ON THE EXPERIMENTATION

SYSIFE was subjected to a small-scale experimentation which was carried out as follows :

- The KB was extracted from an operational ES in brooch[6] design, named CABRI [10], presently in use at the RENAULT car company. It comprised one - third of the total knowledge of the system.
- CABRI being developed in Prolog, the knowledge was translated into SYSIFE's formalisms (described in § 2.1). The first experimentations revealed faults in the KB (and bugs in SYSIFE) which were diagnosed and fixed by the author until his level of incompetence in broach design was reached.

---

[6] A brooch is a tool mainly used for enlarging or smoothing holes in metal.

The results of the experimentation were then as follows :

- Number of constraints tested : 8
- Number of failures from the Student (unsolvable exercises) : 3
- Number of failures from the Examiner (no exercise was difficult) : 2
- Number of difficult exercises solved successfully : 3

Among these results four were presented to the expert during two sessions of half a day each. The following flaws were then detected :

- one constraint was shown to be useless,
- one faulty constraint appeared to be useless but was eventually modified into a more adequate one,
- two missing constraints were detected.

Finally, one of the cases examined was a difficult exercise solved successfully which demonstrated the robustness of the LB towards the constraint under study.

Although limited, the experimentation (on the experimentation) led to the following conclusions :

- The experimentation provides actual assistance in testing the LB. The exercises produced represent extreme but realistic situations which reveal non trivial flaws (sometimes several simultaneously).

- The tasks of results evaluation, including the diagnostic of the fault evidenced by SYSIFE, proved to be long and complex : it took the expert a whole day, assisted by the author, to identify and repair the causes of only five faults.

- Some of the failures of the Examiner revealed useless constraints. Others were due to the limitations of the qualitative dependency model (see §7.2.1). When the response of the constraint does not evaluate monotonously as regards to some input values, the corresponding qualitative dependencies are unknown and the Examiner is unlikely to find the most difficult exercise.

From these experiences, we can draw up the guidelines for future work. First, *enhancing the dependency model* : this could be achieved by introducing other qualitative features, such as orders of magnitude [18], or by switching to quantitative models. *Experimenting on heuristics* : once laws can be considered as reliable, the experimentation can be devoted to validating heuristics. The present framework is suited to testing existing heuristics, it may be enhanced to support learning new ones. Finally, *contributing to the modification phase* : this has been proved complex and fastidious by experimentation. Inspirations can certainly come from previous works on KB refinement, but it is still too early to evaluate their applicability to design domains.

REFERENCES

1. AYEL M., (1987) : *Détection d'incohérences dans les Bases de Connaissances : SACCO*, Thèse d'Etat; U. CHAMBERY.
2. AYEL M., LAURENT J.P., (1987) :SACCO-SYCOJET : Two different ways of verifying Knowledge-Based Systems. in this edition.
3. BOOSE J., (1989) : Knowledge Acquisition Tools, EKAW-89 Tutorial Notes : pp 437-447; Paris, July.
4. BROWN D.C., CHANDRASEKARAN B., (1989) : *Design Problem Solving*, Research Notes in AI, Morgan Kaufman Publishers, San Mateo, California.
5. CLANCEY W., : *Heuristic Classification*, in J. Kowalik (ed.) Knowledge-Based Problem Solving, NY: Prentice-Hall.
6. COSTEA I., (1989) : *Building Expert Systems for Designers* MICAD-89 Tutorial, Paris, February 13.
7. DAVIS R., (1979) : *Interactive Transfer of Expertise : Acquisition of New Inference Rules*, A.I. , Vol 12. pp. 121-157.
8. GAINES B.R., (1988) : *Second generation knowledge acquisition systems*, EKAW' 88, GMD-Studien No 143, pp. 17.1-17.14; Bonn, Germany, June.
9. GINSBERG A., (1988) : *Automatic Refinement of Expert System Knowledge Bases*, Research Notes in AI; Pitman Publishing, London.
10. GLOESS P.Y., MARCOVICH J., (1986) : *OBLOGIS : a flexible flavor implementation of logic and its application to the design of a brooching expert system* In Proc. of First Int. Conf. on Applications of AI to Engineering Problems; vol 1 pp. 1-20. D. SRIRAM & R. ADEY Ed., Springer -Verlag ; April.
11. LENAT D.B., (1983) : *EURISKO : A Program that Learns New Heuristics and Domain Concepts; The Nature of Heuristics III: Program Design & Results*, AI, Vol 21, pp. 61-98; 1983
12. LOPEZ B., MESEGUER P., PLAZA E., (1990) : *Knowledge Based Systems Validation : A State of the Art*, AICOM, Vol 3, No 2, pp. 58-72; June.
13. MARCUS S., Mac DERMOTT J., (1989) : *SALT : A Knowledge Acquisition Language for Propose-and-Revise Systems*, A.I., No 39; pp. 1-37.
14. MAZAS P., (1990) : *Acquisition de connaissances de conception : le système SYSIFE*, Thèse de l'Université de Paris VI; July.
15. MITCHELL T.M., UTGOFF P.E., BANERJI R., (1985) : *Learning By Experimentation : Acquiring and Refining Problem Solving Heuristics*, in Michalski et al. (eds) Machine Learning ; pp. 163-190; Springer Verlag.
16. NGUYEN T.A., PERKINS W.A., LAFFEY T.J., PECORA D. : *Checking an expert system's knowledge base for consistency and completeness*, Proc. IJCAI 1985, pp. 375-378.
17. PIPARD E., (1988) : *Détection d'inconsistances et d'incomplétudes dans les bases de règles*, 8èmes Journées Internationales : Les Systèmes Experts et leurs Applications; Avignon, May, 1988.
18. RAIMAN O., (1986) : *Order of Magnitude Reasonning*, AAAI-86
19. ROSENBLOOM P.S., LAIRD J.E., (1986) : *Mapping Explanation-Based Generalization onto SOAR*, AAAI-86, pp. 561-567
20. ROUSSET M.C., (1988) : *Sur la cohérence et la validité des Bases de Connaissance : Le système COVADIS*, Thèse d'Etat; U. Paris-Sud.
21. SUWA M., SCOTT A.C., SHORTLIFFE E.H. (1982) : *An Approach to Verifying Completeness and Consistency in a Rule-based Expert System*, The AI Magazine; pp. 16-21, Fall.
22. VIGNOLLET L., AYEL M., (1989) : *Constructions de Jeux de Tests pour des Bases de Connaissances*, 9èmes Journées Internationales : Les Systèmes Experts et leurs Applications; pp. 247-257; Avignon 29 May - 2 June.

PART E

COMPLETENESS AND RELIABILITY

10

A Descriptive Model of Predicates for Verifying Production Systems

Philippe LAFON

ABSTRACT

In this paper, we present a new approach for automatic consistency checking of first-order rule-based systems. Most existing approaches consist of verifying a single property, and are strongly related to logic. On the contrary, our system is able to check various kinds of conditions. It is a commonsense knowledge base, which considers rules as physical components that can be matched, transformed (rewritten), assembled, in order to test their behaviour in detected critical situations. Our system requires two kinds of knowledge: on the one hand, the knowledge base to be studied, and on the other hand, specifications of properties of some predicates used in the knowledge base. This latter core of knowledge is some kind of *implicit* knowledge, which must be acquired from the knowledge base designer. This is made possible through a descriptive model of predicates we designed for this task. In summary, our approach comes down to confronting these two partial specifications of a single problem.

1. INTRODUCTION

This paper introduces a new approach to automatic verification of first order rule-based systems. Basically, it comes down to replacing the identity :
Knowledge Base (KB) = Production Memory (PM) {+ Working Memory (WM)}
with **KB = PM + MetaRelations Set (MRS)** {+ **Working Memory (WM)**} where MRS is a set of properties pertaining to the predicates handled by the production memory.

Building of the MRS is designed to improve the knowledge about predicates.

In our context, this knowledge is essential for capturing the issues of the system as well as the steps to address them.

For instance, suppose you are looking at a premise of an expert system based on propositional calculus. If you have the condition: RCV.13VP.ORDERS = 25, you can understand - even if you do not have the slightest idea of what RCV.13VP.ORDERS means - that you are looking at a test on the value of a numerical parameter, and that the number 25 is a significant value of this entity. There is no question that the meaning of this premise is "has the parameter RCV... reached the value 25 ?". The unit of the value is only missing to be fully informed.

On the contrary, suppose you're scanning a first-order condition such as : THING(X) = Y [1] , what can you deduce? "It exists a relation between a "class of object" X and a "class of object" Y". And nothing more! But now suppose that you know that THING represents the predicate IS-NAMED. You can then immediately deduce that (1) X is a complex entity which must be named ; (2) Y is the name of X ; (3) the type of Y is certainly "string of characters"; (4) Y is certainly the only name of X (X has a single name), moreover, X is likely to be the only entity named Y (the link is bi-univocal) ; (5) this predicate can be used (will be used?) to ensure that two objects X1 and X2 of the same type as X are different ; (6) going further, the relation IS-NAMED is certainly provided by splitting up a n-ary relation into binary relations, thus X is the pivot of this operation (for instance it could represent a task with a name, a duration, a starting date, a finishing date, etc... The relation IS-NAMED links the atom which identifies the task, X, to the real name of the task, Y), and so on ...

It stems from the previous paragraph that the name of the predicate implies (for us) a semantic, and that our understanding of a system based on first-order Logic rests on it. We need this information in order to have an insight in the KB which is running. Finally, let us recall that in our language, a predicate is the sole explicit component of knowledge representation. It is the natural support for expressing meta-knowledge.

Here, our purpose is the verification of Knowledge Bases. It dictates that we need to grasp the basic meaning of the system. But we cannot teach the computer the meaning of the words. Thus, we'd rather allow the designer to supply a part of the semantics of his predicates, in order to check that he has handled them conveniently.

In other words, we propose to match two different kinds of knowledge: on the one hand the *inferential knowledge* embodied in the rules, and on the other hand *a deep knowledge about the nature of the predicates* used to structure the universe of discourse.

To be more specific, we have developed a model for the description of predicates. Each part of this description is called a semantic unit, and refers to one feature of the nature of the predicate.

The first semantic units are used to locate the predicate within the universe of

---

[1] It should be noted that the target language in an OPS5-like production language. It is based on relational triples: (object-1 R object-2), where each object-i is either a value or a variable or a triple.

In the proposition (premise or action): R(object-1)=object-2, object-1 occupies the Object position and objet-2 the Value position withing relation R discourse. They are called units of conceptual location of the predicate. They refer to the concepts handled by the predicate and provide two attestants of the "importance" of the predicate for each concept involved (part 2). The next unit (part 3) specifies the physical link between the concepts established by the predicate. The last unit - called the unit of conceptual nature - receives information about the function of the predicate within the process (part 4).

Each and every predicate is described according to this model.

2. SEMANTIC UNITS OF CONCEPTUAL LOCATION

2.1 Description

The first semantic units allow the designer to supply both what the predicate connects with and how it "makes sense". In a sentence including variables, such as F(X) = (Y) - also written (X) F (Y), and called a triple -, we want to delineate what the variables X and Y represent as much as to know whether other triples are necessary to give the meaning of the sentence.

These items of information stem from the semantics of the predicate. Thus we decided to attach different attributes to the predicate. The first ones are called "Object Concept" (resp. "Value Concept") and receive the natural name of what you expect to meet at the object position (resp. the value position) in the triple. The following units, called Object_Covering (resp. Value_Covering) assesses the importance of the predicate for each concept involved. The last ones describe the autonomy degree of the relation, and, if necessary, the name of the complementary predicate.

We use the term concept, which is a generic (and fuzzy) word, rather than class, object, entity or type in order to stress that this notion encompasses both a conceptual model aspect and a more complex and abstract one. For example, a concept can designate either an entity of the real world (a machine) or the association of two concepts through a relation (an ordered sequence of possible actions on a circuit).We want the designer to clarify and make explicit what he has naturally in mind while he is creating his representation. But we don't forget that we are in a ES methodology which puts the predicate forward, and where some "objects" might not be considered either accurately or from a rigid and static viewpoint. Here, accordingly, they are predicates which characterize the concepts.

2.2 Examples

Let us take two examples:

First, suppose you have designed a model of a power plant. The predicate "CONTAINS" connects up items of equipment and the circuits which contain them. Each circuit contains items of equipment, and thus every "instance" of the circuit concept has an image by this relation. Conversely, some items of equipment belong to other parts of a plant. The following is written in the MRS:

CONTAINS Object_ Concept circuit ,
CONTAINS Object_Covering TOTAL
CONTAINS Value_ Concept equipment ,
CONTAINS Value_Covering PARTIAL
CONTAINS Meaning SELF-CONTENT

Here, concepts are entities of the "real" world. Secondly, the meaning of the predicate is self-content: it means that you don't need additional predicates to catch its meaning and its use.

Or, suppose you handle variables, as in our own system, which can be bound to (instantiated by) a single value in a given context. Also, you handle constants which have the same value whatever the context may be. And you wish these two representations to be compatible.

In other words, you need a representation which unifies the two expressions: "X is bound to 3 in a specific context called CONTEXT1" and "3 is equal to 3". Then you write

(X HAS-THE-VALUE 3) IS-VALID-FOR CONTEXT1, local truth
(3 HAS-THE-VALUE 3) IS_VALID-FOR ALL, global truth
CONTEXT1 GOOD-FOR CONTEXT1, the only CONTEXT$_i$ good for CONTEXT1,
ALL GOOD-FOR CONTEXT1, ALL is stated good for each CONTEXT$_i$, but you say it only once for the whole set of constants.

Then, if you want to write that an atom (viz. a instantiated variable or a constant) has the value 3 in a context named CONTEXT1, you write:
((X) HAS-THE-VALUE 3) IS-VALID-FOR (C) *and* (C) GOOD-FOR CONTEXT1
The following shows how this representation is described in the MRS:

HAS-THE-VALUE Object_Concept an_atom
HAS-THE-VALUE Object_Covering PARTIAL
HAS-THE-VALUE Value_Concept a_constant
HAS-THE-VALUE Value_Covering TOTAL
HAS-THE-VALUE Meaning PARTIAL
HAS-THE-VALUE Vector_Of_Extension IS-VALID-FOR,
IS-VALID-FOR Object_ Concept a_valued_atom ,
IS-VALID-FOR Object_Covering TOTAL
IS-VALID-FOR Value_Concept an_extended_context,
IS-VALID-FOR Value_Covering PARTIAL
IS-VALID-FOR Meaning CONTEXTUAL{ VALUE_OBJECT}
IS-VALID-FOR Vector_Of_Extension GOOD-FOR,

and you define:
   * an atom as a variable or a constant and
   * an extended context as a context or the constant ALL.
   * a valued atom as a couple atom-constant through the relation HAS-THE-VALUE.

When you assert that the meaning of HAS-THE-VALUE is partial, you emphasize the inability of the triple in coding a meaningful notion. In other words, you state that the predicate only encodes a part of a n-ary concept, and must be included in another triple (based on the vector of extension relation, here, IS-VALID-FOR) to make sense. Nevertheless, we should specify what a valued atom concept is in order to signal where HAS-THE-VALUE is located inside the extension relation (at the object or the value position in triple x IS-VALID-FOR y).

In the same way, when you assert that the meaning of IS-VALID-FOR is contextual, you say that its meaning depends on a context. To be more specific, it entails that every time you use this predicate in a premise, you have to specify its context by another predicate. This latter is called the vector of extension of the first predicate. You also may specify the nature of the link. Here we have stated that IS-VALID-FOR has the same Value Concept as GOOD-FOR Object Concept.

2.3 Verifying rules

Now, by scanning the rule, we can check that :

> * When a variable appears several times in the same rule, the links are valid:

For instance, if we have the rule:

IF FATHER-OF(X) = Y
THEN NAME-OF(Y) = X

we can discover the mistake since we know that the Value Concept of FATHER-OF
is different from the Object Concept of NAME-OF.

More generally, a given variable is to represent the same concept, or a set of concepts with no-empty intersection between them, wherever it appears in a rule:

Faced with the rule:

IF F(X) = (Y) and G(Y) = b and H(Z) = (Y) and ...
THEN ...

we check that: $Value\_Concept(F) \cap Object\_Concept(G) \cap Value\_Concept(H) \neq \emptyset$
> * When a constant appears in a sentence, it can belong to the involved concept:

To be more specific, it is possible to state all the possible values of a given concept, if they do not depend on the initial working memory. Then, it is easy to check whether a constant belongs to that set: if we meet the sentence F(X) = a and if the Value Concept of F is fully specified, we verify that a belongs to the set of the possible values for F at the value position.

If the concept is not described exhaustively, we check if the constant does not belong to some other incompatible concept: if we find out the membership of two different concepts for a given constant, we ask the user whether it is possible to obtain such an intersection. If the answer is yes, we keep track of it (it is a precious piece of information indeed, see above).

At that stage, we can also find out that a concept is always represented by constants, although it was not stated as a finite set. Conversely we can wonder why a fully specified concept is represented by a variable, whereas we have proved that this variable can only be bound to a single value.

Then, deeper verifications can be dealt with, such as:

* If a predicate supports only a partial meaning, we can first determine the complete set of predicates together, in order to ensure a full meaning, secondly to check that the right-hand side of the rules complies with the computed model. Also, if a predicate has been stated as contextual, it can be checked that the left-hand side of the rules never includes it without its context.

* if a concept must be totally covered by a predicate, the rules asserting its predicate are not contradictory in regard to the properties of the concept.

For instance, when there is only a single rule creating it, the premise - part of the rule should totally cover the concept. To be more specific, the variable that represents the concept must be able to match with each instances of the concept. See the following:

- the concept appears through the variable X in the condition $H(X) = a$,
- H totally covers its object concept ,
- you can only meet either the constant "a" or "b" at the value position of H.

We miss a second rule containing the "complementary part" of the condition on the relation H, i.e. the condition $H(X) = b$, and concluding on the starting concept.

2.4 Structuring the set of concepts

The second kind of results we can extract from matching the production rules and the Meta Relation Set is the building of the dependency graph between concepts.

It provides the user with a view of his universe of concepts as seen from the viewpoint of predicate description. The connections between the concepts are therefore clarified and can be analysed.

This graph gathers different types of links. It contains the _dimensional_ links between concepts, where concept c1 is followed by concept c2 if there exists a relation R between c1 and c2 which totally covers c1, or if c2 is a part of c1, the _attributive_ links, where concept c2 is an attribute (or a property) of concept c1 if there exists a relation R between c1 and c2 which totally covers c2 and partially covers c1, and the _union_ links between concepts.

For instance, we studied the plant processing KB, and built the (partial) graph:

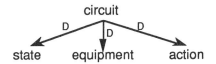

We conclude that circuit is a multidimensional concept, defined by a state, items of equipment, and a set of possible actions to make it work. Each circuit (in the initial working memory) must comply with this model.

From our verification knowledge base, we draw up the following graph:

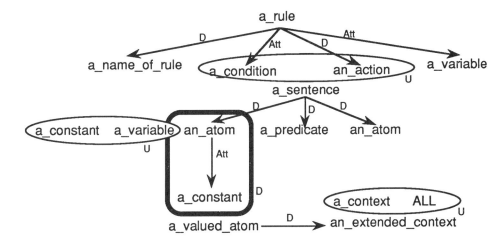

A hierarchy emerges within the universe of concepts. This result is supplied to the user. It brings him a global vision of his universe. Up to now, he used to have a single local and partial view of his model through the rules. Presently, we will provide him with an overall view of his representation.

These graphs are dual representations of the designer's model. At the starting point the concept was implicit, whereas the predicate was explicit. Here, we are in an opposite situation: we forget the predicate to put forward the conceptual objects handled by the system.

3. SEMANTIC UNIT OF PHYSICAL NATURE

3.1 Description

The physical nature of a relation is also an intrinsic part of the semantics of the predicate.

Let us take the relation MUST_FOLLOW(X) = Y. If it is functional, it denotes a precise and fully defined sequence of actions. If it is multivalued, the connection is much less rigid, there may be parallel processing or non-deterministic functioning...

Hence, we have defined a physical nature unit. It makes the kind of link created by the predicate explicit.

*It can be asserted that a predicate is single valued.
More precisely, you can state that a relation is :

right-functional: $R(x) = y1$ and $R(x) = y2 ==> y1 = y2$
and/or **left-functional**: $R(x1) = y$ and $R(x2) = y ==> x1 = x2$

with or without context. When a relation is a contextual function, the functional property depends on a context. For instance, a contextual right-function observes the rule:
If $F(x) = y1$ and $F(x) = y2$
and $[(G(x F y1) = z$ and $G(x F y2) = z)$ or $(G(z) = (x F y1)$ and $G(z) = (x F y2))]$
then $y1 = y2$.
    But $G(x F y1) = z1$ and $G(x F y2) = z2$, with $y1 <> y2$ are both possible if $z1 <> z2$.
    In our plant model, CONTAINS is a left-function. Each item of equipment belongs to a single circuit. In the same way, in our system (see example below), HAS-THE-VALUE is a contextual right-functional predicate: a variable is bound to a single value in a given context, but can be bound to another value in a different context.

*If the relation is multivalued, it may have specific properties. The most frequent ones - of interest for the purpose of verification - are:

antisymmetry: $R(x) = y$ and $R(y) = z ==> z <> x$
symmetry: $R(x) = y ==> R(y) = x$
right-reflexivity: $R(x) = y ==> R(y) = y$, **left-reflexivity**: $R(x) = y ==> R(x) = x$

(here, the point is: if an object has an image through the relation, then it must own itself as an image)
    For instance, the GOOD-FOR predicate of example 2(b) is right-reflexive: we create the two forms: ALL GOOD-FOR CONTEXT$_i$ and CONTEXT$_i$ GOOD-FOR CONTEXT$_i$.

*Lastly, we can specify that an antisymmetry is conceptually symmetrical. We call that **antisymmetrical-symmetry** type. They are often used to reduce the size of the working memory.
    For instance, relation IS-DIFFERENT-FROM is frequently represented in such a way that you create the triple x IS-DIFFERENT-FROM y when y IS-DIFFERENT-FROM x exists. But you must manage the non-oriented side of the relation. Generally, if a property P involving x is deduced from the triple x IS-DIFFERENT-FROM y, the same property involving y may also be deduced. In point of fact, instead of duplicating the working elements, you have to duplicate the rules, establishing a local symmetry inside your production memory.
    This list of properties is not exhaustive. Some properties are likely to be omitted. We just picked what we needed while we studied knowledge bases. One can ask, for instance, why the contextual antisymmetrical property is not taken

into account. My single answer is: up to now, we did not need it, but if I meet it later, I'll deal with it!

3.2 Verifying rules

The verifications related to the functional and antisymmetrical properties are very similar. We are going to detail them, so as to indicate the way we follow to match rules and meta-relations. The other verifications will only be outlined, because of a lack of space, and since they are not yet fully implemented. But we will deal with them in the same spirit as the functional ones.

3.2.1 Checking functional and antisymetrical properties

This consists in examining the rules to find out whether they can deduce instances of relations in contradiction with the property(ies) known about this relation.

For this purpose, one should:

* seek couples of (not necessarily different) rules able to deduce two contradictory instances, together with the necessary conditions for a contradiction to occur. We call these conditions a contradictory context .

Suppose we have the two rules:

r1: IF $F1(a) = X$ r2: IF $F1(U) = Y$
            $F2(X) = Z$ $F2(Y) = T$
            $AS1(Z) = U$ $AS1(b) = T$
     THEN $G(U\ F\ X) = a$ THEN $G(b\ F\ T) = U$

and suppose that each F_i is declared as a right-function, AS1 as an antisymmetrical relation, and F as a contextual right-function. Lastly, let us assume that upper case denotes variables, whereas lower - case denotes constants.

We detect a potential conflict, related to the contradictory context: $U/r1 = b$ (same image), $U/r2 = a$ (same context), $X <> T$ (different values).

* The contradiction occurs whether or not the two rules can fire within this context. In order to settle this problem, we built the resolving rule, defined as the union of the two conflicting rules, after rewriting them within the contradictory context, and renaming the variables conveniently.

The resolving rule related to our example is :

        r1.2:   IF $F1(a) = X$
                                $F2(X) = Z$
                                $AS1(Z) = b$
                                $F1(a) = Y'$
                                $F2(Y') = T$
                                $AS1(b) = T$
                                $X <> T$
                THEN $G(b\ F\ X) = a$
                                $G(b\ F\ T) = a$

* And we check whether or not the resolving rule can succeed, taking into account the properties of the other predicates on the left-hand side of the rule. To detect if a rule is unfirable, we have to examine its premise - part. If it contains a set of logically exclusive (unsatisfiable) conditions, the rule is unfirable. This process is implemented in two steps :

1) Use of the physical properties
- If the rule includes the conditions : (p1): X FUNC x1 and (p2): Y FUNC x2 with FUNC a right-function and x1, x2 two constants or variables such that the condition (p3): $x1 <> x2$ is true, then we add the condition (p4): $X <> Y$.
.if FUNC is a contextual right-functional predicate, the conditions become:

(p1): $G(X FUNC x1) = x3$ and (p2): $G(Y FUNC x2) = x4$
or (p1): $G(x3) = X FUNC x1$ and (p2): $G(x4) = Y FUNC x2$
and we add to (p3) another condition (p3'): $x3 = x4$

.if FUNC is left-functional p1 and p2 become ((p3) does not change):

(p1): x1 FUNC X and (p2): x2 FUNC Y

.if FUNC is contextual left-functional, you add the context to the two previous conditions, as shown for the contextual right-function.

- If the rule includes the conditions : (p1): x1 FUNC X and (p2): x2 FUNC Y with FUNC a right-function and x1,x2 two constants or variables such that the condition (p3): $x1 = x2$ is true, then we add the condition (p4): $X = Y$.
.if FUNC is both right-functional and contextual, the conditions are:

(p1): $G(x1 FUNC X) = x3$ and (p2): $G(x2 FUNC Y) = x4$
or (p1): $G(x3) = x1 FUNC X$ and (p2): $G(x4) = x2 FUNC Y$
and we add to (p3) a second condition (p3'): $x3 = x4$

.if FUNC is a (contextual) left-functional predicate, the sense of the relation (p1) and (p2) is reversed, as above.

- If the rule includes the conditions : (p1) X AS x1 and (p2) x2 AS Y with AS being an antisymmetrical relation and x1, x2 two constants or variables such that the condition (p3): $x1 = x2$ is true, then we add the condition
(p4) : $X <> Y$

2) Transitive closure and detection of nonsense conditions
For example, if the rule contains the conditions (p1): $x1 > y1$ and (p2): $y1 > z1$, we add the condition (p3): $x1 > z1$ (we also use the natural relations between numbers: from $x > 1$ and $y < 0$, we infer that $x > y$). Then, we look at the left-hand side of the rule to detect conditions such as $x <> x$ or $1 = 2$, ...

If a nonsense condition has been established using the physical properties of functions Fi or antisymmetrical relations ASj, the rule is said to be unfirable under control of {..., Fi, ..., ASj, ...}. And the conflict about F (or whose F is the object) is said to be separated under control of {..., Fi, ..., ASj, ...}.

In our example, we deduce from the resolving rule (first step):

F1(a) = X, F1(a) = Y', F1 is right-functional ==> X = Y'
F2(X) = Z, F2(Y') = T, F2 is right-functional ==> Z = T
AS1(Z) = b, AS1(b) = T, AS1 is antisymmetrical ==> Z <> T
then (second step), we deduce from Z = T and Z <> T that Z <> Z and T <> T
The conflict about F is separated under control of {F1, F2, AS1}.

* As the verification process makes use of physical properties, circular proofs should be sought, such as: F1 is a function because F2 is a function, F2 is a function because F3 is a function, ... , Fn is a function because F1 is a function.

Thus, we verify that each conflict is separated by a set of predicates which are not the object of a conflict, or the object of settled conflicts. Then the conflict is said to be settled. Every conflict not settled is supplied to the user.

3.2.2 Checking property of symmetry and reflexivity

Here, the firability (rather than unfirability) of a rule within a given context must be demonstrated. For instance, if R is symmetrical, and if a rule deduces the triple a R b, the triple b R a is also to be deduced. Does thus mean that it must be deduced simultaneously (as a daemon does), by the same rule but triggering later, or by another rule? Up to now, we did not want to take account of the global conflict-resolution strategy. Thus, we are not able to prove that a rule is bound to fire after another. On the other hand, we assume that when a rule is selected, all possible bindings of the rule are triggered consecutively (local saturation strategy). Thus, we have decided to impose the rule: "it must be the same rule which deduces both WM instances", and to verify this restrictive assumption. The proof is established:

* if the rule deduces the two instances of the relation in the same firing. That is, when it owns two actions corresponding to the two directions of the relation.
* comparing the links between atoms in the left-hand side of the rule:
Suppose we have the rule:

R1:   IF   R1(X) = Y
                 S1(Y) = Z
                 R1(T) = Z
       THEN   S2(X) = T
where S1 and S2 are stated symmetrical.

We build the graph:

And we compare it to the same graph, where X and T are inverted, and where the other variables are renamed:

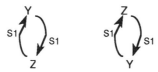

We try to unify these two graphs: first , we deduce that Y = Z', and we delete the link. Secondly, we deduce Z = Y', and we delete the link. It remains the two graphs:

remain and are obviously identical. Then we conclude that S2 is symmetrical if S1 is symmetrical.

Let us note that, if S1 was not stated as symmetrical, it would remain the two graph:

would remain and then we will be able to provide, by joining the two links, the following rule :

Y S1 Z ==> Z S1 Y

which is a sufficient condition to guarantee the symmetrical property of S2.

3.2.3 Checking antisymmetrical symmetry

This consists in verifying that a rule handling such a relation at its left-hand side has a "sister rule" . Generally speaking, if the relation in question appears in the premise x AS_S y, the sister rule is the formed by duplicating the initial one, inverting the role of x and y, except for the x AS_S y premise that stays the same.

For instance, if you meet the rule:

```
IF      AS_S(X) = Y
        F(Y) = a
        G(Y) = Z
        H(Z) = b
        J(X) = T
THEN  P(Y) = c
        Q(Z) = d
        S(X) = T
```

where AS_S is said to be an antisymmetrical symmetry, you are looking for a rule which can be unified with the following rule:

IF   AS_S(X) = Y
        F(X) = a
        G(X) = Z
        H(Z) = b
        J(Y) = T
THEN   P(X) = c
        Q(Z) = d
        S(Y) = T

4. SEMANTIC UNIT OF CONCEPTUAL NATURE

Our current description is rather poor. We are planning on improving it by introducing the notion of the conceptual nature of predicate. Indeed, our experience shows that whatever the production memories may be, there are always various predicates playing a specific conceptual role which is independent of the knowledge domain.

Let us point out the role of Token, which consists in marking objects at the end of a process to isolate them, or, conversely, at the begining, to identify them for the process; the role of Disjunction Operator, to encode a logical OR (such as GOOD-FOR in a previous example) ; the role of "Ordering"...

We hope to determine some patterns of handling, linked to each conceptual nature. And, obviously, we will map the set of rules with these patterns. But it's another story...

5. RELATED WORK AND CONCLUSION

In its "facet" approach of consistency, as well as on some points of the conceptual location units, our system is related to SACCO [2]. Also, our process of a physical nature unit relates to TWAICE [6] and TIBRE [5]. Finally, the idea of matching different levels of knowledge derives from [4] and [3].

In this paper, we have described a system intended for improvement in the reliability of first - order expert system. It contains a consistency checker component, verifying mathematical properties pertaining to predicates (physical units). But it is also a tool destined to enhance completeness, underlining rule unfirability, predicate mishandling, by the way of the conceptual location units. Lastly, it can be considered as a knowledge extraction assistance tool, ensuring the expert to clarify the implicit objects and properties of his system, and supplying him with an external view ensuring that the expert clarifies the implicit objects and properties of his/her system and is supplied with an external view of the universe.

REFERENCES

1.   Most of our examples come from a production system called "Computer-Aided Management for Power Plants" designed by C.M. FALINOWER
      Electricité de France, Direction des Etudes et Recherches, 1990

2.   AYEL M., (1987) : *Détection d'incohérences dans les bases de connaissance : SACCO*, Thèse d'Etat, Chambery, September.

3.   GEISSMAN J.R., SCHULTZ R.D., (1988) : *Verification & Validation of Expert Systems*, AI EXPERT, February, pp. 26-33.

4.   GREEN C., KEYES M., (1987) : *Verification and Validation of Expert Systems Workshop on Knowledge-based System Verification*, NASA/Ames Research Center, Mountain View, Calif., April.

5.   LALO A. (1988) : *TIBRE: un système expert qui teste les incohérences dans les bases de règles*, Proceedings of the Eighth International Workshop on "Expert Systems & their Applications", Avignon.

6.   MELLIS W., RUCKERT M., (1989) : *Checking consistency in expert systems*, Proceedings of the Ninth international workshop on "Expert Systems & their Applications", Avignon, May 29 - June 2, 1989.

11

Estimation of Failure Potential in Knowledge Bases

Sorin GRUNWALD

ABSTRACT

This paper investigates the relationship between the quantity of information contained in a knowledge base and the reliability of an inference based on this knowledge base.

An artificial system is reliable to the extent to which it can be expected that it functions according to its specifications. In the case of knowledge - based systems, it can be said that the system is reliable, if the conclusion that the knowledge based system reaches is the same as the conclusion that this system was expected to reach.

In this paper it is assumed that the reliability of a knowledge based system is related to the quantity of information processed during inference, information which is concentrated in the knowledge base.

The average value of the available quantity of information in the case of the explanatory inference, known as backward chaining, is given by the conditional entropy $H(X/Y)$, where X is the set of possible system states before inference and Y is the set of possible system states after the inference. This entropy is the measure of the failure potential of the explanatory inference.

In the case of predictive inference (forward chaining), the average value of the available quantity of information is given by the conditional entropy $H(Y/X)$, where X, Y have the same significance as above. This entropy is the measure of the failure potential of the predictive inference. The value of the failure potential is related to the incompleteness of the knowledge base. The analysis of the resulting entropies leads to identifying the weak points of the knowldge base, e.g., the most unreliable piece of evidence. Other calculated values, e.g., the discernibility degree, suggest where in the knowledge base the refinement is most needed.

For a better understanding of the concepts, a numerical example is analysed. The example was taken from "A Method for Managing Evidential Reasoning in a Hierarchical Hypothesis Space" by J. Gordon and E.H. Shortliffe and was simplified for the present purposes.

1. INTRODUCTION

1.1 Definitions

Any problem-solving activity requires "knowledge" of the problem domain. There exist many knowledge representation formalisms, each of them optimized for certain types of problem-solving activities.

The domain knowledge, which is used by an artificial intelligence (AI) system in its problem solving activity, is called the knowledge base of the system. The system itself is called "knowledge based". The system considers the actual state of the world stated as facts and analyses these facts based on the knowledge available in its knowledge base. According to this knowledge, conclusions are drawn from the facts in a sequence of inference steps.

An AI system is reliable to the extent to which it can be expected that it functions according to its specifications. It can be said that a knowledge - based system is reliable if the conclusion that the knowledge based system reaches is the same as the conclusion that the system is expected to reach.

There exist many reasons why a system can fail in reaching the expected conclusion. One of the main reasons is related to the fact that in many real systems the knowledge base is incomplete, imprecise, and inconsistent. In such a case, one or another conclusion is characterized by its potentiality, i.e., by its own chance of being drawn. The potentiality distribution of different possible conclusions is related to the failure potential of the knowledge base. By drawing a certain conclusion, new information about the problem is obtained. The quantity of the information obtained depends on the potentiality of the conclusion drawn. Thus the quantity of information processed during inference can be used to characterize the inference failure potential.

1.2 State of the art

Three research areas are related to the present paper. One is concerned with describing and quantifying properties of the knowledge bases [12, 17, 18]. A second research area is concerned with modelling the incompleteness of a knowledge base in order to allow for managing uncertain inference processes [6, 14, 19]. A third area of interest is the one of software engineering. Software reliability plays a major role here [5, 16]. Software properties are defined [3, 9, 15] and their relationship to software reliability is analysed [2, 10, 11]. In estimating software reliability of knowledge - based systems, efforts are still concentrated more on program techniques [13] rather than on knowledge formalization. Work has been done in order to relate the information processed by a program to its complexity [4]. Still, no results are available that relate knowledge - based properties and the information content of the formalized knowledge to the failure potential of knowledge - based systems and to their reliability.

1.3 Theoretical approach and experimental results

This paper is concerned with the reliability of probabilistic reasoning based on incomplete knowledge bases. It addresses some of the above mentioned problems using an information-theoretic framework. The reliability (failure potential) of a knowledge based system is related to the knowledge base incompleteness by assuming that the system reliability depends on the quantity of information available for inference, information which is concentrated in the knowledge base.

The average amount of available information in the case of the explanatory inference, known as backward chaining, is given by the conditional informational entropy $H(X/Y)$, where X is the set of possible system states before inference and Y is the set of possible system states after the inference. This entropy is the measure of the failure potential of the explanatory inference.

In the case of predictive inference (forward chaining), the average value of the available quantity of information is given by the conditional informational entropy $H(Y/X)$, where X, Y have the same significance as above. This entropy is the measure of the failure potential of the predictive inference.

The analysis of the resulting entropies leads to identifying the weak points of the knowledge base, e.g., the most unreliable piece of evidence. Other values suggest where in the knowledge base the refinement is most needed. It is shown, for instance, that pieces of evidence increase the failure potential by decreasing the discernibility of hypotheses. This rule, which is trivial in qualitative thinking, is thus quantitatively experimented with here.

For a better understanding of the concepts a numerical example is analysed. The example was taken from "A Method for Managing Evidential Reasoning in a Hierarchical Hypothesis Space" by J. Gordon and E.H. Shortliffe [6] and was simplified for the present purposes.

2. THE INFERENCE SPACE

The problem solving process can be seen as a sequence of system transformations which are based on certain rule sets and which alter certain value structures in the system memory. The transformation from one system state to another corresponds to a step in the problem solving process and is called inference step. Each such inference step has its own information content. This information content depends on the (un)certainty of the system states before and after the inference step. With other words, the information processed within such an inference step is a measure of the (un)certainty of reaching a new system state starting from an old one under given conditions (constraints). The environment in which the inference process takes place, in which the information is defined and processed with respect to the problem solving activity, is called inference space [7].

2.1 Potentiality

The finite and countable set of all possible system states before an inference step is given by the initial state matrix

$$X = [x_i] = [x_1, x_2, ..., x_n]$$

with x_i, $1 < i < n$, representing the i-th possible initial state for an arbitrary inference step. The system finds itself before the inference step necessarily in one of the initial states x_i.

The final state matrix

$$Y = [y_j] = [y_1, y_2, ..., y_m]$$

contains as elements y_j, $1 < j < m$, which represent all possible system states after an inference step. The system finds itself after the inference step necessarily in one of the final states y_j.

Each of the initial potential situations x_i can be the actual one for the current inference step. Therefore to each of them a value $p(x_i)$ is associated, which represents a measure of the potentiality of the initial state x_i [20]. This value can be an empirical one, based for instance on statistical properties of the set X. It can be a value based on certain fuzzy relationships among the elements of the set. It can also be described by a belief function, i.e., the belief that the initial state for the current inference step is the situation x_i. Thus, the value $p(x_i)$ is the a priori potentiality of the realisation x_i e X.

Let Y be the set of the potential final situations for the current inference step. Each of the final situations y_j, y_j e Y, can be potentially reached by drawing an inference based on the current x_i e X. A measure $p(y_i)$ of the potentiality of an arbitrary state is associated with each final state y_j. $p(y_j)$ represents the a priori potentiality of the state y_j. Let the set

$$[P_x] = [p(x_1), p(x_2), ..., p(x_n)]$$

be the potentiality distribution corresponding to the set X. It is assumed that

$$p(\bigcup_{j=1}^{n} x_i) = \sum_{j=1}^{n} p(x_i) = 1$$

In a similar manner

$$P_y = [p(y_1), p(y_2), ..., p(y_n)]$$

is the potentiality distribution for the set Y with

$$p(\bigcup_{j=1}^{m} y_i) = \sum_{j=1}^{m} p(y_i) = 1$$

When the system reaches the final state y_j from the initial state x_i, it can be said that a piece of information is provided concerning the state transition from x_i to y_j. The amount of information provided by inference is a function of the potentiality of y_j given x_i

$$i\,(y_j/x_i) = F\,[\,p(y_j/x_i)\,].$$

The function F can be chosen from different function classes. One main condition that is imposed on this function for practical applications is that the information must be additive. If an event x_i is the result of two independent events x_{i1} and x_{i2}

$$x_i = x_{i1} \varnothing x_{i2},$$

then the information provided by the realization x_i has to be given by

$$i\,(x_i) = i\,(x_{i1}) + i\,(x_{i2}).$$

This results in

$$F\,[p(x_i)] =$$
$$F\,[p(x_{i1} \varnothing x_{i2})] =$$
$$F\,[p(x_{i1}) \varnothing p(x_{i2})] =$$
$$F\,[p(x_{i1})] + F\,[p(x_{i2})].$$

The solution of this functional equation is

$$F\,(p) = -\,a \log p,$$

where a is a positive constant.

If "$\log_2$" is selected for the logarithmic function, for reasons related to the unity measure of information, then a = 1 and it further follows that

$$i\,(x_i) = -\log p(x_i).$$

Considering X be an ergodic information source, the function

$$I(X) = -n \sum_{i=1}^{n} p_i \log p_i \qquad (1)$$

gives the amount of information that can be provided by all n elements of the set X, i.e., it expresses the amount of infor-mation available in X.

The average amount of information is called informational entropy and is given by

$$H(X) = \frac{I(X)}{n},$$

i.e.,

$$H(X) = \sum_{i=1}^{n} p_i \log p_i \qquad (2)$$

2.2 The failure potential

In order to analyse the failure potential of an inference step it is necessary to consider both the set X of possible initial situations and the set Y of possible final situations of the inference. Therefore a product space [X, Y] is constructed which is defined by

$$[X, Y] = \begin{vmatrix} x_1,y_1 & x_1,y_2 & \cdots & x_1,y_m \\ x_2,y_1 & x_2,y_2 & \cdots & x_2,y_m \\ \cdots\cdots\cdots\cdots\cdots\cdots\cdots\cdots\cdots \\ x_n,y_1 & x_n,y_2 & \cdots & x_n,y_m \end{vmatrix}$$

where the product x_i,y_j represents the conjunction of x_i and y_j, i.e., the realization of both x_i and y_j. No assumption is made regarding the dependency or independency of x_i and y_j. The corresponding two-dimensional potentiality distribution is given by

$$[P(X, Y)] = \begin{vmatrix} p(x_1,y_1) & p(x_1,y_2) & \cdots & p(x_1,y_m) \\ p(x_2,y_1) & p(x_2,y_2) & \cdots & p(x_2,y_m) \\ \cdots\cdots\cdots\cdots\cdots\cdots\cdots\cdots\cdots \\ p(x_n,y_1) & p(x_n,y_2) & \cdots & p(x_n,y_m) \end{vmatrix}$$

Thus three sets can be defined:
X   : the set of the potential initial states
Y   : the set of the potential final states
X,Y : the set of combined potential states.

To each set corresponds an entropy, which represents the average information contained by the set with respect to the inference step:
H(X)   : the entropy of the initial set
H(Y)   : the entropy of the final set
H(X,Y) : the entropy of the combined set.

The formulae for these entropies are correspondingly:

$$H(X) = \sum_{i=1}^{n} p(x_i) \log p(x_i) \tag{3}$$

$$H(Y) = \sum_{j=1}^{m} p(y_j) \log p(y_j) \tag{4}$$

and

$$H(X,Y) = -\sum_{i=1}^{n} \sum_{j=1}^{m} p(x_i,y_j) \log p(x_i,y_j) \tag{5}$$

As already mentioned, if the system state y_j e Y after the inference is known, there still exists an uncertainty concerning the initial state x_i. This uncertainty is a property of the inference and it is measured by an a posteriori potentiality function denoted by $p(x_i/y_j)$. This type of potentiality is called equivocation. It shows that a failure is possible in identifying x_i when already knowing y_j. The failure potential depends on the quantity of information available for the inference.

The average value of the available quantity of information is given by the conditional entropy of the field X determined by the field Y and denoted by $H(X/Y)$. This entropy is the measure for the failure potential of the explanatory inference, known as backward chaining.

Conversely, if the system state x_i e X before the inference step is known, there exists an uncertainty concerning the final state y_j. The uncertainty is a property of the inference and it is measured by an a posteriori potentiality function denoted $p(y_j/x_i)$. This type of potentiality is called prediction error. It shows that a failure is possible in predicting the state y_j out of the state x_i. The failure potential also depends in this case on the quantity of information available for inference. The average value of the available quantity of information is given in this case by the conditional entropy of the field Y determined by the field X and denoted by $H(Y/X)$. This entropy is the measure for the failure potential of the predictive inference, known as forward chaining.

For an arbitrary initial situation x_i, the entropy of the whole final field can be calculated by

$$H(Y/x_i) = -\sum_{j=1}^{m} p(y_j,x_i) \log p(y_j/x_i). \tag{6}$$

For the whole initial field it results that

$$H(Y/X) = -\sum_{i=1}^{n} p(x_i)\, H(Y/x_i),\ \text{i.e.,} \tag{6'}$$

$$X(Y/X) = -\sum_{i=1}^{n}\sum_{j=1}^{m} p(x_i)\, p(y_j/x_i)\, \log p\, (y_j/x_i),\ \text{and} \tag{6''}$$

$$X(Y/X) = -\sum_{i=1}^{n}\sum_{j=1}^{m} p(x_i/y_j)\, \log p\, (y_j/x_i). \tag{6'''}$$

In a similar way

$$H(X/y_j) = -\sum_{i=1}^{n} p(x_i/y_j)\, \log p(x_i/y_j). \tag{7}$$

For the whole initial field it results that

$$H(X/Y) = \sum_{i=1}^{n} p(y_j)\, H\, (X/y_j),\ \text{i.e.,} \tag{7'}$$

$$H(X/Y) = -\sum_{i=1}^{n}\sum_{j=1}^{m} p(y_i)\, px_i/y_j)\, \log p(x_i/y_j),\ \text{and} \tag{7''}$$

$$H(X/Y) = -\sum_{i=1}^{n}\sum_{j=1}^{m} p(x_i/y_j)\, \log p(x_i/y_j) \tag{7'''}$$

With the previous equations the following relations among different entropies may be demonstrated :

$$H(X,Y) = H(X) + H(Y/X) \tag{8}$$

and

$$H(X,Y) = H(Y) + H(X/Y). \tag{9}$$

From (8) and (9) the entropy law of monotonic inference

$$H(X) + H(Y/X) = H(Y) + H(X/Y)$$

results, which yields the failure potential balance for the explanatory and the predictive reasoning.

If $p(y_j/x_i) = 1$, which is the case of no uncertainty concerning the inference it results that

$$H(Y/X) = 0,\ \text{i.e.,}$$

the failure potential is zero in this case.

On the other hand, if no inference knowledge is present, i.e., if the conclusion is independent premises

$$p(y_j/x_i) = p(y_j)$$

then

$$H(Y/X) = H(Y).$$

It can be shown [21] that

$$H(Y/X) \leq H(Y). \tag{10}$$

With relation (10) the maximal value for the failure potential in predictive inference can be determined.

In the case of explanatory inference, similar relations are obtained. The maximal value of the failure potential of the explanatory inference is given by

$$H(X/Y) \leq H(X). \tag{11}$$

3. NUMERICAL EXAMPLE

For a better understanding of the concepts presented here, a numerical example is further analysed. The example was taken from "A Method for Managing Evidential Reasoning in a Hierarchical Hypothesis Space" by J. Gordon and E.H. Shortliffe [6] and was simplified for the present purposes. In the chosen example a "belief" function is considered as a measure for the potentiality. Still this does not influence the generality of the results, since other potentiality measures as, for instance, the fuzzy or the probabilistic ones, would lead to similar conclusions.

Suppose a physician is considering the case of a disease D (cholestatic jaundice). This disease can have four causes : H (hepatitis), C (cirrhosis), G (gallstones), and P (pancreatic cancer). The set { H, C, G, P } is called the frame of discernment as in the in Dempster-Shafer theory of evidence and is denoted by È. The set elements, H, C, G, and P, are assumed mutually exclusive and exhaustive. Each element in È corresponds to a one-element subset called a singleton. The number of all possible subsets of È is 2^N, where N is the number of elements of È. The empty set, ø, is a subset of È, which corresponds to a conclusion known to be false since the elements in È are exhaustive.

The inference process consists in this case in identifying the cause for a disease given certain pieces of evidence. The knowledge needed for the inference can be formalized as inference rules. It is possible to interpret these rules as basic probability assignments (bpa), i.e., each piece of evidence confirms or denies a cause only to a certain degree given by its bpa. The premises of the rules are the pieces of evidence and the conclusion is the disease cause supported by them. If more rules succeed for the same conclusion, then the belief in this conclusion can be calculated using an algorithm of bpa combination.

According to the method presented in [6], the basic probability assignments for the initial pieces of evidence x_1, x_2, x_3, as well as for the combined ones $x_3 = x_1 \bullet x_2$, and $x_4 = x_1 \bullet x_2 \bullet x_3$ are given by :

x_i		i=1	i=2	i=3	i=4	i=5
Y_J						
	A	m_1	m_2	m_3	$m_{12}=m_4$	$m_{34}=m$
	∅	0	0	0	0	0
j=1	{H}	-	-	0.8	-	0.545
j=2	{C}	-	-	-	0.42	0.191
j=3	{H,C}	-	0.6	-	0.18	0.082
j=4	{C,G,P}	0.7	-	-	0.28	0.127
j=5	Θ = {H, C, G, P}	0.3	0.4	0.2	0.12	0.055

Assume that the inference knowledge is stored in a knowledge base in the form of inference rules. The rules are of the form

IF x THEN y,

where x is any subset of X and y any subset of Y with

$$X = \{ x_1, x_2, x_3 \}$$

and

$$Y = \{ H, C, G, P \}.$$

This knowledge base has three primary active rules

P1. IF x_1 THEN $m_{1/C,G,P}$ {C,G,P}, $m_{1/C,G,P} = 0.7$
P2. IF x_2 THEN $m_{2/H,C}$ {H,C} , $m_{2/H,C} = 0.6$
P3. IF x_3 THEN $m_{3/H}$ {H} , $m_{3/H} = 0.8$

and seven secondary active rules deduced with the Dempster-Shafer method of combination out of the primary ones

S1. IF $x_1 \varnothing x_2$	THEN $m_{12/C}$	{C},	$m_{12/C}$	= 0.42
S2. IF $x_1 \varnothing x_2$	THEN $m_{12/H,C}$	{H,C},	$m_{12/H,C}$	= 0.18
S3. IF $x_1.x_2$	THEN $m_{12/C,G,P}$	{C,G,P},	$m_{12/C,G,P}$	= 0.28
S4. IF $x_1.x_2 \varnothing x_3$	THEN $m_{123/H}$	{H},	$m_{123/H}$	= 0.545
S5. IF $x_1 \varnothing x_2 \varnothing x_3$	THEN $m_{123/C}$	{C},	$m_{123/C}$	=0.191
S6. IF $x_1 \varnothing x_2 \varnothing x_3$	THEN $m_{123/H,C}$	{H,C},	$m_{123/H,C}$	= 0.082
S7. IF $x_1.x_2 \varnothing x_3$	THEN $m_{123/C,G,P}$	{C,G,P},	$m_{123/C,G,P}$	= 0.127

The closed world assumption is satisfied with:

CWA1. IF x_1	THEN $m_{1/\Theta}$	Θ, $m_{1/\Theta}$	= 0.3
CWA2. IF x_2	THEN $m_{2/\Theta}$	Θ, $m_{2/\Theta}$	= 0.4
CWA3. IF x_3	THEN $m_{3/\Theta}$	Θ, $m_{3/\Theta}$	= 0.2
CWA4. IF $x_1 \varnothing x_2$	THEN $m_{12/\Theta}$	Θ, $m_{12/\Theta}$	= 0.12
CWA5. IF $x_1 \varnothing x_2 \varnothing x_3$	THEN $m_{123/\Theta}$	Θ, $m_{123/\Theta}$	= 0.055.

If we denote with X the set of premises for the active rules (pieces of evidence) and with Y the set of conclusions, we obtain in a forward chaining reasoning mechanism

$$X = [\ x_1 \quad x_2 \quad x_3 \quad x_1 \cdot x_2 \quad x_1 \cdot x_2 \cdot x_3 \ ]$$

$$Y =$$

		x_1	x_2	x_3	$x_1{\cdot}x_2$	$x_1{\cdot}x_2{\cdot}x_3$
	H	0	0	0.8	0	0.545
	C	0	0	0	0.42	0.191
$[\, p(y_j/x_i) \,]$:	H∅C	0	0.6	0	0.18	0.082
	C∅G∅P	0.7	0	0	0.28	0.127
	θ	0.3	0.4	0.2	0.12	0.055

In order to calculate the failure potential based on a such potentiality distribution, we assume further a random presence of each of the pieces of evidence, i.e.,

$$p(x_i) = \frac{1}{5}, \text{ for each } i \in [1,5]$$

This random presence distribution is the property of only the evidence set and not of the information processing during the inference step.

We also assume a random presence of each of the hypotheses, i.e.,

$$p(y_j) = \frac{1}{5}, \text{ for each } j \in [1,5]$$

In in our particular case H(X) = H(Y) results. From (8) and (9) it results that for the current knowledge base, we obtain the following equation :

$$H(X/Y) = H(Y/X) \qquad (12)$$

i.e., the failure potential in the explanatory inference is equal to that in the predictive inference.

The failure potential H(X/Y), which is a property of the inference step, can be calculated as (7''):

$$H(X/Y) = - \sum_{i=1}^{5} \sum_{j=1}^{5} p(y_j) \varnothing p(x_i/y_j) \varnothing \log p(x_i/y_j).$$

Therefore

$$H(X/Y) = \frac{1}{5} \sum_{i=1}^{5} \sum_{j=1}^{5} p(x_i/y_j) \varnothing \log p(x_i/y_j) = 1.26. \qquad (13)$$

According to (12)

$$H(Y/X) = H(X/Y) = 1.26. \qquad (14)$$

As already mentioned ((10),(11)),

$$H(X/Y) \leq H(X), \text{ i.e., max } [\ H(X/Y) \ ] = H(X)$$

and

$$H(Y/X) \leq H(Y), \text{ i.e., max } [\ H(Y/X) \ ] = H(Y).$$

In our case, according to (4),

$$H(X) = H(Y) = -\sum_{j=1}^{5} p(y_j) \log p(y_j) = 2.33. \tag{15}$$

If H(X) or H(Y) represents 100%, therefore

$$H(Y/X) = H(X/Y) = 54\ \% . \tag{16}$$

These results show, that for the inference knowledge base selected here the failure potential is reduced by a factor of approximately 2 when considering inference knowledge with respect to the case when no inference knowledge is present.

Still, the increased value of the failure potential also shows a need for refining the knowledge base. According to the case study considered, one minor way of improving the reliability of the knowledge base consists of improving the knowledge about the potentiality distribution of the pieces of evidence and thus reducing H(X). Another minor way of improvement is improving the knowledge of the hypothesis potentiality distribution, and thus reducing H(Y).

Thirdly, improvements can be obtained by identifying weak points of the actual knowledge base, i.e., weak points of the information processing inference. In the case of predictive inference, the matrix

$$[H(y_j/x_i)] = \begin{vmatrix} 0 & 0 & 0.052 & 0 & 0.096 \\ 0 & 0 & 0 & 0.106 & 0.092 \\ 0 & 0.088 & 0 & 0.09 & 0.06 \\ 0.072 & 0 & 0 & 0.104 & 0.076 \\ 0.104 & 0.106 & 0.094 & 0.074 & 0.046 \end{vmatrix}$$

helps in identifying the components having the most significant contribution to the global failure potential. According to (6)

$$[H(Y/x_i)] = [\ 0.176\ \ 0.194\ \ 0.146\ \ 0.374\ \ 0.37\ ], \tag{18}$$

and

$$[H(Y/x_i)]\ [\%] = [\ 14\ \ 15\ \ 12\ \ 30\ \ 29\ ]. \tag{18'}$$

These entropies are an indicator of the reliability of the individual pieces of evidence. The maximum value shows the most unreliable piece of evidence with respect to the defined conclusion set:

$$H(Y/x_4 = x_{12}) = 30\%. \tag{19}$$

As a rule, it can be said that pieces of evidence increase the failure potential by decreasing the discernibility of the hypothesis.

This rule, which is trivial in qualitative thinking, is thus here quantitatively experimented with here.

In a similar way, the entropies

$$[H(y_j/X)]' = [\ 0.148\ \ 0.198\ \ 0.238\ \ 0.252\ \ 0.424\ ], \tag{20}$$

where ' denotes the matrix transposition, and

$$[H(y_j/X)]' \, [\%] = [\, 12 \quad 16 \quad 19 \quad 20 \quad 33 \,]. \qquad (20')$$

refer to individual conclusions and their influence on the failure potential with respect to the whole initial field X.
    The entropy

$$H(y_5=\Theta/X) = 0.424 \qquad (21)$$

shows a major source of failure referring to the hypotheses set Θ . The pieces of evidence assign too much uncertainty to Θ. The failure potential is increased by not being able to offer a cor - responding conclusion to the premises. The value of the failure potential is then a measure of the incompleteness of the knowledge base and indicates a need for refinement.

4. CONCLUSIONS

This paper is concerned with the reliability of probabilistic reasoning based on incomplete knowledge bases.

    The reliability (failure potential) of a knowledge based system is related to the knowledge base incompleteness by assuming that the system reliability depends on the quantity of information available for inference, information which is concentrated in the knowledge base.

    The average amount of available information in the case of the explanatory inference, known as backward chaining, is given by the conditional informational entropy H(X/Y), where X is the set of possible system states before inference and Y is the set of possible system states after the inference. It has been shown that this entropy is a measure of the failure potential of the explanatory inference.

    In the case of predictive inference (forward chaining), the average value of the available quantity of information is given by the conditional informational entropy H(Y/X), where X, Y have the same significance as above. It has been shown that this entropy is the measure of the failure potential of the predictive inference.

    Relative measurement scales were introduced in order to estimate the failure potential in practical cases.

    The analysis of the resulting failure potential values lead to identification of the weak points of the knowledge base, e.g., the most unreliable piece of evidence. It can be thus seen where in the knowledge base, the refinement is most needed. It has been shown that pieces of evidence increase the failure potential by decreasing the discernibility of hypotheses. This rule, which is trivial in qualitative thinking, was quantitatively experimented with here.

    One particular value of the failure potential, H(Θ/X), was used to measure the completeness degree of the hypotheses set Θ.

    The numerical example taken from "A Method for Managing Evidential. Reasoning in a Hierarchical Hypothesis Space" by J. Gordon and E.H. Shortliffe [6] exemplified the methodology introduced here.

REFERENCES

1. ACZEL J., DAROCZY Z., (1975) : *On Measures of Information*, Academic Press, New-York.
2. BASILI V.R., SELBY R.W., PHILLIPS T.-Y., (1983) : *Metric Analysis and Data Validation Across Fortran Projects*, IEEE Trans. SW Eng., SE-9 (1983), 6, pp. 652-663.
3. CONTE S.D., DUNSMORE H.E., SHEN V.Y., (1986) : *Software Engineering Metrics and Models*, Benjamin/Cummings, Menlo Park, California.
4. COULTER N.S., COOPER R.B., SOLOMON M.K., (1987) : *Information-theoretic Complexity of Program Specifications*, The Computer Journal, 30, 3, pp. 223-227.
5. FERRARI D., (1978) : *Computer Systems Performance Evaluation*, Prentice -Hall.
6. GORDON J., SHORTLIFFE E.H., (1985) : *A Method for Managing Evidential Reasoning in a Hierarchical Hypothesis Space*, Artificial Intelligence, 26, pp. 323-357.
7. GRÜNWALD S., (1988) : *A Contribution to the Construction and Use of Decision Spaces with Respect to Knowledge Representation in Expert Systems*, 4th Intl. Conf. on System Research, Informatics and Cybernetics, Baden-Baden, August 1988, West Germany, THD-Report, PU1R12/88.
8. GRÜNWALD S., (1988) : *The Selection of Expert System Development Environments*, EUROMICRO-88, Zürich, August 1988, Elsevier.
9. HALSTEAD M.H., (1977) : *Elements of Software Science*, Elsevier, New York, 1977.
10. IANNINO A., MUSA J.D., OKUMOTO K., LITTLEWOOD B., (1984) : *Criteria for Software Reliability Model Comparisons*, IEEE Trans. SW. Eng., SE-10, 6, pp. 687-691.
11. LEW K.S., DILLON T.S., FORWARD K.E., (1988) : *Software Complexity and its Impact on Software Reliability*, IEEE Trans. SW Eng., 14, 11, pp. 1645-1655.
12. MARCOT B.G., (1987) : *Testing the Knowledge Base*, AI EXPERT, July 1987, pp. 43-47.
13. MARKUSZ Z., KAPOSI A.A., (1985) : *Complexity Control in Logic-based Programming*, The Computer Journal, 28, no 5, pp. 487-494.
14. MARTIN-CLOUAIRE R., PRADE H., (1985) : *On the Problems of Representation and Propagation of Uncertainty in Expert Systems*, Int. J. Man-Machine Studies, 22, pp. 251-264.
15. MCCABE T.J., (1976) : *A Complexity Measure*, IEEE Trans. SW Eng., SE-2, no 4, pp. 308-320.
16. MUSA J.D., (1975), : *A Theory of Software Reliability and Its Application*, IEEE Trans. SW. Eng., SE-1 (1975) 3, pp. 312-327.
17. NAZARETH D.L., (1989) : *Issues in the Verification of Knowledge in Rule-based Systems*, Intl. J. Man-Machine Studies, 30, pp. 255-271.
18. NGUYEN T.A., PERKIND W.A., LAFFEY T.J., PECORA D., (1985) : *Checking an Expert System Knowledge Base for Consistency and Completeness*, IJCAI-85, Vol. 1, pp. 375-378.
19. PRADE H., (1985) : *A Computational Approach to Approximate and Plausible, Reasoning with Application to Expert Systems*, PAMI 7 (1985), No.3, pp. 260-283.
20. ROBERT F.S., (1979) : *Measurement Theory*, Addison-Wesley, 1979.
21. SPATARU AL., (1973) : *Theorie der Informationsübertragung*, Vieweg, Braunschweig.

12

Using Interactive Concept Learning for Knowledge-base Validation and Verification

Luc DE RAEDT
Gunther SABLON
Maurice BRUYNOOGHE

ABSTRACT

We describe how the interactive concept-learning environment CLINT can be used for knowledge-base validation and verification. There are two contributions of interactive concept learning to this area : (1) it can be used to generate relevant tests in a systematic way, which verify or validate the knowledge base if they succeed ; (2) if a test does not succeed, or in case an error is signalled by the user, CLINT can be used as an intelligent debugger, which locates the source of the error and replaces the incorrect rules by new rules that are automatically constructed from the tests and the existing knowledge base. First, the learning environment of CLINT is sketched and then it is shown how CLINT contributes to the area of knowledge base validation and verification.

1. INTRODUCTION

The use of machine learning techniques in knowledge - acquisition systems has been demonstrated in the past (e.g. [14], [13]). Most of the existing Machine Learning approaches to knowledge acquisition use machine learning to construct a knowledge base. In contrast to these approaches, we propose to use machine learning to verify or validate a *given* knowledge base. The idea of applying machine learning to this purpose is not new. It has been suggested many times in panels and lectures on applications of machine learning (by Yves Kodratoff amongst others). Despite these proposals, there has not been much work in this area. Some exceptions can be found in this volume, e.g. [3] and [12], and [11]. The key idea of applying machine learning to the area of knowledge base validation and verification is, however, quite simple :

• A given knowledge base can be used to construct facts that are true, or that are not true according to the knowledge base. In machine learning terms we will call these facts examples.

• Examples can be considered as local tests, or experiments, for the correctness of the knowledge base, when they are shown to the user for confirmation. If the user confirms that a test has the desired truth value (true or false), the test partially validates or verifies the knowledge base.

• To verify or validate the knowledge base completely, one should verify all possible examples.

• On the other hand, machine learning can be used to construct (i.e. *learn*) new knowledge from examples. This knowledge is correct, i.e. complete and consistent, in the examples. Completeness guarantees that all examples that are true according to the user (the *positive examples*), are true in the constructed knowledge. Consistency guarantees that all examples that are false according to the user (*negative examples*) are false in the constructed knowledge. When the user does not make mistakes in the classification of examples, the new knowledge is automatically validated and verified. The power of machine learning lies in the fact that usually there will be more facts true (resp. false) in the learned knowledge base, than there will be positive (resp. negative) examples needed to learn this knowledge base.

• Consequently : given an existing knowledge base to be validated or verified, it can be used to construct examples that are shown to the user for confirmation. If the confirmed examples allow us to learn a knowledge base that is equivalent to the given one, the knowledge base is considered to be validated or verified, since the learned knowledge base is correct in the constructed examples.

• An additional advantage of using machine learning techniques for validation and verification is the possibility of using the learned knowledge instead of the given knowledge when the latter is found to be incorrect. The given knowledge base is incorrect when the user classifies an example in a different way than did the given knowledge base . Using this feature machine learning can be used to modify incorrect knowledge bases [3].

In this paper we propose to use our interactive concept-learning environment CLINT [7] as the machine learning component of a validation and verification technique. The advantages of CLINT are three fold :

- CLINT is a system that generates examples in a systematic way.

- CLINT is able to cope with integrity constraints. Integrity constraints are a very useful and general form of knowledge : they specify properties that have to be satisfied in the desired target-knowledge base.

- CLINT has sound theoretical properties, which guarantee the soundness of the approach.

Notice that the outlined idea can be used for validation as well as for verification (see [1]). If the user is the system-builder, our approach realizes knowledge - base *verification*. If she is the end-user, the system realizes *validation*.

The paper is organized as follows : in section 2 we will summarize CLINT. In section 3 the application of CLINT to knowledge base validation and verification will be presented. In section 4 we show how CLINT can be used to *modify* a knowledge base that is incorrect. In section 5 we briefly touch upon related work and conclusionsf are given in section 6.

2. THE USE OF CLINT AS MACHINE LEARNING ENVIRONMENT

CLINT [4-9] uses a first-order logical framework [10] for its knowledge representation. Within this framework, a *concept* is a predicate, which is defined by a set of Horn clauses. Horn clauses in CLINT are organized into sets satisfying certain syntactical restrictions. These sets are called *languages*. A *language bias* is a set of restrictions a Horn clause must satisfy to belong to the language. For example, in the language L_0 all variables occurring in the head of the clause must also occur in the body, and vice versa. Because each language allows only the formulation of certain concept descriptions, it is necessary to devise a series of languages (L_0, ..., L_m). For example, in L_0 it is impossible to formulate the concept 'grandparent' in terms of the concept 'parent', because this requires the use of existentially quantified variables. When CLINT discovers that it cannot describe the concept in L_i, it will try to describe it in L_{i+1}. This process is called *shift of bias* [7]. *Examples* in CLINT are "ground" facts. *Integrity constraints* are represented by general first-order logic clauses. CLINT also assumes an *oracle* (the *user*) to answer membership questions, i.e. questions that ask for the truth value of examples. Figure 1 shows an example knowledge base. It is used in the example session of the application of CLINT for knowledge-base validation or verification in the appendix.

The problem specification of CLINT can now be formalized as follows :
Given :

- an initial knowledge base ;
- a set of positive and negative examples ;
- a set of integrity constraints ;
- an oracle to classify examples as true or false ;
- a series of languages $L_0, ..., L_m$, such that $L_{i+1} \supset L_i$, i.e. all clauses in L_i are
L_i is a subset of L_{i+1} also expressible in L_{i+1} ;

Find :

an updated knowledge base such that
- all positive and no negative examples are implied by the knowledge base ;
- all integrity constraints are satisfied ;
- all clauses in the knowledge base are expressed in L_i for some i.

There are two cases in which CLINT has to modify the knowledge base : a true fact (i.e. a positive example) that is not implied, or a false fact (i.e. a negative example) that is implied by the knowledge base. We now discuss how these cases are handled.

2.1 An unimplied positive example

When CLINT receives an unimplied positive example, it will derive a clause that *covers* the example, i.e. a clause that, once asserted in the knowledge base, will make the example implied. To derive a clause that covers the example, CLINT uses two steps :

- In the first step it computes a starting clause. This is a most specific clause that covers the example.
- In the second step the starting clause is generalized carefully by asking membership questions.

The starting clause is computed by means of an algorithm SC, that computes for a knowledge base KB, an example e and a language L a most specific clause SC(KB, e, L) expressed in L and covering e in KB. CLINT first considers L_0, then $L_1, L_2, ...$ If there exists no clause SC(KB, e, L_i) that covers no negative examples, the concept is not expressible in L_i. CLINT will then shift the bias, and compute the next clause SC(KB, e, L_{i+1}), until it finds an i such that SC(KB, e, L_i) is consistent, i.e. does not cover any negative example. This starting clause is then passed to the second step for generalization.

In the second step, the starting clause is made the current clause. For the current clause a minimal generalization is computed by dropping literals in the body and/or turning constants into variables. Then an example is generated that is covered by this minimal generalization, but not by the current clause. The user is asked whether the example is positive or negative. If the example is classified as positive, CLINT generalizes : the new clause becomes the current one. Then the generalization process on the current clause is repeated. Otherwise, if the example is negative, the new clause is an over-generalization. Therefore the system backtracks, to find other possible candidate generalizations. If there are no backtracking points left, the current clause is asserted in the knowledge base.

2.2 An implied negative example

Whenever there is an implied negative example, there must be an incorrect clause in the knowledge base (see [15]). This clause is located and retracted using an adapted version of Shapiro's contradiction backtracking algorithm [15]. After the retraction of the clause, positive examples that were covered by the facility clause are re-examined as in the previous subsection. This may yield new clauses to be added to the knowledge base. All concept definitions that rely on the modified definition have to be verified. The order in which the concept definitions are revised, is based upon a dependency graph for predicates. Following a bottom up approach starting from the modified predicate, we first verify the predicates which directly depend on the modified predicate, then the ones which directly depend on these, and so on... A predicate p is *directly dependent on* a predicate q if and only if q occurs in a clause of the definition for p. The relation *dependent on* is the transitive closure of the relation directly dependent on. This relation organizes the predicates of the knowledge base in a graph structure, called the *dependency graph*. For an example graph based on the knowledge base of Figure 1, see Figure 2. It states e.g. that in Figure 1 the predicate liftable_box is expressed in terms of the predicates color, material and box.

table(t1).	color(t1, yellow).	material(t1, wood).
table(t2).	color(t2, red).	material(t2, metal).
table(t3).	color(t3, red).	material(t3, plastic).
box(b1).	color(b1, green).	material(b1, plastic).
box(b2).	color(b2, yellow).	material(b2, wood).
box(b3).	color(b3, yellow).	material(b3, plastic).

object(X) <-- box(X).
box(X) <-- table(X).
liftable_box(X) <-- box(X), color(X, green), material(X, plastic).
same_color(X , Y) <-- color(X, C1), color(Y , C2), eq(C1, C2).

A simple knowledge base

liftable_box(b1).   box(X) & table(X) --> false.
same_color(t1, b2).   material(X, M1) & material(X, M2) --> M1 = M2.
             color(X, C1) & color(X, C2) --> C1 = C2.

Examples of Integrity constraints

Figure: 1

All examples that are generated by CLINT are relevant, i.e. they bring useful new information to the system. The use of integrity constraints is another way to provide CLINT with additional knowledge about properties that have to be satisfied in the learned knowledge base. When provided with integrity constraints, CLINT takes care that these are theorems in the learned knowledge base. This process is interleaved with the learning process. Examples are just a special kind of integrity constraint : e.g. the positive example 'same_color(t1,b2)' can also be represented by the integrity constraint 'true → same_color(t1,b2)', and the negative example 'same_color(t2,b3)' by 'same_color(t2,b3) → false'.

CLINT has some problems learning facts. This is not a major problem : facts just have to be told to the system CLINT one by one (see [9] for more details).

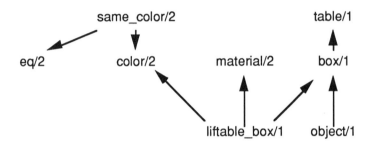

Figure: 2

CLINT identifies concepts in the limit, i.e. it converges to a correct definition of a predicate provided that the predicate is expressible in one of the languages used by CLINT. Together, these languages have almost the expressive power of pure PROLOG [9].

For an example session with CLINT, we refer to the appendix, where CLINT is used in the context of knowledge base validation and verification.

3 USING CLINT FOR VALIDATION AND VERIFICATION

As we already stated in the introduction, CLINT can be used to validate and verify a given knowledge base. We will now indicate how this can be achieved. The key idea can be summarized as follows :

To validate or verify a given knowledge base KB, an attempt will be made to learn a knowledge base KB' that is equivalent to KB. This will be realized by generating examples, which have to be classified by the user. If the classification of an example e by the user is the same as the truth value in the given knowledge base KB, the example is a confirmation of the correctness of KB. Otherwise, KB is found to be incorrect. In section 4, we will show how to modify incorrect knowledge bases. So, if and only if the attempt to construct KB', such that KB is semantically equivalent to KB', succeeds, KB is considered to be validated or verified, since KB' is then correct in the examples.

To derive the knowledge base KB', we will use CLINT to learn for each predicate p in KB a predicate p' in KB'. We will assume that before learning p', all predicates q in KB on which p depends, have already been validated or verified. If the definition of p in KB is correct, the process of generating examples for p in KB and providing them for CLINT, will converge to a definition p' in KB' that is semantically equivalent to p in KB. p in KB is *semantically equivalent* to p' in KB' if and only if we have for all ground substitutions Θ that

$$KB \vdash p\Theta \Leftrightarrow KB' \vdash p'\Theta.$$

When no functors are used, this is decidable.

Finally, in case one only wants to validate or verify a certain set of predicates R, the above method can be straightforwardly modified. For each r in R one can copy all predicates t in KB on which r depends, to t' in KB' and verify r. The dependencies between predicates of R must still be respected.

The algorithm to validate or verify p in KB by learning p' in KB' is shown in figure 3.

We will now elaborate on some particular aspects of the algorithm.

(1) The first two lines state that whenever an inconsistency is found during the while loop, the loop is terminated immediately, and the algorithm for modification of KB is called (see section 4).

(2) In the initialization all facts of p are to be confirmed by the user as being positive examples. If one of the facts is not positive, an inconsistency is found (see (1)). Then the definition of p' is initialized to the set of the facts. This is because CLINT cannot really learn facts, so they are put in KB' explicitly. All definitions on which p depends should have been validated or verified already at this point. Recursive definitions can be handled by learning sets of predicates. As this is quite technical, we refer to [9] for more details.

(3) The test whether the predicates p and p' are semantically equivalent can be solved by two queries. As a matter of fact, p and p' are not semantically equivalent, if a ground substitution Θ can be found such that $(KB \vdash p\Theta) \wedge \neg(KB' \vdash p'\Theta)$, or if a ground substitution Θ can be found such that $(KB' \vdash p'\Theta) \wedge \neg(KB \vdash p\Theta)$. In fact both conditions can be verified by queries of the form $g \wedge t$, where g is a generation part and t is a test. Queries of this form can be optimized using logic programming techniques. If the queries both fail, p and p' are semantically equivalent. If one query succeeds, we have automatically generated an example e (i.e. $p\Theta$ in the former case, or $p'\Theta$ in the latter) on which the two definitions do not agree, and for which the truthvalue will be asked the user.

(4) If the classification of the user is not consistent with KB (the else part of the if-structure), the predicate p is found to be incorrect and an inconsistency is apparent (see [1]).

(5) If the classification of the user is consistent with KB (the then part of the if-structure), the predicate p' has not yet been identified. Therefore CLINT will be used to learn from the example e, which can be positive or negative. In this learning process, CLINT will also generate examples and ask their truth value the user, in order to generalize the starting clause it constructs from the example (see section 2). For each of the generated examples e' the truthvalue of e' in KB

has to be the same as the answer of the user. In case it is not, an inconsistency will be apparent (see (1)) after CLINT has finished learning p'.

(6) If the predicate p' in KB' is constructed, such that p in KB and p' in KB' are semantically equivalent, the user still has the opportunity to give additional examples and/or integrity constraints that have to be satisfied in KB. Whenever these are not satisfied, an inconsistency is apparent (see (1)).

An example session with the knowledge base of figure 1 is given in the appendix. Notice that in this knowledge base the definition of box and object are not what is expected by the user, and that the knowledge base therefore will have to be modified during validation / verification.

> **on** inconsistency
>   **do** modify the definition of p in KB by means of the definition of p' in KB'
>
> initialize the definition of p' in KB'
> **while** the definition of p' in KB' is not semantically equivalent with the
>   definition of p in KB
>   **do**
>   generate an example e
>   ask the user to classify e
>   if the classification is consistent with KB
>   **then**   learn p' in KB' from the example e
>   **else**   **raise** inconsistency
>   **end if**
> **end while**
> let the user input examples or integrity constraints if she wants to, and check them
>
> **Verification or validation of a predicate p in KB**

Figure: 3

4. MODIFYING THE KNOWLEDGE BASE

When inconsistencies in the original knowledge base KB have been found, the concept learner can be used further to derive the new concept definition p', which is complete and consistent with the given examples and integrity constraints. The user can then decide to use the newly derived concept definition p' instead of p in the knowledge base KB during the phase of validation and verification of predicates depending on p. The new concept definition p' will be complete and consistent with respect to all known examples.

In case the user decides to replace p with p', a new criterion for validation and verification will have to be used for p'. We will now describe such a modified criterion.

Using the algorithm of [15] (see also section 2) we can detect for each inconsistency in the predicate p which clause of p is incorrect. The clauses of p are divided in two classes : the set I of incorrect clauses and the set O of all the other clauses. Examples that are covered in KB by the subconcept p_O of p described by O, should still be covered by p'. In other words, the criterion for p' to be validated or verified is now restricted to the implication for all ground substitutions Θ : KB $\vdash p_0\Theta \Rightarrow$ KB $\vdash p'\Theta$.

On the other hand p' must also cover all examples and must satisfy all integrity constraints from the user. The algorithm for modifying the knowledge base can then be summarized as follows :

- examples are generated using the clauses of p in KB that are not incorrect ;
- the user classifies the examples ;
- the examples are then used to modify the definition of p' in KB' by means of CLINT. CLINT can ask other relevant examples during the generalization of its starting clause ;
- when no further examples are generated, the user still has the opportunity to provide CLINT with examples or integrity constraints ;
- the definition of p in KB is replaced by the definition of p' in KB'.

5. RELATED WORK

To the best of our knowledge, there are only a few approaches to knowledge base validation and verification that use machine learning techniques.
These include :

Thomas Hoppe [11] who describes a related approach to generate systematically relevant tests or examples. His approach is based on partial evaluation techniques. He does not address the problem of how to modify the knowledge base when an inconsistency is found, nor how to use integrity constraints.

Susan Craw's approach [2, 3] generates a new knowledge base from an existing one and a given set of examples, such that the learned knowledge base best fits the examples. However, she does not address the problem of how to generate examples nor how to use integrity constraints. An important difference with our technique is that the role of the user is limited to supplying the training set. Whereas there are situations in which this is an advantage, the opposite can also be true, because the user has only minimal control over what happens to the knowledge base.

6. CONCLUSIONS

We have shown how a technique based on interactive concept - learning can be used to systematically validate a knowledge base or part of it. The main advantage of our technique is that it systematically generates relevant tests for the knowledge base. If errors are found during validation and verification or testing, concept-learning techniques can be used to propose modifications to the given knowledge base. The proposed method is quite general, as it is applicable to knowledge bases that satisfy the syntactic restrictions imposed by the languages of CLINT (this is almost pure PROLOG) and integrity constraints can be used.

ACKNOWLEDGEMENTS

This work was inspired by Luc's listening to a presentation of Yves Kodratoff on applications of machine learning and suggestions of Katharina Morik and Thomas Hoppe. The authors are also grateful to all participants of the ECAI Workshop, especially Marc Ayel, Susan Craw and Thomas Hoppe. We also thank Hilde Adé for her constructive comments on earlier drafts of this paper.

REFERENCES

1. AYEL M., (1990) : *SACCO and SYCOJET : two ways for verifying Knowledge-Based Systems*, Proceedings of the First Workshop on "Validation, Verification and Test of KBS", ECAI 90, Stockholm.

2. CRAW S., SLEEMAN D., (1990) : *Automating the refinement of Knowledge-Based Systems*, Proceedings of the 9th European Conference on Artificial Intelligence, ECAI 90, Stockholm 1990, Pitman, pp. 162 - 172.

3. CRAW S., (1990) : *Judging Knowledge Base Quality*, Proceedings of the First Workshop on "Validation, Verification and Test of KBS", ECAI 90, Stockholm.

4. DE RAEDT L., BRUYNOOGHE M., (1988) : *On interactive concept-learning and assimilation*, Proceedings of the 3rd European Working Session on Learning, EWSL 88, Pitman, pp. 167-176.

5. DE RAEDT L., BRUYNOOGHE M., (1989-a) : *Towards friendly concept-learners*, Proceedings of the Eleventh International Joint Conference on Artificial Intelligence, IJCAI 89, Detroit 1989, MI : Morgan Kaufmann, pp. 849-854.

6. DE RAEDT L., BRUYNOOGHE M., (1989-b) : *On explanation and bias in inductive concept-learning*, Proceedings of the 3rd European Knowledge Acquisition for knowledge based systems Workshop, EKAW 89, Paris 1989, pp. 338-353.

7. DE RAEDT L., BRUYNOOGHE M., (1990-a) : *Indirect relevance and bias in inductive concept-learning*, Knowledge Acquisition, Vol. 2, pp. 365-390.

8. DE RAEDT L., BRUYNOOGHE M., (1990-b) : *On negation and three-valued logic in interactive concept-learning*, Proceedings of the 8th European Conference on Artificial Intelligence, ECAI 90, Stockholm, Pitman, pp. 207-212.

9. DE RAEDT L., (1991) : *Interactive Concept-Learning*, Ph.D. thesis, Katholieke Universiteit Leuven.

10. GENESERETH M., NILSSON N. (1987) : *Logical Foundations of Artificial Intelligence*, Morgan Kaufmann.

11. HOPPE T., (1990-a) : *Hypotheses Generation for Knowledge Validation*, Proceedings of the 9th European Conference on Artificial Intelligence, ECAI90, Stockholm 1990, Pitman, pp. 354-356.

12. HOPPE T., (1990-b) : *Aspects of Incremental Knowledge Validation*, Proceedings of the First Workshop on "Validation, Verification and Test of KBS", ECAI 90, Stockholm.

13. MICHALSKI., DAVIS., BISHT., SINCLAIR., (1985) : *Plant/ds : an expert consulting system for the diagnosis of soybean diseases*, Progress in Artificial Intelligence, Ellis Horwood.

14. MORIK K. (1989) : *Sloppy Modeling*, Knowledge Representation and Organization in Machine Learning, Vol. 347 of Lecture Notes in Artificial Intelligence, Springer-Verlag.

15. SHAPIRO E.Y., (1982) : *Algorithmic Program Debugging*, The MIT Press.

APPENDIX

The appendix shows a session with CLINT used as a tool for validation / verification of a knowledge base with the knowledge base of figure 1. The program output is adapted in two ways : some intermediate output is left out because of paper length constraints and some steps are commented (preceded by ##).
CLINT is completely implemented on Sun. At the moment we are working on an implementation on Apple Macintosh. The integration of CLINT with the validation and verification algorithm is not yet completed.

    ## The basic predicates color, material and table have already been learned. For
    ## the predicate box the facts box(b1), box(b2), box(b3) have already been told to
    ## CLINT. However, the definition of box in KB is not yet semantically equivalent to
    ## the one of box in KB' (the reason is the incorrect clause box(X) <-- table(X)).
    ## Therefore an example is generated, and the user is asked to classify it.
Checking equivalence... Not equivalent
Generating example in old KB
Example : box(t1).
Is box(t1) positive ? [y/n] @n.
Inconsistency found :
box(t1) is false
but covered by
    box(b1). box(b2). box(b3).
    box(X) if
       table(X).
Replace clauses by new definition ?
    box(b1). box(b2). box(b3).
Examples covered by old, not by new : [box(t1), box(t2)]
Examples covered by new, not by old : []
    ## Now the user can admit the modification of the old knowledge base KB using the
    ## new definition proposed by CLINT. All examples that were covered by this
    ## definition and not by the old one, must be checked, and if necessary, asked to
    ## the user.
Replace ? @ y.
Checking examples...
Is box(t2) positive ? [y/n] @n.
No more unchecked examples
    ## The same result could have been achieved earlier if the integrity constraint
    ## box(X) & table(X) -> false
    ## would have been input before.
Equivalent !
Concept definition for box is
    box(b1).
    box(b2).
    box(b3).
Example, Integrity Constraint or Stop ? @stop.
Continue other preds or abort ? [c/a] @c.
    ## Box is validated / verified. Then the definition for object is to be validated /
    ## verified. No special things happen in learning the existing clause for object.
    ## However, the example object(t1) is not covered neither by the old (but
    ## modified) knowledge base, nor by the learned knowledge base. Therefore the
    ## user has to let CLINT learn the new definition clause for object by providing this
    ## example. The resulting clause can then be added to both knowledge bases.
    ## The starting language is L0, in which all variables occurring in the head of the
    ## clause also occur in the body of the clause, and vice versa
    ## [7].
Next concept ? @object/1.

Determining language...   Starting language is L0
Checking equivalence... Not equivalent
Generating example in old KB...   Example : object(b3).
Is object(b3) positive ? [y/n]   @ y.
　　## Since the user confirms that the example is positive, CLINT starts learning from
　　## this example.
Starting clause :
　　object(b3) if
　　　box(b3).
　　## CLINT tries to generalize the starting clause by turning the constant b3
　　## into a variable. Generalizations are represented by a list of literals to be
　　## dropped, and a list of constants to be replaced by a variable.
Generalization tried : [], [b3 / X]
Is object(b1) positive ? [y/n]   @ y.
Next clause :
　　object(X) if
　　　box(X).
No more valid generalizations
Generalized clause :
　　object(X) if
　　　box(X).
Checking equivalence... Equivalent !
Concept definition for object is
　　object(X) if
　　　box(X).
　　## Since both object in KB is now semantically equivalent to object in KB', the
　　## system does not generate more examples. However, there are still uncovered
　　## examples : e.g. tables are also objects. Therefore the user has to provide a not
　　## yet covered example of object, from which the missing clause object(X) <--
　　## table(X) is derived.
Example, Integrity Constraint or Stop ?   @ object(t1).
Learning from positive example...
Starting clause :
　　object(t1) if
　　　table(t1) ,
Generalization tried : [], [t1 / X]
Is object(t2) positive ? [y/n]   @ y.
Next clause :
　　object(X) :-
　　　table(X).
No more valid generalizations
Generalized clause :
　　object(X) :-
　　　table(X).
　　## The next predicate is liftable_box. For liftable box the starting language is
　　## determined. The language is L2 [De Raedt & Bruynooghe 90a] because there
　　## are constants in the body that do not appear in the head.
Next concept ?   @liftable_box/1.
Determining language...   Starting language is L1,1
Checking equivalence... Not equivalent
Generating example in old KB...   Example : liftable_box(b1).
Is liftable_box(b1) positive ? [y/n]   @ y.
　　## Since the user confirms that the example should be covered by liftable_box,
　　## CLINT will now start learning from this example.
Starting clause :
　　liftable_box(b1) if

```
    object(b1),
    box(b1),
      material(b1,plastic),
      color(b1,green).
```
CLINT will try to generalize this clause by dropping the literal box(b1) and
turning the constant b1 into a variable X. Then an example is generated
that is covered by this generalization, but not by the starting clause.
Generalization tried : [box(b1)], [b1 / X]
Is liftable_box(t3) positive ? [y/n]   @ n.
    ## The generalization tried was an over-generalization, therefore CLINT tries
    ## another generalization.
Generalization tried : [color(b1,green)], [b1 / X]
Is liftable_box(b3) positive ? [y/n]   @ y.
Next clause :
    liftable_box(X) :-
      object(X),
      box(X),
        material(X,plastic).
Generalization tried : [], [plastic / M]
Is liftable_box(b2) positive ? [y/n]   @ n.
Generalization tried : [material(X,plastic)],   []
No more valid generalizations
Generalized clause :
    liftable_box(X) if
      box(X),
        material(X,plastic).
    ## Now CLINT has finished learning. During the learning phase an inconsistency
    ## has been found which is now raised.
Inconsistency found :
liftable_box(b3) is true
but not covered by
    liftable_box(X) if
      box(X),
        color(X,green),
          material(X,plastic).
Replace clauses by new definition ?
    liftable_box(X) if
      box(X),
        material(X,plastic).
Examples covered by old, not by new : []
Examples covered by new, not by old : [liftable_box(b3)]
Replace ? @ y.
Checking examples...
No more unchecked examples
Equivalent !
Concept definition for liftable_box is
    liftable_box(X) if
      box(X),
        material(X,plastic).
Example, Integrity Constraint or Stop ? @stop.
Continue other preds or abort ? [c/a] @c.
    ## In the following concept we shortened the text by eliminating intermediate
    ## clauses. We still show which generalizations are tried, and resulting questions.
Next concept ? @same_color/1.
Determining language...   Starting language is L2
Checking equivalence...   Not equivalent

Generating example in old KB...   Example : same_color(t1,b3).
Is same_color(t1,b3) positive ? [y/n] @ y.
   ## Here CLINT starts learning from the example same_color(t1,b3)
Starting clause :
   same_color(t1,b3) if
      object(t1),
      table(t1),
      object(b3),
      box(b3),
       material(t1,wood),
       color(b3,yellow),
        material(b3,plastic),
       color(t1,yellow),
       eq(yellow, yellow).
Generalization tried : [table(t1)],   [t1 / X]
Is same_color(b2,b3) positive ? [y/n] @ y.
Generalization tried : [],   [wood / M2]
Is same_color(b3,b3) positive ? [y/n] @ y.
Generalization tried : [color(X,yellow)],   []
Is same_color(b1,b3) positive ? [y/n] @ n.
Generalization tried : [color(b3,yellow)],   [b3 / Y]
Is same_color(b2,b1) positive ? [y/n] @ n.
Generalization tried : [material(Y,plastic)],   [b3 / Y]
Is same_color(b2,b2) positive ? [y/n] @ y.
Generalization tried : [box(Y)],   []
Is same_color(b2,t1) positive ? [y/n] @ y.
   ## In the next step the constant yellow is replaced by a variable in two places. In
   ## fact it is replaced by C1 in the literal color(Y,yellow) and by C2 in the literal
   ## color(tX,yellow).
Generalization tried : [],   [yellow / C1, yellow / C2]
Is same_color(b1,b1) positive ? [y/n] @ y.
Next clause :
   same_color(X,Y) :-
      object(X),
      object(Y),
       material(X,M2),
      color(Y,C1),
      color(X,C2),
      eq(C1,C2).
No more valid generalizations
Generalized clause :
   same_color(X,Y) :-
      color(Y,C1),
      color(X,C2),
      eq(C1,C2).
Checking equivalence... Equivalent !
Concept definition for same_color is
   same_color(X,Y) :-
      color(Y,C1),
      color(X,C2),
      eq(C1,C2).
   ## CLINT has now identified the concept same_color. No inconsistencies
   ## are found, and same_color is equivalent with the old definition, which is
   ## now considered to be validated / verified.
Example, Integrity Constraint or Stop ?   @stop.
Continue other preds or abort ? [c/a] @a.

13

CONKRET : A Control Knowledge Refinement Tool

Beatriz LOPEZ

ABSTRACT

In this paper we introduce CONKRET, a tool to refine control knowledge. In particular, CONKRET checks the metarule functionality which is responsible for the dynamic generation of goals and strategies of a knowledge-based system when solving a given case. CONKRET deals with different types of deficiencies that can be found while solving a case, as for example: goals that are pursued unnecessarily, goals that are not considered but should be pursued, etc. In the paper it is shown how, in different stages, CONKRET is able to detect deficiencies, identify their causes, and suggest repairs to avoid them.

1. INTRODUCTION

We introduce CONKRET, a tool to refine control knowledge. Control knowledge has a wide meaning and the scope of CONKRET does not cover all the aspects. For example in [7] a distinction between implicit control and explicit control is made. Implicit control is embedded in the inference engine of a knowledge-based system (KBS). It reflects how a rule is selected among the set of rules fireable in a given time. Implicit control is out of the scope of CONKRET even though there are some shells (like PROLORD [3]) that allow the users to provide such implicit control.

Explicit control is represented by metarules that are formulated while building a specific expert system. Explicit control represented by metarules will be the focus of our refinement process. In particular CONKRET checks the metarule functionality, which is responsible for the dynamic generation of goals and strategies during the execution of a KBS for a given case.

Before using CONKRET, we assume that the domain knowledge of the KBS has already been checked and structural problems like circularities cannot be found during a case execution[1]. That is, the KBS is able to achieve a correct solution and with CONKRET the user is trying to improve the way this solution has been found, i.e. to improve the problem solving strategies. Problem-solving strategies avoid exploring the whole search space, and focus the inference on the most likely solution as soon as relevant evidence is known (as human experts are able to do), and reduce the number of questions posed to the user (low cost solution). CONKRET deals with problem solving strategies used to achieve a solution. This is the main contribution of CONKRET since most of the refinement tools built up to now have as their main objective that the KBS reach solutions to problems and do not pay so much attention to the strategic knowledge used to achieve solutions.

1.2 CONKRET overview

The aim of CONKRET is to verify and refine the metarule functionality of a KBS, as has been stated in the introduction. However, before describing how CONKRET performs the metarule refinement, we introduce the environment in which CONKRET works. CONKRET deals with KBS represented in VETA [4], a metalanguage developed in the Valid project. VETA allows us to have a standard representation of different KBS in order to validate them with the same set of tools. Knowledge base (KB) static structures (facts, rules, metarules, rule sets, cases...) and dynamic structures (strategies, traces) of different expert system shells can be mapped into VETA through an interface.

Since strategies, metarules, rule sets, cases an traces play and important role in CONKRET, we will describe them in the framework of the VETA metalanguage. A strategy in VETA is defined as a sequence of goals that the inference engine should pursue to reach a solution. A metarule in VETA consists of a *name*, a *premise*, a *conclusion*, a *certainty factor* and a *rule set* (see for example figure 1).

Name is the metarule identifier. Premise consists of a set of conditions under which the metarule is fired. *Conclusion* is the action performed by the metarule when it is fired. The *certainty factor* of the metarule is used by the inference engine to select the metarule with the highest certainty when more than one is fireable. *Rule set* is the rule set identifier to which the metarule belongs. A rule set, also called blocks or modules in the literature, is defined in VETA as a set of either rules or metarules and a set of criteria against which these rules or metarules will be evaluated (see for more details document [4]). Rule sets of rules

---

[1]The Valid project, to which this tool is involved, attempts to provide solutions for a wide spectrum of structural and functional validation problems of KBS, like checking of inconsistencies and circularities, domain knowledge verification and refinement, etc.([10], [6]).

also have a sequence of goals that can be deduced by applying the rules it contains. Cases and traces are described in section 2.

```
METARULE structure :
Name:        M23015
Premise:              (aids)
Conclusion:   (create-goals (bacterian-atypical
                             pneumocistis-carinii
                             tuberculosis
                             citomegalovirus
                             criptococcus
                             nocardia
                             aspergillus
                             pneumococcus
                             enterobacteriaceae))
Certainty factor:     possible
Rule set:       pneumonia
```

Figure 1 : A metarule of PNEUMON-IA application (a pneumonia diagnosis system implemented in the MILORD shell [9]) mapped in the VETA metalanguage.

The actions allowed as conclusions of metarules are the following :

(a) actions on rules: inhibit a set of rules to be fired.
(b) actions on goals: create, add, remove or reorder goals from the current strategy.
(c) problem solving termination.

Metarules are therefore responsible for the strategy generation along the problem solving process. They add, remove or reorder goals in the current strategy. For example, suppose that the current strategy is the following sequence of goals g_1, g_2, g_3, and a metarule M is fired. Suppose that the conclusion of M is to add the goals (g_i, g_j, g_3) to the current strategy. The current strategy will then become a combination of g_1, g_2, g_3, g_i and g_j, depending on how the addition is performed by the kbs (for example the goals can be added at the beginning of the current strategy).

Sometimes, however, metarules do not work as expected, causing different types of deficiencies in the problem-solving strategy for a case. For instance, when the metarule M is fired but the goals it provides are eventually found not to be relevant to the solution of the current case, it means that the firing of M wastes resources trying to achieve goals g_i, g_j and besides, the user has been asked unnecessary extra questions. We call deficiencies the goals added by M, and M the cause of the deficiency that should be repaired to prevent its firing for the current situation. Other types of deficiencies can be produced while solving a case, as for example goals that should be considered, but they are not, etc. The aim of CONKRET is to analyse such deficiencies and propose repairs in order to improve the problem-solving strategy.

In the course of solving a case the KBS generates different strategies that are reflected in a trace of the execution (see section 2). CONKRET examines the information stored in traces to detect deficiencies, to find their causes and repair them. In fact, CONKRET does not automatically update the kb. It suggests to the user which repairing actions better fit the given inputs.

Basically CONKRET consists of five main blocks (see the control flow diagram in figure 2). The two first blocks are the deficiency detection block and the deficiency cause identification block that constitute the deficiency analysis cycle. In the deficiency detection block traces are inspected in order to find possible deficiencies and if any are found they will be identified as the cause of the deficiency in the deficiency cause identification block. The selection block chooses one identified deficiency *di* among all deficiencies identified (one for each trace) to be repaired.

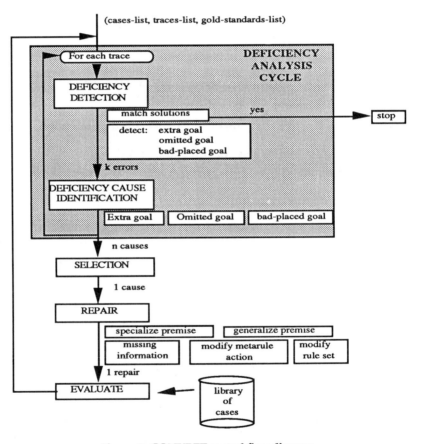

Figure 2 : CONKRET control flow diagram

The repair block takes *di* and suggests a repair to fix the deficiency *di*. Finally in the evaluation block the repair suggested in the former block is evaluated. We will begin by describing in section 2 what are the inputs to CONKRET and then, in the rest of the paper, we will explain in detail the above-mentioned blocks.

2. INPUTS

The input to CONKRET are a **case**, a **trace** and a **gold standard**. The case represents the input data (observable data of an expert system). The trace is a file containing information about the KBS execution the case. The gold standard will be our model of functionality, that is, a generally accepted correct answer with which the KBS results can be compared (in the following section we will expand on what the format of the gold standard should be). Moreover, CONKRET accesses the interfaced KBS, to obtain information about the static structures (metarules, facts, etc.).

However, the inputs described above are not enough to improve a KB. CONKRET also works with a library of cases (and its corresponding traces), since a repair suggested from a set of cases will be more informative than the one produced from a unique case. This is the reason for distinguishing two working modes in CONKRET: single-case mode and multiple-case mode. Depending on the mode, the call to CONKRET will be

        (CONKRET   *case*
                   trace
                   gold-standard)   for the single-case mode, and
        (CONKRET   *list-of-cases*
                   list-of-traces
                   list-of-gold-standards)   for the multiple-case mode

In the second situation, the elements of list-of-cases will correspond one-to-one to the elements of the list-of-traces and also to the list-of-gold-standards. If for some trace the gold-standard is not provided, the corresponding place should be filled by a null value, and then CONKRET will take the default gold-standard associated with to the case that, as we will see in the following section, is stored in the respective case.

2.1 Gold standard

In the literature it is not clear enough what a gold - standard should be for a given expert system application (see, for example [5] regarding the current state of the art in KBS evaluation and verification). We define a gold - standard sufficient for our purposes, that is, to refine control knowledge. For CONKRET in particular the gold standard is the correct sequence of goals that should follow the KBS inference mechanism for efficient solving of a case.

However, this gold - standard may not be easy to obtain. The Valid project also plans to develop an assistant tool to obtain the gold standard for a given case and trace based on optimality criteria such as simplicity, path focus, etc. We assume that whatever criterion of optimality is given the corresponding sequence of goals can be constructed and passed to CONKRET. We plan to use the work on deductive paths done by Meseguer [8] and the work on modelling user interaction done by Valiente [11] for building this "assistant". Meanwhile we assume that the user can provide the gold standard, for instance by mock-up sessions in which he explains the goals pursued while solving a case.

This is an example of a case taken from the pneumonia diagnosis application using the shell MILORD [9] and expressed using VETA:

CASE
Name "Llorenç Tremoleda":
CONTEXT
    Context-name: ...
    Table-of-attribute-value:
    ((community-acquired-pneumonia *true*) (state-of-the-patient *unknown*)
    (days-since-the-beginning *14*) (days-since-the-diagnosis *0*)
    (initial-data *14/11/86*)(sex *(f)*) (coma *false*) (confused *false*)
    (existence-pathological-record *true*) (pathological-record *(smok advp)*)
    (heroin-abstinence *false*) (preliminary-antibiotic *false*)
    (establishment *(subacute)*) (cough *true*) (expectoration *true*)
    (sputum *unknown*) (pleuritic-pain *true*) (temperature *37.5*) (cardiac-rate *110*)
    (consolidation *(buft cr)*) (associated-clinical-data *true*)
    (clinical-data-associated-pairs *(hemlimf res)*)
    (hematopoietical-clinical-data *unknown*) (respiratory-clinical-data *(catarro)*)
    (x-rays *true*) (x-rays-data *(braeri vmaldef)*)
    (distribution-pattern-infiltrate *(brneum)*)
    (certainty-of-bronchopneumonic-infiltrate *certain*) (lab-results *true*)
    (leucocyte *11100*) (%polynuclear *56*) (%bands *31*) (evolution *(ag)*)
    (jaundice *unknown*) (tuberculin-converted *false*)
    (tuberculosis-contact *unknown*)
)
Gold-solution:
    (((bacterian > *possible*) (estaphylococcus > *possible*) (pneumococcus > *very-possible*))
    ()
    (acquire-general-data bacterian-atypical staphylococcus pneumococcus enterobacteriaceae tuberculosis))
Keywords: : ((typicality . typical) (completeness . incomplete))

The gold solution of a case is composed of three elements. The first two elements of the gold solution respectively specify the conditions that a correct solution should satisfy and should not satisfy. For instance, bacterian for bacterian-type disease should have an evidence degree bigger than "possible". The third element contains strategic aspects of the solution. The information referenced in this third element of the gold - solution is the information that CONKRET takes, by default, as gold standard. For instance, to solve the case of this example the KBS should start pursuing the goal *acquire-general-data,* and then successively the goal bacterian-atypical, the goal *staphylococcus,* the goal *pneumococcus,* the goal *enterobacteriaceae* and finally the goal *tuberculosis.*

The first process performed upon the inputs to CONKRET takes place in the deficiency detection block that belongs to the deficiency analysis cycle (see figure 2). It is time to describe such analysis.

3. DEFICIENCY ANALYSIS CYCLE

The first two blocks of CONKRET perform the deficiency analysis cycle where deficiencies are detected (deficiency detection block) and, if any, the culprit objects that causes the deficiencies to be identified (deficiency cause identification block). Both blocks work sequentially for a given case, trace and gold standard (see figure 2).

3.1 Deficiency detection block

Inside the deficiency detection block a test comparing a trace against its gold standard is performed. The process of matching the trace against the gold standard is based on the comparison functions described in [4]. They are application-dependent and we can get them by using the following VETA primitives:

(current-solution-comparison)   it returns the comparison function by default for the current application

(case-solution-comparison trace) if it exists, it returns the comparison function specific to the trace

We assume that comparison functions are able to deal with comparison related to the gold standard of control knowledge. The arguments of the functions are :

arg-list = (KBS-solution gold-standard   &allow-other-keys &rest)
In the detect deficiency block the comparison functions will be called with
KBS-solution = sequence of goals followed by the trace.
gold-standard = current gold standard.

The sequence of goals followed by the trace can easily be obtained by looking in the VETA format of the traces. Traces in VETA consist of different kinds of steps storing information about the actions that change the KBS state: rule firings, metarule firings, new goals, new strategies, procedure calls, interruptions ([1] gives detailed definitions).

Once CONKRET has the comparison function retrieved and the arguments instantiated, it evaluates the aforementioned function. A boolean result is obtained :

- true if the trace is accepted,
- false otherwise.

The problems arise when the strategy of the solution is rejected (the comparison function returns false). CONKRET should evaluate the solution and try to detect the possible causes of the trouble. CONKRET is able to detect three main deficiencies: a extra goal in the sequences of goals followed by the trace, an omitted goal, and a bad-placed goal in the sequence of goals with respect to the gold standard.

Example 1 : Suppose we are testing the trace of the pneumonia case described above. The sequence of goals followed is S and the gold standard is (*acquire-general-data, bacterian-atypical, staphylococcus, pneumococcus, enterobactericeae, tuberculosis*)

1.a   Example of extra goal: *virus* is an extra goal since it does not appear in the gold standard and appears in S:

S = (*acquire-general-data bacterian-atypical staphylococcus <u>virus</u> pneumococcus enterobacteriaceae tuberculosis*)

1.b   Example of omitted goal: *bacterian-atypical* is an omitted goal since it appears in the gold standard and does not appears in S:

S = (*acquire-general-data staphylococcus pneumococcus enterobacteriaceae tuberculosis*)

1.c   Example of bad-placed goal: *pneumococcus* is a bad-placed goal since there are some goals behind it in S that appear in the gold standard in front of it.[2]

S = (*acquire-general-data bacterian-atypical <u>pneumococcus</u> staphylococcus enterobacteriaceae tuberculosis*)

Combinations of more that one deficiency can hold, and the algorithm of CONKRET is also able to detect them:

1.d   Example of bad-placed goal plus extra goal:

S = (*acquire-general-data bacterian-atypical staphylococcus virus pneumococcus tuberculosis enterobacteriaceae*)

1.e   Example of bad-placed goal plus omitted goal:

S = (*acquire-general-data staphylococcus pneumococcus tuberculosis enterobacteriaceae*)

1.f   Example of bad-placed goal plus extra goal plus omitted goal:

S = (*acquire-general-data staphylococcus virus pneumococcus tuberculosis enterobacteriaceae*)

The following algorithm detects the deficiencies:

```
procedure DETECT (St Sg)
Let St the strategy followed by the trace
Let Sg the gold standard
i = 1, j = 1
While i ≤ (length St)
    let gi the goal in the i position of St
    let gj the goal in the j position of Sg.
    1- if gi = gj, next i, next j, go to 1
    2- if gi is not in Sg, gi is an extra goal, next i, go to 1
    3- if gj is not in St, gj is an omitted goal, next j, go to 1
    4- if gj is in S, where
            S = {gk}, gk belongs to St, k<= i,
            then gj is a bad-placed goal already detected, next j, go to 1
    5- if gi is in Sg, gi is a bad-placed goal, next i, go to 1
```

The result of the deficiency detection block is a set of deficiencies (extra goals, omitted goals, or bad-placed goals), if any. This set of deficiencies constitutes the input to the deficiency cause identification block.

---

[2] G is a 'bad-placed' goal if any other goal that occurs after it in the strategy, occurs before it in the gold standard.

3.2 Deficiency cause identification block

When entering this block, CONKRET knows that the strategy of the solution is not accepted, and it has the information provided by the previous block. That is, a report containing the omitted goals, the extra goals and the bad-placed goals (see figure 3). The aim of this block is to identify the causes of the wrong solution.

Virus is an extra goal
Bacterian-atypical   is omitted
Tuberculosis is bad-placed

Figure 3 : Example of report (of example 1.f.)

The report provided by the detect deficiency block points out some initial start points to analyze the causes of the deficiency. It is important to note that the detect deficiency block outputs all the deficiencies starting from the beginning of the case execution. More than one deficiency is possible for a given trace, although in many cases the first one causes the rest.

Depending on the type of deficiency, CONKRET applies a specialized algorithm to identify the cause of each deficiency: the extra-goal algorithm, the omitted-goal algorithm or the bad-placed-goal algorithm. Each algorithm outputs an error identifier (a summary of errors is provided in table 1) and points out the metarules or rule sets causing the error. All errors are detected, accumulated, and finally passed to the selection block.

In the following subsections we will describe the specific algorithms (one for each type of deficiency) and the main procedure for the deficiency identification block.

3.2.1 Extra-goal algorithm

This algorithm identifies the causes of the presence of extra goals.

1. Starting from the end of the trace, look for metarule firings that introduce the extra goal in the current strategy (error E1).

Table 1. Table of errors. Each row describes an error that can be detected in the deficiency cause identification block. Column *error ident* contains the error identification. Next column indicates the _amount_ of metarules or rule sets than can be related to the error. Third column describes the _action performed_ by the metarule which causes the error of the current row. Finally there is an _explanation_ of the behavior expected by the KBS upon the metarule.

Error Ident.	Am	Action Performed	Explanation
E1	1	create or add an extra goal	Should not be fired
E2	1	inhibit an omitted goal	should not be fired
E3	1-n	create or add an omitted goal	should be fired
E4	-	any metarule create or add an omitted goal	should exists
E5	-	any metarule create or add an omitted goal and any rule set contains it	should exists
E6	1	create or add a goal in a bad place	metarule action should be rewritten
E7	1	sort (bad) goals of current strategy	should not be fired
E8	-	a goal is bad place in the sequence of goals for a given rule set	sequence of goals for the rule set should be rewritten
E9	-	affects goal ordering	sort criteria should be changed

By creating a goal we mean including a goal in the current strategy, or to set a new strategy with the goal.

3.2.2 Omitted-goal algorithm

This algorithm identifies the causes of the omission of a goal.

> 1- Starting from the end of the trace, look for metarule firings that could create at some moment the omitted goal.
> 2- Two possibilities
>   2.1   If the omitted goal has appeared once, then look from this point at the end for a metarule that
>   - inhibits the goal (error E2)
>   - performs a filter action that eliminates the omitted goal (error E2)
>   2.2 If the omitted goal has never appeared, then gather from the KB all the metarules that create the omitted goal (error E3).
>   If no metarule is found, then
>   - if there is no metarule that creates the goal then
>   then there will be an error E4
>   - if there is neither a metarule that creates the goal nor a rule set that contains the goal in its sequence of goals
>   then there will be an error E5

3.2.3 Bad-placed-goal algorithm

This algorithm identifies the causes of the bad-placed goal position.

> 1-Starting from the end of the trace, look for changes of goals
>   1.1   If the goal disappears, then there will be:
>   - error E6, if there is a metarule fired after this step that creates the goal in a bad place
>   - error E8, if there is a rule set containing the goal ordering in a bad place.
>   1.2   If the bad-placed goal changes its position because some goal has been added, then go to 1.
>   Explanation: no new information is obtained. The inclusion of this goal will not be the cause of the deficiency since the goal has been eliminated before being pursued (it does not appear in the final sequence of goals followed by the trace)
>   1.3   If the goal changes its position because some goal G has been removed, then two situations are possible:
>   -   The goal fills the correct place (well-placed),
>   then there will be error E9
>   Explanation . there is a metarule fired after this step that creates G affecting the position of the bad-placed-goal
>   -   Otherwise, go to 1.
>   1.4   If the goal changes its position without any goal addition or removal, then two situations are possible:
>   -   The goal fills the correct place (well-placed).
>   Then the error will be error E7 or E9.
>   Explanation: there is a metarule fired after this step that changes the order of the goals
>   -   The goal fills the wrong place (bad-placed).
>   Then keep as error E7, go to 1.
>   Explanation: That means that there is a metarule fired after this step that changes the order of the goals, that may or may not be the cause of the deficiency.

3.2.4 Main procedure

This is the main procedure for the deficiency cause identification block. Its aim is to gather information about the deficiencies provided by the reports of the deficiency detection block for a given case C_i.

The variables EG_i, OG_i and UG_i are lists composed of triplets $<e_{ij}, c_{ij}, k_{ij}>$ of error identifiers, metarules and the number of times that the metarule has appeared as a possible cause of the deficiency identified by the error. EG_i will accumulate error E1, OG_i will accumulate errors E2 through E5, and UG_i errors E6 through E9.

> For each g in the report of detect deficiency block
> - if extra-goal then apply extra-goal algorithm, and accumulate the result in EG_i
> - if omitted-goal then apply omitted-goal algorithm, and accumulate the result in OG_i
> - if bad-placed goal then apply bad-placed goal algorithm, and accumulate the result in UG_i

In the deficiency cause identification block one EG_i, OG_i and UG_i is obtained for C_i, after which the deficiency analysis cycle restarts again in the detect deficiency block to check the case C_{i+1}. When the deficiency analysis cycle (i.e. the deficiency detection block plus the deficiency cause identification block) is run over the n cases, three sets of variables, $S_{EG} = \{EG_i\}_{i=1,..,n}$, $S_{OG} = \{OG_i\}_{i=1,..,n}$ and $S_{UG} = \{UG_i\}_{i=1,..,n}$, are obtained. The sets S_{EG}, S_{OG} and S_{UG} are passed to the selection block in order to select only one culprit object to be repaired.

4. SELECTION BLOCK

The objective of the selection block is to choose the KB object (metarule or rule set) whose modification will correct the highest amount of deficiencies among the deficiencies detected for the complete set of cases entered in CONKRET.

At this stage CONKRET knows the deficiencies and their causes from the information gathered in the set of variables S_{EG}, S_{OG} and S_{UG} that have been provided by the deficiency analysis cycle. A variable EG_i in S_{EG} contains triplets $<e_{ij}, c_{ij}, k_{ij}>$ that retain information about extra goals detected for the case C_i. Analogously the variables OG_i in S_{OG} and UG_i in S_{UG} store information about respectively omitted goals and bad-placed goals detected for C_i. Based on these triplets $<e_{ij}, c_{ij}, k_{ij}>$ and on the *typicality* and *completeness* of the cases CONKRET attempts to select only one object by using a credit assignment process.

The *typicality* of a case informs us on the frequency of its occurence. For example, a case with *typicality* "typical" indicates that the case occurs very often. KBS is expected to work at least for typical cases. Therefore repairs based on typical cases will be more relevant than repairs based on atypical cases. *Completeness* indicates the degree of information the case contains related to the information needed for the KBS to solve the case. For example, the case shown at the beginning of the paper have several data with *unknown* values ; so the case cannot be considered as complete. Repairs based on complete cases will be preferable since the KBS execution for them is more precise and accurate than for incomplete cases. *Typicality* and *completeness* of cases is provided by the VETA environment .

Two phases are performed to select the culprit object. In the first phase a metarule or rule set is selected over all the metarules or rule sets gathered as causing the deficiencies for a single case C_i. After applying the first phase for the n cases entered to in CONKRET a set of n metarules or rule sets, one for each case C_i, is obtained. In the second phase only one metarule or rule set will be chosen among the n culprit objects selected in phase one. However it is also possible for CONKRET to enter in a dialog with the user and allow him to select the one that he considers more likely to eliminate all the bugs. The culprit object will be passed to the repair block.

Selection criteria of phase 1 :

For each C_i,
(1) Select the metarule with the highest frequency associated over the sets EG_i, OG_i, and UG_i.
(2) If none can be selected then select one by using the following criteria:
- select a metarule among the metarules causing extra goals (i.e. metarules in EG_i).
- select a metarule among the metarules causing omitted goals (i.e. metarules in OG_i).
- select a metarule among the metarules causing bad-placed goals (i.e. metarules in UG_i).
(3) Together with each criterion CONKRET can also apply the following rules to choose a single culprit object:

- among metarules that should have been fired
- the metarule with the premise most partially matched
- the one that most satisfies the conflict resolution mode
- among metarules that should not have been fired

Selection criteria of phase 2 :

(1) Take the metarule or rule set that appears with a predetermined percentage (given by the user) over all the traces belonging to typical cases.
(2) If this percentage is not satisfied by any metarule or rule set, then select the metarule or rule set that appears most frequently.
If, on the contrary, more than one metarule or rule set is selected in step 1), then take the metarule or rule set that appears most frequently in the traces belonging to complete cases.

Note that when working in the single case mode, CONKRET does not perform the second phase.

The output of the selection block consists then of a single metarule (or rule set) that should be repaired. To repair the metarule some suggestions are proposed to the user as we will describe in the next section.

5. REPAIR BLOCK

In this block, CONKRET is able to automatically suggest some repairs for the faulty metarule chosen in the selection block. Depending on the error associated with this metarule or rule set a different repair can be suggested. It is possible that more than one repair fits. But CONKRET has a conservative strategy: it tends to make the smallest changes. Only one modification is allowed in the repair block, after which CONKRET leaves this block without allowing further modifications. The user can easily run the KBS again to check the results of the changes he has introduced. (This is managed automatically by the VETA environment capabilities for multiple KB-versions and trace-handling.)

It is possible to partition the causes of trouble into five groups according to the source of failure: a metarule that was expected to be fired but did not (errors E1, E2, and E7) missing information (errors E4 and E5), a metarule that was fired but should not have been (error E3), the incorrect action of a metarule (errors E6, and E9), and some modifications should be carried out on a rule set definition (error E8). For each situation there is a method for repairing:

(a) a metarule should not have been fired
  • specialize the premise by adding a condition (note that the user should be sure that the condition he adds holds).
  (It is interesting to note that if the domain knowledge has an organization as for example, semantic nets, the condition to add can be taken from a specialization of a condition that still holds [12]. However it is up to the user to select the new condition.)
  • specialize the premise by turning a variable into a constant
  • specialize by decreasing the certainty degree attached to the metarule

The last one is the more conservative. So CONKRET will suggest it first of all. However, it will be effective depending on the conflict resolution mode of the KBS shell.

(b) a metarule should have been fired
  • generalize the premise by removing the condition(s) that did not hold
  • generalize by turning a constant into variables
  • generalize by extending the conditions of the premise
  (e.g. = to <= or >=)
  • generalize by increasing the certainty degree attached to the metarule

As in (a), the last suggestion will be effective depending on the conflict resolution mode.

(c) missing information
  • Error E4: in this case CONKRET will advise that there is no metarule in the KB creating the expected goal
  • Error E5: in this case CONKRET will advise that there is no metarule in the KB creating the expected goal and there is no rule set containing the expected goal.

(d) rewrite the action part of the metarule
- Error E6: rewrite the goals in the expected way.
- Error E9: rewrite the sorting function of the action part.

e) rule set modification
- Error E8: rewrite the goals of the list of goals in the expected order.

The repair is effected on the metarule or rule set, and as result the KBS has a new, refined version of its KB.

6. EVALUATION

The evaluation block involves executing the new KB version on the library of cases and judging the new outcomes. An evaluation is needed to guarantee that strategies already refined are not lost. For example, the specialization of a metarule could mask another metarule, and prevent the successful solving of old cases. CONKRET evaluation consists, then, of testing cases.

First it is necessary to check if the modification really improves the case execution. And if this improvement is obtained, then it is necessary to check the execution of a library of cases that have been correctly solved until now, to verify that no unexpected situation can arise. If some problem arises in a certain number of cases correctly solved up to now, then CONKRET recovers the previous KB version, and will take into account the suggested repair to avoid it in the future. If, on the contrary, cases correctly solved continue being correctly solved but there are still cases that require some improvement, then CONKRET will restart its process again.

Special care has to be taken when working in the single-case mode. Modifications of some metarule or rule-set which are based on a unique case can be dangerous. Even when the case is a typical case, it is difficult to determine how the modification performed to improve that case will affect the rest of cases that have been correctly executed up to now.

When working with the multiple-case mode a metarule or rule-set is modified according to the analysis of all the traces. Although this mode of working is safer than the single case mode, there is no guarantee that the new KB version will have a better performance than the old one. For this reason CONKRET stores information about the number of cases correctly solved by each KB version. This information allows CONKRET to recover the previous KB version when the expected improvements are not achieved in the evaluation of the new traces (executed in the new KB version) in the next cycles of the tool. Thus CONKRET behaves as a hill-climbing optimizing strategy. Automatic support for maintenance and organization of multiple KB versions is provided by the VETA environment.

Besides, when working with the multiple-case-mode, CONKRET informs the user about :

- the percentage of traces upon which the modification was built,
- the percentage of typical cases entered into CONKRET,
- the percentage of complete cases entered into CONKRET,

- the percentage of typical cases among the traces that suggest the repair,
- the percentage of complete cases among the traces that suggest the repair,
- the percentage of typical cases that were not involved in the modification, that is, that have not been taken into account to build the modification, and
- the percentage of complete cases that were not involved in the modification, that is, that have not been taken into account to build the modification.

From this data the user can decide to restart CONKRET with a previous KB version or continue refining the current one (see figure 4).

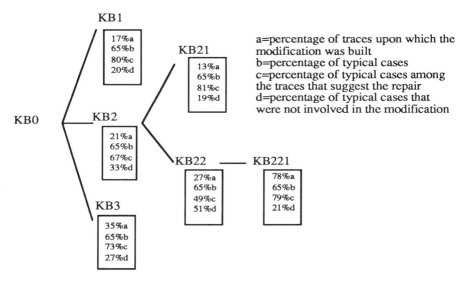

Figure 4 : A tree of KB versions. The root contains the original KB (KB0) before performing any repair. KB1, KB2 and KB3 are different refinements for KB0.

7. CONCLUSIONS

We have seen in the paper how CONKRET can refine control knowledge represented by metarules. Four main phases are described. First CONKRET detects three types of deficiencies (extra goal, omitted goal and bad-placed goal) by using the comparison function particular to the given application. Then CONKRET identifies a cause of the deficiency by executing a particular algorithm for each deficiency type. Third it selects the most probable cause of the failure. Finally, CONKRET suggests to the user repairs based on what is expected to be corrected.

An evaluation process that sometimes relies on the user final decision is performed to check that the new modification will really improve the KB. This is perhaps the weakest part of CONKRET, but it is difficult to assure that the modification will really improve the KB since it depends on the percentage of traces that suggest the modification, and the typicality and completeness of the cases to which the traces belong. To make evaluation more bearable, it will be interesting to develop a utility that runs a library of cases, testing the results in order to detect any significant change. This utility should take into account the typicality and completeness of the case being tested.

CONKRET is written in the VETA language. That means that the KBS mapped on VETA can be refined by CONKRET. However, given that CONKRET requires the control knowledge declared using metarules, only these kbs whose control can be represented using such metarules could be refined effectively by CONKRET.

One critical point is the availability of a gold standard for a given case. As shown in [2], in the course of solving a problem, an expert can tell what to do next. Besides facilitating the elicitation of a correct strategy we intend to develop an assistant tool in the framework of the Valid project that, together with other tools like a refinement tool for domain knowledge (also being developed in the Valid project [6]) is expected to provide a complete package for functional verification of kbs.

ACKNOWLEDGEMENTS

I am in indebted to Enric Plaza, Carles Sierra and Thomas Hope who read previous versions of this paper, providing many useful suggestions fand comments.

REFERENCES

1.   ARMENGOL E., LOPEZ B., MAÑA F., SANGÜESA R., (1990) : *External format of cases and traces*, document CEAB/W/22.4.
2.   GRUBER T.R., (1989) : *The acquisition of strategic knowledge*, Academic Press, Inc.
3.   LOPEZ B., (1989) : *Control and inference in the PROLORD system*, document CEAB/W/9.1.
4.   LOPEZ B., LOPEZ DE MANTARAS R., MAÑA F., MESEGUER P., PLAZA E., BOUTELDJA N., LARSEN H.L., NONFJALL H., LESAFFRE F.M., VAUDET J.P., (1989) : *VETA definition*, document CEAB/D/1.1 (Deliverable D4).
5.   LOPEZ B., MESEGUER P., PLAZA E., (1990) : *Knowledge based systems validation: a state of the art*, AI Communications, vol. 3, no 2, June.
6.   MAÑA F., (1990) : *Domain knowledge refinement tool specification*, document CEAB/W/27.1.
7.   MESEGUER P., (1989) : *Inconsistency detection in rule-based systems*, document CEAB/W/2.1.
8.   MESEGUER P., (1990) : *Inconsistency checking in rule-based expert systems with uncertainty and control features*, submitted to the International Symposium on Methodologies for Intelligent Systems (ISMIS) to appear.
9.   SIERRA C.A., (1989) : *MILORD: Arquitectura multinivell per a sistemes experts en classificació*, Tesi Doctoral, Universitat Politècnica de Catalunya, Maig.
10. *VALID (1988) : Validation methods and tools for knowledge-based systems.* Technical Annex, Esprit II VALID Project 2148.
11. VALIENTE G., (1990) : *Specification of user interaction for modular rule-based systems*. CEAB Report GRIAL 90/10.
12. WILKINS D.C., CLANCEY W.J., BUCHANAN B.G., (1987) : *Knowledge base refinement by monitoring abstract control knowledge*. Int. J. Man-Machine Studies, 27.

14

Judging Knowledge - base Quality

Susan CRAW

ABSTRACT

Empirical validation is one approach to judging the goodness of knowledge in a knowledge base (KB). But, what is a good metric? In this paper we suggest a metric for KB quality based on performance. As the KB is run on a set of cases, we collect statistics for rules which are responsible for incorrect diagnoses. Instead of simply blaming rules which include misdiagnoses and rewarding rules which diagnose correctly, our method investigates all rules which claim to give the diagnoses. In this way we assign blame to rules at **all** levels of the KB.

The blame assignment algorithm identifies rules by using a refinement generator which suggests **all** possible refinements to fix a misdiagnosis. Statistics are collected to attribute blame to rules which appear in refinements. The average blame for the rules in a KB is used as a metric for its quality.

1. INTRODUCTION

This work on judging quality was designed as a component of a knowledge refinement system. KRUST[1] is an automated refiner which refines the original KB in as many ways as possible. KRUST finally **judges** its refined KBs by ranking them so that a single KB can be recommended as the best replacement for the original, faulty KB. KRUST has been implemented to refine KBs which use a

---

[1] KRUST was developed as a PhD thesis under the supervision of Professor D. Sleeman, Aberdeen University, [2].

backward-chaining inference engine and a conflict resolution strategy which fires the first rule to be satisfied. Figure 1 illustrates KRUST's refinement philosophy of generating many refinements and choosing the best.

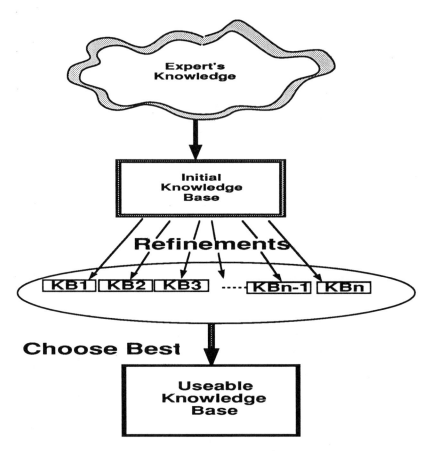

Figure 1: KRUST's Approach to Refinement

Our approach to judging quality applies a statistical blame assignment algorithm which attaches a measure of blame to the rules in a KB as a result of empirical testing. We rate the quality of the KB by calculating the average blame for a rule in the KB. The metric for KB quality is the average blame.

We allocate blame to rules by running a simplified version of KRUST's refinement generator for each of the task-solution pairs which are misdiagnosed (Figure 2). The refinements identify changes to the KB rules which improve the performance of KB for the case. Note that the existence of a suggested change to a rule can count as evidence against that rule. We can use KRUST's refinements in this way because KRUST suggests all possible refinements.

In this section we have introduced our blame assignment method and indicated the source of our problem, knowledge refinement. Section 2 describes those components of the KRUST refinement system which are relevant to the blame assignment method. The details of using multiple refinements for blame assignment is discussed in Section 3. Testing results appear in Section 4 and the final section, 5, contains a summary.

2. GENERATING REFINEMENTS IN KRUST

In KRUST, a single training task-solution pair triggers the refinement process, if the KB's conclusion conflicts with the expert's solution. Although the training case suggests the refinements, they are empirically tested using other task-solution pairs. Figure 3 shows the architecture for KRUST. A description of KRUST as a refinement system appears in [4]. The main components of KRUST are

- a Rule Classifier to select interesting KB rules,
- a Refinement Generator to generate as **many** sets of rule changes as it can,
- a Refinement Filter to remove refinements which are unlikely to be good,
- a Rule Changing Mechanism to implement the refinements as refined KBs,
- a Refined KB Filter to remove KBs whose performance is unsatisfactory,
- a Judgement Module to rank the refined KBs according to the quality of their performance.

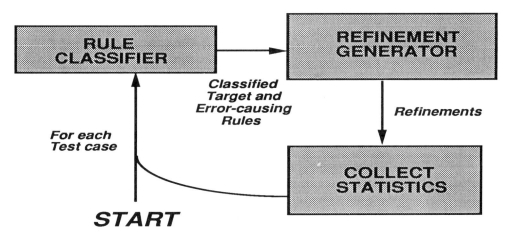

Figure 2: Using KRUST to collect statistics

The **Rule Classifier** uses POKER's approach [11] to select and classify target rules which should be allowed to fire and **(potentially) error-causing** rules which must be prevented from firing. The **Refinement Generator** assembles a set of refinements based on the rule classification. Rules can be changed by allowing them to fire **(enabling)** or preventing them from firing **(disabling)**. A rule can either be enabled/disabled directly or by **recursively** applying enable/disable to rules whose conclusion matches the premise which must be enabled/disabled.

This is similar to TEIRESIAS's exploitation of HOW explanation [5].

2.1 Rule classification

A case comprises a task of case facts together with the expert's solution, C+.
We use C- for the KB's conclusion.
  • the **Error-causing** rule wins the conflict resolution
Target rules fail to fire for several reasons:

  • **No Fire** rules have a high enough priority to fire, but must be enabled.
  • **Can Fire** rules need a higher priority to fire.
  • **NoCan Fire** rules must be enabled **and** have their priority increased.
  • **Potentially Error-causing** rules may preclude the firing of a target rule; they must not fire.

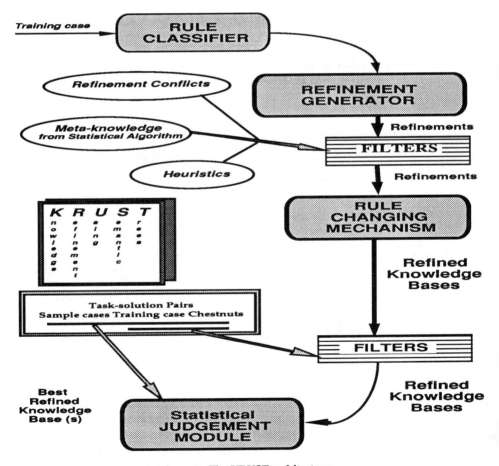

Figure 3 : The KRUST architecture

2.1.1 A simple single level example

This first example uses a simple, backward-chaining KB to make the explanation easier; see figure 4(a). The conflict resolution strategy fires the first rule which is satisfied; here, a rule's priority is determined by its position in the list of rules forming the KB. The propositions, p_i, form the rule premises.

Suppose that for a particular training case it is known that p_2, p_3, p_5, p_6 and p_7 are true, and p_1 and p_4 are false. Let t_i and f_i represent p_i being true and false respectively. Figure 4(b) represents these rules instantiated for this training case.

R_1:	$p_1 \, \& \, p_2$	$\rightarrow$	C_-		R_1:	$f_1 \, \& \, t_2$	$\rightarrow$	C_-
R_2:	$p_2 \, \& \, p_3 \& \, p_4$	$\rightarrow$	C_+		R_2:	$t_2 \, \& \, t_3 \, \& \, f_4$	$\rightarrow$	C_+
R_3:	$p_1 \, \& \, p_3$	$\rightarrow$	C_+		R_3:	$f_1 \, \& \, t_3$	$\rightarrow$	C_+
R_4:	$p_2 \, \& \, p_5$	$\rightarrow$	C_-		R_4:	$t_2 \, \& \, t_5$	$\rightarrow$	C_-
R_5:	$p_3 \, \& \, p_5$	$\rightarrow$	C_-		R_5:	$t_3 \, \& \, t_5$	$\rightarrow$	C_-
R_6:	$p_4 \, \& \, p_5 \, \& \, p_6$	$\rightarrow$	C_+		R_6:	$f_4 \, \& \, t_5 \, \& \, t_6$	$\rightarrow$	C_+
R_7:	$p_5 \, \& \, p_6 \, \& \, p_7$	$\rightarrow$	C_+		R_7:	$t_5 \, \& \, t_6 \, \& \, t_7$	$\rightarrow$	C_+

Knowledge Base (a)   Instantiated Knowledge Base (b)

Figure 4 : Knowledge base for example 1

Let us consider each of these rules in turn to decide how they behave for the training case.

- Rule R_1 is not satisfied and so may be a No Fire rule. However, it does not conclude C_+ and so is of no further interest.
- Rule R_2 is not satisfied, however, since it concludes C+, it is a **No Fire** rule.
- Similarly Rule R_3 is a **No Fire** rule.
- Rule R_4 is satisfied for the training case and so it fires, being the first rule which is satisfied. It is the **Error-causing** rule.
- Rule R_5 is satisfied and so its classification depends on its conclusion. Since it does not conclude C_+, it is a **Potentially Error-causing** rule.
- Rule R_6 is not satisfied and does not have a high enough priority to fire anyway. We are only interested in this rule because it concludes C+. Since it fails to fire for two reasons it is a **NoCan Fire** rule.
- Rule R_7 is satisfied but does not have a high enough priority to fire. Therefore, since it concludes C+ and this time it is satisfied, it is classed as a **Can Fire** rule.

The full classification is

No Fire R_2 and R_3
Error-causing R_4
Can Fire R_7
No Can Fire R_6
Potentially Error-causing R_5.

2.2 Refinement generation

For blame assignment to rules, we are interested only in changes to the **content** of rules. (Potentially) Error-causing rules are prevented from firing and target rules are allowed to fire. Other possible refinements allowed by KRUST, such as changing rule conclusions and adding new rules, are not relevant.

A rule is **enabled** by generalising **all** unsatisfied premises so that it becomes a member of the conflict set. Premise p in rule R is generalised by:

- weakening p directly in R
- enabling **any** rule whose conclusion is p.

A rule is **disabled** by specialising **any one** premise so that it is no longer satisfied; it is prevented from being a member of the conflict set. Premise p in rule R is specialised by:

- strengthening p directly in R
- disabling **all** rules whose conclusion is p.

We can picture the effect of the rule classification on refinement generation as shown in Figure 5.

2.2.1 Example 1 Completed

We complete Example 1 by generating the set of refinements which are relevant to blame assignment; i.e., those that contain specialisations and generalisations for rules. The headings show the rule classification and the target rule which now fires. Tags have been attached to indicate how many refinements are produced; [1] labels the first refinement; [2] labels the 2nd; [3-6] labels the 3rd, 4th, 5th and 6th; etc. We note that KRUST uses additional refinements to these; e.g., those containing priority changes, adding a new rule, etc. For this example, the full KRUST generates 24 refinements, [3].

No Fire - R_2 or R_3 fires

- [1] Weaken p_4 in R_2.
- [2] Weaken p_1 in R_3.

Can Fire - R_7 fires

- [3-6] Disable R_4 by specialising p_2 or p_5 and disable R_5 by specialising p_3 or p_5.

No Can Fire - R_6 fires

- [7-10] Enable R_6 by weakening p_4 **and** do **any** of the changes listed above under

Can Fire with all references to R_7 being replaced by R_6, of course.

	ENABLE	
No Fire rules		by generalising the premises

	DISABLE	
		by specialising a premise
Error-causing rule	OR	
		by decreasing its priority

	DISABLE	
Potentially Error-causing rules		by specialising a premise
	OR	
		by decreasing its priority

	ENABLE	
CAN FIRE rules		by increasing its priority

		by generalising its premises
NOCAN FIRE rules	AND	
		by increasing its priority

Figure 5 : Refinements for classified rules

2.2.2 A simple two level example

This example shows the effect of allowing chains of rules in the KB. Figure 6(a) shows the set of rules for Example 2.

Suppose that for a particular training case it is known that p_1 and p_2 are true and p_3 is false. Hence, p_4 can be deduced to be true and p_5 is assumed to be false. Again let t_i and f_i represent p_i being true and false respectively. Then Figure 6(b) represents these rules instantiated for this training case. We use the same conflict resolution as in Example 1. These rules form a multiple level set because chains of rules can produce conclusions. For this training case, R_2 and R_3 fire to conclude C_-. The Rule Classifier gives:

R_1 :	p_1 & p_3	->	p_5	R_1 :	t_1 & f_3	->	f_5
R_2 :	p_1 & p_2	->	p_4	R_2 :	t_1 & t_2	->	t_4
R_3 :	p_1 & p_4	->	C_-	R_3 :	t_1 & t_4	->	C_-
R_4 :	p_1 & p_5	->	C_+	R_4 :	t_1 & f_5	->	C_+

Knowledge Base (a)   Instantiated Knowledge Base (b)

Figure 6 : Knowledge base for example 2

No Fire { }

Error-causing R_3

Can Fire { }

No Can Fire R_4.

Using the same notation as Example 1:

No Can Fire - R_4 to fire

Enable R4 by weakening p5

and

      [1-2]   disable R_3 by strengthening p_1 or p_4,

      [3-4]   disable R_3 by disabling R_2 by strengthening p_1 or p_2 in R_2,

Enable R_4 by enabling R_1 by weakening p_3 in R_1

and

      [5-6]   disable R_3 by strengthening p_1 or p_4,

      [7-8]   disable R_3 by disabling R_2 by strengthening p_1 or p_2 in R_2.

Note that in this example p_5 in R_4 can be generalised by directly weakening the premise or by enabling R_1. Similar changes are appropriate for p_4. Therefore, we have used recursive applications of disable and enable to generate more refinements than those affecting simply R_3 and R_4. This example is too simple to see the effect of multiple rules at the lower level. Remember that whenever R_1 is enabled an **alternative** change would be to enable any other rule concluding p_5. Also, whenever R_2 is disabled **all** other rules concluding p_4 must also be disabled. The full KRUST refinement generator suggests 14 refinements for this example, [3].

3. BLAME ASSIGNMENT

Our blame assignment algorithm is an extension of SEEK's statistical method [7, 9]. SEEK allocates a measure of likelihood of error to individual rules, on the evidence of past cases. The statistics highlight those rules which commonly fail during routine testing of the KB on a set of task-solution pairs. For each rule SEEK counts occurrences of:

- True Positive cases where the rule fired correctly,
- False Positive cases where the rule fired when it should not have fired,
- True Negative cases where the rule did not fire and this was correct,
- False Negative cases where the rule did not fire when it should have fired.

As an extension to SEEK, our process collects more statistics by considering **all** rules at **all** levels of the proof trees. By investigating rules at **all** levels, we may focus attention on low-level rules which are used in a variety of proof trees. In

KRUST's refinement generator, conflict cases in the task solution pairs supply a list of refinements. These refinements are stripped so that they contain only specialisation or generalisation changes, because we wish to attach blame only to rules whose **contents** are changed.

Each KB rule is represented as a frame containing slots called gen_weight and spec_weight which store weighting evidence on the suitability of the rule for generalisation or specialisation of its premises. The evidence is accumulated from the list of simplified refinements; each specialising change increments the spec_weight slot of the frame for that rule, similarly for generalising changes. Thus, the blame assignment has taken account of SEEK's False Positives and False Negatives, but at all levels of the proof structures. The True Positives and True Negatives have merely contributed zero to all these counters. In this way we blame rules which cause conflicts but do not reward successful rules; however, there may be an argument for non-conflict cases reducing the weights. Our blame assignment method takes account of non-conflict cases in a normalisation factor, but, the importance of correct rule behaviour may need to be given more significance in KRUST. A multiplicative, normalising factor takes account of the way that the number of task-solution pairs, the number of conflict cases and the total number of refinements affect the raw weights. The normalising factor was chosen to be

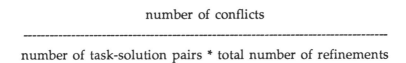

The task-solution pairs allocate a normalised measure to the gen_weight slot of each rule to indicate how likely it is to need generalising; similarly the spec-weight measure indicates the likelihood of specialising. We have taken the **larger** of these two measures as the likelihood of changing; it measures the "poorness" of the rule. An alternative approach might assign the **absolute value** of the difference of the two measures as the rule's "poorness". The rating of the KB is calculated as the **average** "poorness" by summing the **larger** weight for each rule and dividing by the number of rules.

The blame assignment method used in KRUST was chosen as a compromise between

- a simple SEEK-like tally for misdiagnoses, which blames those rules whose
  conclusion matches the diagnoses; it does not allocate blame to rules further down the chain,
- BB, a more sophisticated weighting (described below), which shares the blame for failure among rules which contribute to the failure.

Our method fits between these extremes. Instead of simply identifying only those rules whose conclusion matches the expert's diagnosis or the conclusion of the KB, we investigate chains of rules and rule interactions. Our method is more finely tuned than counting failure and success cases, but less complex than the BB approach.

3.1. An alternative empirical approach - BB

BB extends our approach to blame assignment. Suppose in a refinement to disable a particular rule, R, it is necessary to disable a set of n rules concluding one of the premises of R. In this case, there is some merit in using a smaller increment by **sharing** the original increment equally among the n rules. This sophisticated allocation of weighting increments can be explained using a bribing metaphor. We assume that bribing is a non-profit-making occupation! We use p_+ for a premise that should be satisfied, p_- is a premise that should not be satisfied.

3.1.1 Generalisation bribes

To persuade a premise p_+ to be satisfied, **any** rule which concludes p+ should be bribed to fire. Thus, p_+ can pass its **full** bribe on to any one of these rules. The rule can use the bribe to change itself directly, or it must persuade **all** of its premises which are not satisfied to be satisfied by **dividing** its bribe among them.

3.1.2 Specialisation bribes

To persuade a premise p_- not to be satisfied, **all** satisfied rules which conclude p_- must be bribed not to fire. Thus, p_- must pass **equal shares** of its bribe on to each of these rules. The rule can use its bribe to change itself directly, or it can persuade **any** of its satisfied premises not to be satisfied by passing its bribe to the premise, which in turn bribes each of the rules concluding it in equal shares.

The way that this algorithm divides a bribe among suitable rules is reminiscent of the Profit Sharing Plan and Bucket Brigade algorithms for credit assignment [1].

3.2 Justifications as blame

We have described empirical ways of ascribing blame to individual rules in a KB. Alternatively, the evidence could consist of justifications concerning the content of the rules directly. The justification structures used by Smith et al [10] could be adapted to determine areas of suspicion in the support for individual rules. The belief network can propagate error types across the dependency links and so assign a belief category to each rule. One disadvantage to this justification method is the problem of acquiring the knowledge in the belief network. In some circumstances the acquisition of justifications may be easy, but we feel in general that it is an intolerable burden. Certainly for the Wine Advising KB, which was used to test KRUST, such justifications did not seem appropriate, so we favoured our statistical blame assignment for this domain.

4. PERFORMANCE

The performance of this metric has been documented during the testing of KRUST on a wine advising KB. This KB contains approximately 200 rules; the proof trees have an average branching of 3 and solution length of 4. Combinations of 60 task-solution pairs formed 60 test runs for KRUST. Each KRUST test run implemented a small number of refined KBs which were then judged for quality.

For each test run of KRUST we calculated the AVErage, MINimum and MAXimum ratings for all the refined KBs in that test run. We also calculated the RANGE as the difference between MAX and MIN, and the percentage range. The range allows us to quantify the spread of ratings, an important idea for ranking our refined KBs. Figure 7 shows the averages of these figures over all the test runs. The final column shows the average number of refined KBs selected as best by the judgement module. We note that in only one test run, test 13_3, was the **original** KB judged as best. These figures have been scaled by a factor of 1000. Tables of data for individual test runs appear in [2].

SUMMARY of RATINGS for REFINED KBs in a TEST RUN
AVERAGED over ALL TEST RUNS (X 1000)

AVE	MIN	MAX	RANGE	% RANGE	Number of Best KBs
3.9528	3.8352	4.1139	0.2787	7	1.12

Figure 7: Summary of test run ratings

Although all the range magnitudes are small, we can see from the % range column that the rating range is **significant**. It is also important for KRUST that the judge usually recommends a **single** refined KB. During testing a single best refined KB was suggested in 85% of the test runs. This indicates that the sensitivity of our judging algorithm is appropriate. The SEEK-like and BB blame assignment algorithms were implemented, but the SEEK-like algorithm was too coarse to select a **single** best KB, and BB's increased sensitivity was at the expense of increased complexity, and hence reduced speed. Also, neither of these algorithms was able to cope with the interaction of target rules; but KRUST's refinement generator was designed specifically to achieve this. Testing suggests that KRUST's blame assignment algorithm is preferable since it has combined discrimination with the ability to delve deeply into rule chains.

We are not content with the execution time of our judgement algorithm; judging the quality of a refined KB takes on average approximately 31 minutes CPU time on a 4 MIP, 16 Mbyte, SUN 3/280! Our judging was done with 30 task-solution pairs, at least 11 of whom were correctly diagnosed. The slow execution time is a problem, particularly for KRUST, where, on average, it judges 8 such KBs per test run. We have investigated the causes of this slow execution and have found that this is caused by a long individual query time. Any gains in the speed of querying would be reflected in corresponding gains for KB judging, because KRUST's classification and generation algorithms use KB queries extensively.

Alternatively, instead of improving the speed of individual queries, we could process the queries in parallel. In fact, the judgement module in KRUST is ideally suited to a coarsely-grained parallel approach; the tasks could even be distributed among the processors in a conventional computer network. Each task-solution pair would be used by a processor to generate refinements, and hence assign its portion of blame to a single representation of the KB. Only after all the task-solution pairs had been processed would the normalisation and averaging processes be executed.

5. SUMMARY

During testing, the KBs judged on each test run of KRUST are necessarily **similar**, because each refined KB is a refinement of a single original KB, and the refinement cures a single conflict case. Also, the rating is based on a single set of consistent test cases. For KRUST's purposes the judgement has proved quite successful, because it seems able to distinguish between these similar KBs. But we are using the judge as a relative quality measure in order to **rank** the KBs. One interesting question is whether the method could be used outside the field of refinement, as an **absolute** judge of KBs; i.e., any KB with a rating below a certain threshold is taken to be satisfactory. It seems possible that we could alter the normalisation factor to take account of KB and case features, so that it could be used as an absolute judge.

KRUST applies empirical testing on a set of task-solution pairs to allocate blame to rules and hence judge the quality of KBs. We should investigate how well this metric predicts the **actual** performance of the KB in **routine** use. Our method is biased towards blaming faulty rules, so we should investigate how to balance the blame factor, by rewarding well-behaved rules which give correct diagnoses. Because opinions vary on the equality of the status of positive and negative examples [8], we must rely on testing to indicate a suitable method to assign blame and credit. Current research favours a blame assignment where a rule's performance is moderated by the contents of the rule itself; e.g., it has been argued that more general rules should be given more blame, Macdonald rewards the brevity and clarity of rules [8], Prodigy [6] gathers statistics on rule utility, cost of testing, frequency of applicability and resulting savings as a way of rewarding success. KRUST's blame assignment could adopt analogous adaptations to its statistical approach.

This work on judging the quality of KBs occurred during research on knowledge refinement. We are also interested in investigating other validation tools, which may be suitable as a way for KRUST to rank its refined KBs. Our requirements are that the method is sufficiently discriminating to distinguish between very similar KBs. However, our application does not require an **absolute** judgement metric, because we wish only to **rank** the refined KBs so that we can choose the best.

REFERENCES

1. BOOKER L.B., GOLDBERG D.E., and HOLLAND J.H., (1989) : *Classifier systems and genetic algorithms*, Artificial Intelligence, vol. 40, pp. 235-282.

2. CRAW S., (1990) : *Automating the Refinement of Knowledge Based Systems*, PhD Dissertation University of Aberdeen.

3. CRAW S., and SLEEMAN D., (1990) : *Automating the refinement of knowledge-based systems*, Aberdeen University Technical Report AUCS/TR9002.

4. CRAW S., and SLEEMAN D., (1990) : *Automating the refinement of knowledge-based systems*, in Proceedings of the ECAI90 Conference (Stockholm, Sweden), ed. L.C. Aiello, pp. 167-172, Pitman, London.

5. DAVIS R., (1984) : *Interactive transfer of expertise*, in Rule-based Expert Systems, ed. B. Buchanan and E.H. Shortliffe, pp. 171-205, Addison-Wesley, Reading, M A.

6. ELLMAN T., (1989) : *Explanation-based learning: a survey of programs and perspectives*, ACM Computing Surveys, vol. 21, pp. 163-222.

7. GINSBERG A., (1988) : *Automatic Refinement of Expert System Knowledge Bases*, Research Notes in Artificial Intelligence, Pitman, London.

8. MACDONALD C., (1989) : *Machine learning: a survey of current techniques*, Artificial Intelligence Review, vol. 3, pp. 243-280.

9. POLITAKIS P.G., (1985) : *Empirical Analysis for Expert Systems*, Research Notes in Artificial Intelligence, Pitman, London.

10. SMITH R.G., WINSTON H.A., MITCHELL T.M., and BUCHANAN B.G., (1985) : *Representation and use of explicit justifications for knowledge base refinement*, in Proceedings of the Ninth IJCAI Conference (Los Angeles, CA), pp. 367-374.

11. WATERMAN D.A., (1970) : *Generalization learning techniques for automating the learning of heuristics*, Artificial Intelligence, vol. 1, pp. 29-120.

Some of this information
may be unreliable